D0615917

Advance praise for
Double Helix: A Memoir of Addiction, Recovery, and Jazz in Two Voices

"In this gripping, gut-wrenching, knock-your-socks-off memoir,
Diane and Ed Reed tell their shared, unsparing story of addiction
and betrayal, forgiveness and redemption. Their two voices, point/
counterpoint, are entangled and illuminating. Their happy ending,
when it finally comes, is well-earned and thrilling. They show
how it's never too late to be what you might have been."

— **Elizabeth Fishel, author of *Getting To 30:
A Parent's Guide to the 20-something Years***

"A story of the universal human experience and a journey
of two souls walking through the dark night as partners and
sometimes utterly alone. It will be a relief to those of us who
have been stifled (or worse) by shame and trauma."

— **Galen Ellis, Community Health Planning Consultant**

"An honest, thoughtful, and touching chronicle of two very different but
totally intertwined lives. Always fascinating—and at times horrifying—
Ed and Diane's stories unfold in tandem, sometimes joyful, sometimes
poignant, sometimes almost unbearably sad. They hold nothing back
in this recounting, but eventually it becomes a story of triumph and
fulfillment. A compelling and satisfying read, hard to put down."

— **Steve Allen, Addiction Psychologist**

"A tough and frank account with a compelling presentation of co-dependency and how it develops. There were times reading that I didn't see how Ed *possibly* could turn it all around, and that made the story so harrowing and suspenseful."

— **Heather Pegas, Essayist**

"In his late 70s Ed Reed emerged suddenly on the national scene as an extraordinary jazz singer whose performances revealed new emotional depths to familiar standards. *Double Helix* not only details his anguished but ultimately triumphant sojourn from self-sabotaging addict to uncommonly self-aware artist; it offers the braided tale of Diane Reed, a resilient force in the fight for women's rights who navigated the treacherous path with Ed over five decades and two marriages. A brave, unsettling, and deeply human story."

— **Andrew Gilbert, Jazz Journalist, *SF Chronicle***

"It reads like a great jazz gig: call and response, maybe not knowing the changes and improvising, blowin' some clams, not knowing how the tune might end, but trusting the musicians to take you there. All that's left after every falsehood has been peeled away is love and music—and two lives well examined."

— **Alisa Clancy, KCSM**

Double Helix

A Memoir of Addiction,
Recovery, and Jazz
in Two Voices

Ed & Diane Reed

ReedsWrite
B O O K S

RICHMOND, CA

Double Helix is a memoir. It reflects the present recollections by each author of their experiences over time. Some names and characteristics have been changed, some events have been compressed, and some dialogue has been recreated.

Published 2021
Printed in the United States of America on SFI Certified paper
Print ISBN: 978-1-09838-220-9
eBook ISBN: 978-1-09838-221-6

Cover design by Ian Carey
Cover photo by Irene Young

For information and permission requests:
Ed and Diane Reed
ReedsWrite Books
421 30th St.
Richmond, CA 94804

reedswrite.com

First Edition

ReedsWrite
B O O K S

For Ruth and Simonne

It may be that when we no longer know what to do,
we have come to our real work
and when we no longer know which way to go,
we have begun our real journey.

The mind that is not baffled is not employed.
The impeded stream is the one that sings.

— Wendell Berry

There are two means of refuge from the
miseries of life: music and cats.

— Albert Schweitzer

Table of Contents

Prologue

DIANE

December 17, 2015

It was between sets on the last of Ed's three nights of sold-out shows when we read the online review by Nate Chinen titled "An Interpreter Draws from a Deep Well," which would be published in print in the *New York Times* the next day. We were at Dizzy's Club Coca-Cola on the fifth floor of Jazz at Lincoln Center in New York City. Through the towering window behind Ed and his band was the magically dazzling New York skyline. Chinen wrote:

> Every jazz singer who reaches a certain age is granted a turn as the voice of experience. Ed Reed, who will be 87 in February, takes that covenant more seriously than most. "I spent so many years being unhappy," he said, confidingly, early in his first set at Dizzy's Club Coca-Cola on Wednesday night. He waited a beat. "Anybody out there read my bio?"
>
> An appreciative laugh rippled through the room: Why yes, of course. But for the benefit of anyone who hadn't, Mr. Reed

sketched a basic outline over the course of the night: his struggles with addiction, to heroin and other substances; his cycles of incarceration, including several stints at San Quentin State Prison in California. ... Mr. Reed is clear-eyed about what he has had to overcome.

It is a unique feature of Ed's concerts that through song and the spoken word he tells painful stories about his journey through heartbreak and hopelessness. This is something that many jazz artists of his era shy away from talking about publicly.

Ed's first CD release in 2007, his voice, and his story took the jazz world by storm. Jazz journalist Andrew Gilbert wrote, "He has released a ravishing album at the age of 78. ... It's Reed's coming out party and he gives the performance of a lifetime."

One year later, in 2008, the legendary Marian McPartland invited Ed to one of the last of her iconic *Piano Jazz* radio shows on NPR that she would record. She joked with him, "You're only 80 [*sic*]? Well, I'm 90. You're just a baby!" In one of the letters they exchanged after the show, she wryly observed, "It's so great that you were able to put out a record and do *Piano Jazz* after you were in prison. That's something [prison] you can now put behind you and concentrate on your career!"

The *Times* review continued:

Mr. Reed sings in a dark-mahogany baritone with careful diction, evoking the midcentury styles of Billy Eckstine and Nat King Cole. The tunes in the set—drawn from each of Mr. Reed's four albums—seemed chosen partly for their dramatic potential, amplifying his narrative and persona. ... Still, he isn't a miserablist. His banter, earnest and encouraging, often had the ring of therapy: "I'm the choice-maker in this experience I call me."

Ed's message is always consistent: Change is possible. It's never too late to have your dreams.

That night, at Dizzy's, Ed was in the middle of one of those dreams. He said it felt like he was on the set of a Bogart-Bacall movie.

I was so proud of him.

ED

I would never have imagined I'd be performing at Jazz at Lincoln Center. Certainly not when I was shooting heroin and overdosing, spending the better part of 16 years at San Quentin and Folsom Prisons and, for 20 years more, rotating in and out of 25 drug treatment programs, five mental hospitals, and fleabag hotel rooms in San Francisco's Tenderloin district.

I certainly had many low points during my 40 years of addiction, but perhaps few as hard as in late 1971. Five years after coming out of prison I had been hired as a consultant to a county medical administrator. That ended when they found out I was using heroin. By then, my wife, Diane, had left me and I had no income. I saw no way out but to kill myself.

I wrote a series of bad checks and bought an ounce of the best heroin in Northern California—I was detoxifying from methadone and knew it would take a lot to kill me. Then I went to a low-down, snake-in-the-grass dope dealer's house. He lived in the projects in Stockton and I made a lot of noise as I entered, waving and hollering at people. Everybody on the block saw me going in there. Because, you see, I intended to overdose and die there so he would get in trouble. As I was dying, I was going to handcuff myself to the gas pipe in his living room so he would have a big problem getting rid of the body.

I offered him and his slimy girlfriend some of the dope. They were salivating to get some free drugs. We sat at the dining room table as he cooked up a huge greedy spoonful. They fixed and then one after the other overdosed and fell to the floor. I shot up and hardly felt anything because of the methadone still in my system. Nothing happened.

I started to freak out. Not only did I fear that I could have a stroke, be paralyzed, and *not* die if I continued, but the courts, at that time, were charging persons with murder when they used drugs with someone who overdosed and died. Then I *really* freaked when it sank in that I could be charged with a double homicide. I spent the next 12 hours reviving them and then slunk out of the projects, filled with despair. I couldn't even kill myself right.

It would get much worse before it ever got better.

DIANE

Ever since Ed got into recovery in 1986, people have said we should tell our story because it could help others in their struggles with addiction and relationships.

Then, when Ed's first CD was released in 2007 and the story about his addiction, recovery, and dreams come true grabbed the imagination of jazz journalists across the country, several writers approached us with offers to write his story. It sounded like a great idea, but had shortcomings because people see through their own lenses. Ed's story isn't just about drugs and prison, lies and betrayal, recovery and music, but also about a decades-long relationship. And that story—about how our lives have continually spiraled around each other, like a double helix, through the worst and the best of times—is really two stories that we both agreed should be told in our own voices about our own journeys.

Telling our own stories in our own voices was the only way we *could* have done it. After our first 18 years of marriage, divorce, lies, and loss of trust, the truth was we didn't really know each other very well. The failures, fighting, revolving door of separations and temporary reconciliations had been relentless. Despite therapy, encounter groups, and treatment programs, neither of us understood what was driving the other until we each got into our own recovery program. And even then, we never really talked about it in any depth.

There's a reason we keep our darkest memories buried. What we don't expect is their staying power. During the harsh years of addiction, we couldn't articulate why we continued the unending sad dance that had each of us stuck. Even when it was over and we re-created our lives as seemingly "normal" people, we only really began connecting all the dots when we started writing.

The complexity of our relationship would change each of us forever. In his 2009 *Wall Street Journal* review of Ed's first CD, the great jazz critic, historian, and social commentator Nat Hentoff ended with a thought that, unbeknownst to him, applied perfectly to our journey: "If you never give up," he wrote, "it's a strangely, sometimes revivingly, unpredictable world. Like jazz itself—and Ed Reed."

How did we get to Jazz at Lincoln Center, one of the most venerated venues in the jazz world, after so many years of struggle through the darkest of times?

It *is* an unpredictable world.

We have got to create dreams. We have to practice keeping our dreams in focus or we cannot experience living the dream. Without our dreams, we are lost — Ed Reed

Part One:

We Become Ourselves

1

Razor Blades for Breakfast

My early upbringing in Cleveland, Ohio was a very joyful time for me. Great things were expected from my coming into the world. My first name, Edward, was taken from Edward VIII, the Duke of Windsor, who would abdicate the throne for love, and my middle name, Lawrence, was from T.E. Lawrence of Arabia, another romantic English figure. No one ever explained how my mother's fixation with English heroes ended up naming me, an African American child, after them.

My mother worked for the Morrison family who were very wealthy and had managed to maintain their affluence during the Great Depression. In 1927, my mother's beautiful voice motivated the Morrisons to look into the possibility of sending her to study opera at La Scala Theatre Academy in Milan, Italy. This offer was made at a time when women—all women—much less African American women, had few choices and little freedom. My grandmother, who had been born into slavery, was scandalized and terrified. Gramma convinced my mom, Ruth Veal, to marry Dad, John Reed, who was already smitten by her and worked for the Morrisons as their chauffeur. Though my mother had a very hard time letting go of such a stupendous offer, she acquiesced and married my dad. I was born two years later in 1929.

Dad drove the Morrisons' huge, beautiful, purple-colored Pierce Arrow. I often was, so proudly, allowed to ride along with him. By the time I was five, I had learned the name and model designation of nearly every car on the road, and I was hardly ever mistaken. Dad used to try to trip me up but was seldom successful, which made him very proud of me.

Around that time, when I was five years old, Dad left Cleveland for Los Angeles to work for the railroad, leaving Mom and me at home until he got settled. By the time he sent for us, two years later, she had convinced me that there was no future in yelling out the complete nomenclatures of passing cars, besides it was ungentlemanly and undignified and made people stare. I understood her to mean that study and practice of a profession wherein I could become "somebody respectable and admired" would prove a more profitable venture. The implication was that presently I was nobody, and yelling out the names of cars made me even less so.

I spent my early days in Cleveland in the care of Aunt Lois, who ran a laundry in her home. The women who worked there were church choir members, and the whole house was continuously filled with song. Aunt Lois was a jazz fan. She had a Victrola phonograph in the sitting room and taught me how to stand on a chair and play records (under threat of death if I broke anything). I became surprisingly adept at playing and listening to her recordings of jazz greats like Duke Ellington, Louis Armstrong, Bing Crosby, and Lester Young. Someone was always reading poetry, lines from a play, scriptures, and Shakespeare and my mother always had me reading, reciting, or singing in front of people.

I was the only kid in that house—except for an occasional visiting cousin or two—and those women kept me singing all the time. They treated me like royalty. I could have anything I wanted. All I had to do was sing. They gave me presents of money and treats of all kinds. I learned to save like my Uncle Monroe who had escaped from a Virginia chain gang (about which there was never any elaboration). He was a model of industry and thrift and was always counting and handling money earned from his parking garage business. I began to imitate him. I saved every penny I acquired and at some point had a big bank with almost $200 in it. I had never considered spending that money. I was into saving it for its own sake.

My mother, her sisters, the ladies of the laundry, and their friends were the main figures around which my childhood revolved, and they, in turn, did their spins around church, their families, books, art, and, most especially, music. Of course the music of family and church was heavily laden with Negro spirituals, accompanied by classical music, popular music, and jazz.

Church was a place for me to get bored, hot, scared, and excited by the music. Mom, her two sisters, Ruby and Lois, and Dad were in the choir and all were soloists. Church was also the place where much of the conflict between my mother and me began. When I asked her questions about things our pastor would say that didn't seem to follow his actions or those of the flock, she would respond physically, with an elbow on my arm, and sharply tell me that children should be seen and not heard, or that children shouldn't question their elders.

Our pastor was Reverend Alexander R. Schooler. "Elder" Schooler was a very beautifully dressed, tall and handsome scholar, orator, and kind man. His church at 77th and Kinsman in Cleveland was a huge beautiful building with a giant pipe organ. But Elder Schooler did something, about which I won't speculate, that caused him to have to leave the church. He and his family and my parents were very close and when he decided to start over in California he convinced my Dad to do the same. Dad was not very religious, but he was a friend and he stuck by Elder Schooler.

From my earliest memory I was constantly and consistently given instructions in etiquette, like do not touch the property of other people unless you have permission, always dress properly, stand erect, speak to people directly with good diction, mind your manners, be polite. So imagine my shock when one night before my father left with Elder Schooler I was awakened by the unmistakable sound of my bank being violently shaken. I jumped out of bed to find my parents robbing it.

I wanted to know how they dared touch my savings bank without asking my permission. It went against everything they had taught me. I said that taking my money was theft. My mother said that they were borrowing my money and would repay me soon.

I retorted, "You can't borrow without asking the lender."

Mother then slapped my face and I started screaming. "Help! I'm being assaulted and robbed."

We lived upstairs in a duplex, so the neighbors were soon at the door. I cannot recall ever receiving an apology, or being repaid. It seemed so hypocritical to me that it was okay for adults to take from a child without asking, but if I took something from them, I would have been punished.

Not long after the "robbery," my father drove to Los Angeles with Rev. Schooler and got a job as a dining car waiter on the Southern Pacific Railroad where he became active in the Brotherhood of Sleeping Car Porters. By then, still in Cleveland, I had started kindergarten. It wasn't as bad as I expected. I got a lot of teacher approval because I was already a fairly good reader, having gotten a library card on my fifth birthday. Time passed quickly.

Child that I was, I didn't yet understand the racially charged environment I was growing up in, but I would soon learn to remember that every time you walk out the door you are colored, Negro, "Nigger." There was something at risk but my parents didn't know how to explain it to a small child. Things happened that no one would or could explain to me, like why my dad wouldn't take me to the Cleveland Air Races before we moved to Los Angeles.

The first book I took out when I got my library card was about the Douglas DC2 transport. It was the coolest looking aircraft, sleek, no wires holding the wings together, and it was big in the news that year. I had a burning desire to see the airplanes and the air races and my dad kept promising he would take me. Maybe he hoped it was a passing notion and I would eventually forget about it, but I didn't. To this day, I still can't be in a taxiing aircraft and not strain to see the parked or landing planes. I pinned him against the wall and got his solemn promise that when the next Cleveland Air Races began he would have me and my two friends, Alfred Hall Jr. and "Snooky," sitting in the best seats available. The day finally arrived, along with the excuses.

"I have to work today, we'll go next time," said Dad, avoiding eye contact.

Then he turned quickly and walked away He was deeply chagrined, I'm sure, by his inability to be the father he wanted to be, a man who could escort the son he loved wherever he might choose. But that was not the reality for my father or for any other Black man in America in 1935. It would not have been wise for us to attend the grand parade down beautiful Euclid Avenue to the Cleveland Municipal Airport. I think Dad felt, or experience had taught him, that we would not be welcome. Nor could he assure our safety in those crowds.

In retrospect, I think this incident changed my relationship with my father for the rest of our lives. Before this, he treated me like a little man, but afterwards I felt he had become uncomfortable with the sensibilities of the child that I was and somewhat wary of my overly literal tendencies in believing that everything he told me was a done deal that could not be casually retracted.

My mother was upset with both of us. I heard her tell him that he too was acting like a child.

It had to be heartbreaking for my parents, but they would not talk to me, a six-year-old, about the racial pain of Blacks. It was still fairly common for African Americans to be lynched in America. Although the great Black newspapers, *The Chicago Defender* and *The Pittsburgh Courier,* were common around the laundry, I never understood the significance of the abrupt conversational silences and the rustling disappearances of the front pages with pictures of Black bodies swinging in American trees that I wasn't allowed to see (though occasionally I would see one of those pictures in a newspaper that had been left on a table). Nor was I permitted to know about the fear, anger, and heartbreak of the Black adults in my life.

Because I didn't know about or understand the significance of what was happening, I was left with feelings of not being worthwhile or good enough to be let in on the secrets those unexpected silences hid. Those feelings have had profound consequences in my life. Shortly after the air races disappointment, I was sitting on the curb in front of Aunt Lois's house and Alfred Jr. walked up and asked me what was wrong. I scrambled to my feet and screamed through my tears that nothing was wrong with me. I threw a wild punch at him and chipped his tooth. Then I ran upstairs and hid in a closet and cried myself to sleep.

I awoke much later hearing my parents and others calling me, terrified because I was nowhere to be found. I now believe they were also afraid to call the police because of Uncle Monroe's chain gang history. The family needed to keep a very low profile. When I came out hours later, I got slapped and hugged and nearly drowned in tears.

What I heard in Alfred's question was an implication that I had done something wrong. Of course he had no such intent, but it was what my mother would say when I displeased her. It started when I was four and she caught me playing with matches under the bed. She screamed, "What's wrong with you?" Her voice was filled with acid and it frightened me because in my small child's brain, I thought that if she didn't know the answer it must be awful.

When I started first grade at six years old, my life changed forever. At the time, we lived in an all-white neighborhood on Baldwin Road, in view of a large beautiful reservoir. It was a very pretty area, hilly, with large open spaces. There was only one other Black family who lived nearby, with a female child that I never met.

It was quite shocking to learn that that I was a hated "little nigger." Every morning after I was dressed in my fancy, three-piece "Little Lord Fauntleroy" tweed, short pants suit, and tie, I picked up my fancy little book bag and began my walk up the steep hill of Mt. Carmel Road which took me through Little Italy to get to school. Unfortunately for me, Mussolini had just invaded Ethiopia and the war was not going well for the Italians. So to prove their patriotism, Italian adult males on Mt. Carmel Road saw it as their sacred duty to help the Ethiopian war effort by hitting little Black six-year-old Edward and calling me names. Fortunately, their women folk did not agree and came to my rescue. They protected me from the abuse and waited for me every morning and afternoon to assure my safe passage. But then I would arrive at school and it would start all over again, *nigger, nigger, nigger,* and I would get punched and ironically have to run to safety in Little Italy.

When I arrived home, my mother would ask me what happened, and when I tried to explain, she interrogated me about what I had done to earn such treatment. Her fear led her to assume that I had provoked some wrathful consequence, and sometimes I had. My mother, who had been born in Alabama, wanted to believe that we were living in the "promised land" of the "North" where the behavior that I had endured as a child could not occur. But now I believe she often laid the blame on me because she couldn't take on the real perpetrators.

My mother never learned to drive a car, so she and I walked everywhere. Whenever she felt any displeasure about anyone, she would only say, "Let's cross the street, Edward, here come those people."

There seemed to be myriad classes of "those people" and I seldom understood Mom's method of classification. But they were mainly small groups of men, regardless of color, and I think that my mother felt it was safer not to get too close to them. Anyway, I didn't care to understand because I was tired of walking and it seemed to me, after crossing the street 150 times, that we had walked 500 miles to go two blocks!

My mother used no expressions of racial blame or hatred and never, to her dying day, did I hear her speak against people of any race, class, or gender. If anything, my mother, who was no religious zealot, would pray for them. But I think she also knew that she could not really protect her little boy, and that must have brought her no end of heartbreak. She chose to focus on the idea borne by the pre-amble to the Declaration of Independence—life, liberty, and the pursuit of happiness—and that if she applied to me all of the trap-pings of gentility, perhaps I, or we, could escape the hatred of the cultural norm.

Even at that young age, I refused to be cornered or bullied. My cousins and the kids who lived around the laundry had taught me how to fight and not let myself be pushed around. So in response to what kept happening in the schoolyard, I took a hatchet to school to protect myself. The next time the bullies threatened me, the only Black kid in the school, I pulled out my hatchet and swung at them. Of course, the teacher sent me home with a note pinned to my coat. My mother, horrified at my behavior, had to go to school and prom-ise I wouldn't do it anymore.

As you might imagine, the hatchet incident did not go over well at all. I cannot recall much of what followed, or was said next, but my dad convinced Mom to transfer me to Bolton School on Carnegie Avenue in my aunt's neighborhood, where I didn't stand out so much. But this success was to be short-lived because my dad had settled into his new job in California, and Rev. Schooler came back to Cleveland to drive me and my mother to Los Angeles in his Model A Ford.

In California, we lived in Watts which, in 1936, was a work-ing-class Anglo community with a sprinkling of African Americans, Latinos, and Japanese people. We lived there because Watts was one of the few areas in Los Angeles where African Americans were allowed to live and buy property.

Mom and I both suffered from the move. She was unhappy because she had to leave her sisters Lois and Ruby, her social life, musical community, and her musical ambitions. Plus, Watts was far from the city and public transportation. To her, California lacked culture and decorum compared to the more refined people in Cleveland. There were many places where there were no sidewalks in Watts. The suits, dresses, hats, and white gloves she had proudly worn in Cleveland did not go over well in the mud, heat, and dust. And I had lost the comfort of those women who worked in the laundry, along with the kids who were my best friends.

Despite the stark change in our environment, Mom continued to send me to school in suits, ties, short pants, a cap, and a proper book bag when everyone else was simply wearing blue jeans. Needless to say, I was always in fights with kids who laughed at me. I didn't want to be there, dressed in Little Lord Fauntleroy suits, or go to school where I had to constantly defend myself. I was so angry and unhappy that every time she looked at me, I was mad, especially at breakfast before I had to go off to school.

She would look at me and say, "You act like an old bear that had razor blades for breakfast."

My father finally stepped in and got me into long pants.

My brother James was born in December 1938. In the 10 years between my birth and his, Mom had suffered a series of miscarriages and stillbirths, including James's twin brother who did not survive the birth. Today I understand that during those years, my mother had to be in a nearly constant state of grieving those lost babies. Knowing about those losses helps explain how all her hopes and dreams for me so weighed me down as a child and beyond childhood. It also helps explain her fear that something might happen to me if she let me leave the yard to play in the street with other kids.

We had a Japanese neighbor, 18-year-old Nobus Oki, who taught me some martial arts to help me take better care of myself against the other kids. That gave me the confidence to know I could avoid being pushed around physically. Then one sad day in 1942, not long after Pearl Harbor, my friend and his family and all the other Japanese families in the neighborhood disappeared. I never saw them again.

I was a pretty lonely child and vulnerable to peer pressure. As I got older, I would do things that I knew were crazy, but I did them anyway because I didn't want to be left out.

When I was 11 or 12 and "they" said, "We're going to Sam's house and get drunk," I replied, "That's the stupidest thing I ever heard."

They said, "If you ain't gon' get drunk, you cain't hang wid us."

I said, "Okay, man. I'll get drunk."

They all sat around sipping with their legs crossed, like adults. I had tasted alcohol and I did not like it, nor did I like being around adults who had been drinking. There was never any drinking in my home, or the homes of my parents' friends. So sipping wasn't working for me. I began to guzzle. When that stuff hit my stomach, I became belligerent. I didn't mean to be but I was angry that those kids had insisted on my drinking, so I drank until I was unconscious. I think I freaked them out; they had never seen me like I had become. But what did they know? They thought having a drink was "getting drunk." They took me home, knocked on the door, and left me there on the porch. My mother called the ambulance. The paramedics said it was a close call. I was sick and drunk for three days.

In years to come, I would still claim a hatred for alcohol but I would drink all you had on hand if there was no heroin around.

And, given the proper amount of self-disgust, I would get drunk, shoot heroin, stop breathing, and fall down. For some unknown reason, people, some of whom I'd never seen before, would sometimes spend hours reviving me.

From my earliest memories, I liked to talk to Elder Schooler's son, Alexander Jr., who, after moving to California, became a policeman and married Vivian Mingus. They lived across the street from us with his parents. Alex Jr. was always playing music; he loved Duke Ellington and Count Basie. Vivian's younger brother, then 19-year-old Charles, came over often to see his sister, and sometimes he'd take care of their kids. He carried his huge bass with him everywhere and was always playing the piano. I'd hang out by the screen door to listen until he invited me in and let me ask him questions. He taught me how to hear chord changes and how they related to melody. Charles Mingus went on to become one of the most renowned jazz bassists and composers.

In 1942, when I was 13, the Plantation Club, which billed itself as California's largest Harlem nightclub and attracted all the top Black talent visiting Los Angeles, opened on 108th and Central in Watts. Most of the jazz I'd heard was on the radio—Ellington, Basie, Andy Kirk, Benny Goodman, Nat Cole, and many others. One day a friend told me that we could see and hear the bands from the roof of the Plantation Club. So enthralled with the music, but too young to get into the club, and out of pure hunger to see what it was all about, I would climb up to the roof with some friends to see the shows. We also used to cut school to go to the 10 a.m. show at the Orpheum Theater when bands like Duke Ellington or Lionel Hampton came to L.A. We sat in the side boxes just over the stage where Hamp could see us and, when he did, he always waved.

2

Keep Off
the Grass

DIANE

I was born in 1944 to a lower-middle-class, liberal Jewish family in the Fordham-Bedford section of the Bronx. Our neighborhood was a mix of cultures, religions, and languages—Italian, Irish, Jewish. I was the first of two daughters. My younger sister, Miriam, or Mimi as we called her, was born three years later. I was shy and introverted, and starting kindergarten at age 4 and a half, considerably younger than the rest of my classmates, didn't help. One day, feeling invisible and overwhelmed, I left the playground during lunch and, without telling anyone, just walked home.

We lived on the fifth floor of a faded brown brick apartment building on Briggs Avenue, half a block from P.S. 46, my six-story public elementary school, where each grade meant going up to the next floor. The city closed one of the streets bordering the building every day after school to give us kids a place to ride bikes, skate, and engage in the innumerable games passed down or invented by city children limited to sidewalks and cement. We played ball, jump rope, and hopscotch, chalking up the sidewalk in pastels after school, only to find the colored squares rubbed out by the next morning. In the winter, we made snowmen on the sidewalk and in the summer we never missed a day getting coconut-covered vanilla ice cream bars—the revolutionary new ice cream on sticks—from the Good Humor man riding around the neighborhood in his iconic truck. Every few days, the vegetable man would come through the streets in a cart pulled by a horse which, to our delight, left real horse droppings. As a child, I inexplicably attributed feelings to just about everything, alive or not, including the building across the street where our babysitter lived with her parents. When a fire left its outside walls scorched black, I worried for a long while about the pain it was in.

My parents slept in the living room on twin beds, which doubled as day beds, pushed up against eggshell-colored walls. Mimi and I shared the only bedroom in the apartment. That room was our fantasy world where we enacted thousands of stories, under the table, between the beds, anywhere so as not to have to look out our fifth-story window into someone else's bedroom. We played with dolls and made a world where living things grew tall and free, where fresh sea breezes cooled the world on hot summer nights, where we could pick apples right off the tree and watch kittens being born, where we didn't have only cement and dark scary basements to play in, where we could breathe.

I longed to be out of the city. We used to go to tiny Poe Park, a few blocks away, named for Edgar Allan Poe who had lived in the small white house on that site in the mid-1800s. But every single one of its smallish lawns had "Keep Off the Grass" and "Curb Your Dog" signs posted, so all we could really do was sit on benches and look at the trees. Some summers my mom, sister, and I would spend a week or two in the Catskills at the Hotel Capital, which catered to Jewish families, where we swam, learned to row boats in the small lake, took hayrides through the countryside, and sometimes rode a horse. Like most of the other fathers, my dad would drive up from the city on weekends. One summer we rented a house in New Canaan, Connecticut, where we walked through the woods to town, following the railroad tracks, inhaling the hot, sweet fragrance of wildflowers and grasses.

To escape the oppressive heat and humidity during those Bronx summers, my mother, sister, and I would take the subway and then a bus to Rye Beach, a few miles from the New York/Connecticut border on Long Island Sound. We'd make our way through the crowds of beach blankets and umbrellas until we found a spot to squeeze our blanket in between all the other families, and run to the shore where, during low tide, the water would be knee deep for a long way out. Then the trek back on the bus and the subway to the Bronx, returning hotter and sweatier than when we had left.

On unbearably hot humid summer nights, my mother and I would sit on the fire escape outside the kitchen eating ice cream. We talked about a lot of things on that fire escape. One of those nights, when I was about 11, she explained why my best friend, Mona, who lived on the third floor, suddenly had fuzzy brown hair under her arms. I listened in awe, watching the orange Sears sign flash on and off in the distance on Fordham Road. I guess Mona's mother told my mother that Mona got her period and mom was trying to prepare me for the changes I would soon have in my own body—unlike the way my grandmother had handled it. When my mom went to her mother in tears, fearing that she was bleeding to death, my grandmother, following one of the more distressingly confounding Jewish traditions, slapped her face and exclaimed, "Mazel tov! Now you're a woman!"

My mother had a high school degree and worked as a secretary, with the main purpose of saving money to send me and my sister to college. Born in Paris in 1913, she was the oldest of three girls. When she contracted polio at age four, her father insisted that she have intensive physical therapy which saved her affected leg from wasting away. Despite lifelong muscle weakening in that leg, my mom was typical of many polio survivors—tough, fiercely independent, unstoppable, and always refusing to be treated like an invalid.

I have a cherished photo of my three- or four-year-old mother in an elegant white ermine jacket that my grandfather, who was a furrier, had made for her. In the picture, she is standing next to her child-size baby carriage. When my aunt—my mother's middle sister—saw it, she laughed. "Mom and Dad didn't have two dimes to rub together during those years," she said, "but he could dress Simonne in an ermine jacket!"

My grandparents had a somewhat confusing dynamic for a child. Grandma was very orthodox, kosher, and rigid. She was critical of just about anyone or anything that wasn't Jewish, and her prejudices created a lot of conflict between us as I grew older. My grandfather, on the other hand, had a great sense of humor and, in my childhood experience, was a lighthearted breaker of rules. When I was eight, he took me out to lunch one day and ordered ham sandwiches, an act which would have been unforgivable had my grandmother known. I don't know what other secrets he might have kept from her, but I loved that it was our secret and—who knows?—maybe that was the beginning of a series of rules I would break in my life, sometimes with dire consequences. It was a huge loss when Grandpa died from colon cancer at age 64 when I was just 11.

My father was a gentle, soft-spoken, cautious, and self-made man who loved to collect rare four-leaf clovers and tape them onto our baby pictures. Lacking a high school diploma, he learned by doing. When he met my mother, he was a bookkeeper, and later, when we were children, he worked as an assistant to his pharmacist brother-in-law, my mother's middle sister's husband, in Stamford, Connecticut.

We moved to Stamford in 1955, when I was 11. The decision was made so Dad wouldn't have to commute from the Bronx every day and could spend more time with the family. But other factors were also at play. The neighbors, and even my grandparents who lived on Long Island, encouraged us to move. "The Puerto Ricans are coming!" they warned.

At 11, I didn't even know who or what Puerto Ricans were, and no one would explain why this would be so terrible. While our neighborhood was a dense patchwork of European ethnicities, religions, and languages, I don't remember seeing too many, if any, people of color—not even at school.

The neighbors turned out to be right. The great migration from Puerto Rico to the mainland was underway. Forty years later, when my sister and I took our mother to revisit her roots in New York City on her 80th birthday, we found our old Bronx neighborhood transformed from the grays and faded brick tones I remembered as a child into buildings and signs reflecting the bold and vibrant colors of Latino culture.

As an apprentice, Dad learned every aspect of pharmacology, but without a license he couldn't be left alone in the store. In those years, he could have taken the state exam to become a licensed pharmacist, since people without degrees who passed the licensure exam by a certain time were "grandfathered" in. Sadly, by the time he felt ready to take the exam, it was too late. The deadline had passed. He had already decided it was time to leave my uncle's business, but without a license he couldn't get a job in another pharmacy. So he and my mom bought a convenience store that they ran together every day of every year until they retired.

My dad was a worrier. From my earliest memories, we struggled over how he exaggerated normal childhood mishaps, scrapes, and colds that in my mind were not a big deal, but in his mind were emergencies. Maybe becoming a first-time father at age 40 had something to do with it, but his overprotectiveness was oppressive. When my sister was born in 1947, my dad had some sort of "nervous breakdown" and spent a couple of weeks at a rest home in the country, leaving my mother alone with a 3½-year-old and a newborn.

Even at four years of age, when I somehow cut my finger as he and I walked home from the corner delicatessen featuring a huge barrel filled with the best dill pickles in the world, I had already seen enough of how he overreacted to relatively insignificant events. So I hid my hand behind my back until we got home and Mom put a Band Aid on it. Every single night when he came into our room to say goodnight, he would look under the bed with a flashlight. One night, when I was 12 or 13, I couldn't stand it anymore and asked him what he thought he'd find there. He finally stopped.

My sister once saw a psychic who, as part of the reading, talked about the struggle between me and my dad. "Your father," the psychic told her, "always tried to stuff both your sister's feet into one shoe." That analogy resonated perfectly with how suffocated I felt by his overprotectiveness and why, from such an early age, I had rebelled against it. Sometimes, to my own detriment, in trying to keep his fears from stifling me, I ignored my own common sense. If it was raining and he told me to take an umbrella and put on my galoshes, I would deliberately leave the house without them. I once sat under a neighbor's sunlamp too long and then refused to let him put anything that would have provided relief on my burned and burning face. It only got worse as he grew older. In his late seventies, he would not leave their apartment on the 15th floor until he had closed and locked all the windows, even in the stifling heat.

My parents, like many other liberal Jewish families, instilled a strong sense of social consciousness in us. I grew up aware of social justice issues, and the connection that we, as Jews, have with other oppressed people. Despite having no real-life memory of the atrocities of World War II, I always understood the burden that every living Jew carried. "After thousands of years of persecution," my mother said many times as we were growing up, "we have a responsibility to do what we can to fight injustice experienced by other groups."

In the U.S., that meant African Americans. During my preteen and adolescent years, my mother and I read many of the leading Black writers of the time—Richard Wright, John Howard Griffin, Ralph Ellison. We used to talk at length about the experiences and injustices they described and, even though I didn't know any African Americans (or Negroes as they were called then), I felt a bond.

3

Heroin

ED

Having come from the more rigid scholastic standards of Eastern schools, I had an easy time with my studies in Los Angeles and got very good grades. But that didn't last. By the time I got to high school in the 1940s, I started not caring that much about school. The last straw was when I asked to join the Debate Society and the teacher told me I would be better off taking a shoe shop class because colored people didn't need to know things like elocution; after all, what would we debate? That did it for me. I started ditching school and hanging out with a rough element at about the same time my mother's sister, Alzena, along with her husband and seven children, moved in with us. I lost my room, my privacy, and my sense of self. I altered my birth certificate and joined the Army in May 1946. I was 17.

I went to basic training at Fort Lewis, Washington and learned very quickly that to be Black in the U.S. Army in 1946 was a bad idea. We were living in tar paper shacks in a swamp at Fort Lewis, with no amenities, while the white soldiers lived in beautiful two-story brick barracks with trees and lawns. In September, I was given a nine-day delay en route to Kobe, Japan. I went home to L.A. and didn't go back until my father figured that I had overstayed my leave. I had not returned because the rumor was that Gen. MacArthur was hanging Black soldiers like Christmas tree ornaments in Japan for the most racially bigoted reasons. I never discovered if that was true, but it terrified me.

By the time I got to Camp Stoneman in Pittsburg, California— an Overseas Replacement Depot (ORD) with thousands of soldiers coming and going at all hours of the day and night—my company had already left, and my records went with them. Records were routinely misplaced or lost because of the sheer numbers of people cycling through the ORD. So they told me to go find a bunk in a barracks. I was there for about 30 days and they put me on another shipment to Yokohama, but I didn't show up for that one either. I had figured out that when the shipment left, you leave the barracks, find another one, tell them you lost your papers, and get on that roster. I played that game over and over and ultimately escaped being sent overseas. I also somehow escaped any punishment for my behavior.

I smoked weed and hung out with a bunch of crap-shooting, jazz-loving soldiers who would go to the center of the parade ground as ships were about to be boarded by thousands of soldiers, each with a new $20 bill given to them by the ORD team for the voyage. My pals would shoot crooked dice. I had never heard of such a thing. On a pair of crooked dice, one die has only five dots on each side, and the second one has only two dots on each side. No matter how you throw them, the total is always seven, the winning number. So there's no way for the person who owns the crooked dice to lose on a throw. Once thrown, we would quickly snatch the dice up and leave.

Fortunately for us, the area was so crowded that it was hard for anyone to really know what was happening. We tied our pants legs with
condoms like paratroopers, stretching them around our boot tops,
and we would leave the parade ground with our pants legs stuffed
with $20 bills. Some days we'd make three or four thousand dollars.

Finally I was assigned to the 9206 Harbor Craft Detachment
and stationed on a houseboat anchored under the Antioch Bridge
at the mouth of the Sacramento-San Joaquin River Delta, east of
San Francisco. One of my jobs was to be sure that FDR's mothballed
yacht was safe and dry. We were on the water all the time; the duty
was light.

One of the guys, who called himself Kilroy, was a "sneak thief."
Since so many people coming back from overseas were owed back
pay, many of the officers just landing were paid large sums—as much
as several thousand dollars in checks and cash. They also tended
to drink too much, so glad they were to be alive. Kilroy used to
sneak into the officers' quarters at night and steal their checks, cash,
watches, rings, and other valuables. He got me to forge the names
and he cashed the checks. I was caught almost immediately and sent
to San Francisco County Jail, where I was tried, convicted, and put
on probation.

Strangely enough I was allowed to reenlist, got a $2,000 reen-
listment bonus, and bought a '39 Ford convertible. I was transferred
to the 43rd Truck Company at Oakland Army Base where I met Jesse
and Smitty, enlisted men like myself. We started selling weed on 7th
Street in what was then a thriving Black middle-class community in
West Oakland. I went to jazz concerts on 7th Street and in greater
Oakland and Berkeley where I saw the Billy Eckstine Band, Stan
Kenton, Miles Davis, Ernestine Anderson, and others.

On Labor Day 1947, I went to a Stan Kenton concert with Jesse and Smitty. Afterward, we went to our weed connection, who also dealt heroin. There, we met the great alto saxophonist Art Pepper, who walked in rolling up his sleeve. The dealer handed him an eye-dropper full of heroin, which Art promptly injected into his arm. I wanted to run out of there but Smitty and Jesse started talking about shooting heroin. I thought it was one of the stupidest ideas I had ever heard. But on that Labor Day in 1947, I tried it for the first time, never dreaming that 40 years later I would still be paying for that choice.

The feeling I got from the heroin that first time was amazing. For a while I kept throwing up. But strangely, I didn't feel sick, and each time I had to vomit, it felt so good that I thought I might fly away. All of my anxiety and need to please people disappeared. For the first time in my life I felt free. Smitty, who was from New York, was about 5'4" in height, very handsome and claimed to know everything about everything. I always felt inferior to him even though I often thought he was an idiot. I walked away to throw up because I wanted to feel good on my own without anyone else's commentary. Strangely enough, I still thought it was a stupid thing to do. Though I was only 18 years old and knew absolutely nothing about hard drug use or addiction, I was sure I was smart enough that I could control it. So I continued to shoot heroin whenever I had the chance.

One day in May 1948, I overdosed and don't know how I got back to the base. My job required me to light the fires in the kitchen in the morning for breakfast. That morning I was so knocked out that when the Charge of Quarters (CQ), who oversees the company during the night, came to wake me, I didn't get up. After a number of attempts to rouse me, the company commander (whom I called Captain Maggot) was informed; he came and flipped me out of my bunk onto the floor. I jumped up, flipped my cot back over, snatched my blanket out of his hands, and went back to bed.

Captain Maggot started yelling, "He's crazy. Call the MPs!"

They took me to the dispensary where the shrink sent me to Letterman Hospital in San Francisco to be evaluated. Letterman was so backed up with people that I didn't get an appointment for months. All I did was read books, go out on pass, hang around the Palace of the Legion of Honor, smoke grass, shoot dope, chase girls, and hang out with the guys in Oakland. I finally got to see one of the psychiatrists there, and we had about ten weeks of sessions, at the end of which, he asked me if I'd like to go home. I guess after looking over what he could find of my record, it was clear to him that I wasn't much use as a soldier. I had demonstrated that quite clearly.

So after two and a half years, the Army finally got it and gave me a General Discharge under Honorable Conditions in December 1948. I later learned that my outfit of Black truck drivers and cooks had been put on the front lines in Korea even though they had never received any training to fight. When most were killed in combat, the Army called them cowards.

I returned to Los Angeles, lived with my parents, worked at various jobs, and "chippied" around with heroin on weekends. I had become a well-dressed, drug-confident adult, but still didn't have much self-confidence in my interactions with others.

I began to sing with a combo led by my neighbor, now-legendary trumpeter, the late Dupree Bolton, who became my friend, my music mentor, and my crime partner. His trumpet playing was so beautiful that I now refer to Dupree as "Clifford Brown before Clifford Brown" (another great trumpeter). Dupree was one of the best jazz trumpet players, but he never got the attention that he deserved because of his addiction and his time in prison.

I met Dupree when I went to buy dope one day and found out he lived around the corner from my parents. He used to come to our house and he was always hungry. My mother loved him. He charmed her. He was filled with charm. My mother once asked him, as she was making lunch for us, why he always seemed hungry. When he said he didn't have money to waste on food she was stunned. But she kept inviting him to the table and worried about him. She'd ask me where he was if she hadn't seen him in a couple of days. My mom, my dad, my younger brother, and I all loved him.

Dupree, my longtime friend pianist George Lewis, and I spent a lot of time together. They used to dare me to sing at the Lincoln Theater Amateur Night where comedian Dewey "Pigmeat" Markham would charge out from the wings with a gigantic stage prop pistol that made the loudest sound, and he would "shoot" the losers. Pigmeat always "shot" me, and George and Dupree would fall out laughing and dare me to do it again the next week. I hardly ever made it through a song. It took me a long time to figure out that smoking marijuana made me tone deaf.

One night we went to a Hollywood jazz club called the Trophy Dash. Hampton Hawes was in charge of the open mic session. Art Farmer's brother, Addison, the bassist, and drummer Billy Higgins were on the bandstand. Dexter Gordon was in the room, but without his horn, along with Teddy Edwards, Harold Land, Ornette Coleman, and others too numerous to recall. As always, we had been smoking weed. As I stumbled through the first chorus, Hampton interrupted me. Standing up from the piano, he asked the audience, "Are there any singers in the house?"

Despite all the booing and getting shot by Pigmeat, for some unknown reason I kept trying to become a "jazz singer." I had been singing all my life. Some of my earliest memories are of my mother

and me singing duets. As I grew older, she began training me to sing
with professional intention. She taught me how to use my voice, how
to perform with dignity. My need to keep singing was stronger than
the embarrassment of getting laughed at. I knew that I could carry a
tune, but I didn't understand about being tone deaf until years later
when I took a hit on a joint and couldn't finish the tune.

Hampton pulled a similar stunt on Ornette who already was
listening to a different drummer. He wore bib overalls while the rest
of us wore suits and ties, and he had shoulder-length hair, which
was unheard of in the 1950s. Black people had just started coming
to Hollywood and felt we had to be at our very best with our dress
and language—everything had to be impeccable. You could feel
Hampton bristle at the sight of Ornette and, when he got up on stage
to play, Hampton ordered him off the bandstand.

A few days later, Dupree and I had yet another one of our routine struggles. I always had a day job and had to keep something for
lunch and gas, but Dupree never understood. His main objectives
were getting high and playing music. I was still trying to sing and we
played some "bucket of blood" gigs in and around Watts where people were always fighting and cutting and shooting each other. These
places had chicken wire between the bandstand and the audience
to protect the musicians. One time, Dupree and I even got as far as
Phoenix, Arizona before it fell apart over drugs and money.

Dupree and I had ongoing struggles over my not wanting to
spend all my money on junk (heroin), but if I stayed with him too
long, he'd always talk me into buying more dope. One day we got into
an argument over some money I needed to keep. Dupree felt I was
being stingy and socked me on my head. I was driving and I stopped
the car to duke it out with him.

As I was getting out of the car he said, "Just a minute, we're going to fight but you can't hit me in the chops, okay? I got a gig tonight."

He was relentless. He'd say, "Why don't you come on and buy dope?"

And I'd say, "I already said I don't want to."

He'd say, "Okay then, I want to go cop some dope, why don't you take me?"

Then he'd come out loaded and say, "This is the best shit in the world, I never had anything this good…okay, I understand you don't want to buy dope, but can you lend me $2?"

I'd take my wallet out and he'd see my money, and he'd say, "You have all that money and you don't want to buy dope?" And before I knew it, I had bought dope and used all my money.

After the early 1950s, I didn't see Dupree until 1968 when he had already recorded with Harold Land in 1959 and Curtis Amy in 1963. Both recordings received high acclaim. And then Dupree dropped out of sight in the jazz world. When we met up again in 1968, we were coppin' some dope in Watts and I was interning in a program at UCLA. We promised to get together, but we never did.

Then in 1987, I saw him playing on a street corner in San Francisco's Chinatown. I had been clean for only about a year and knew that I could not hang out with Dupree and stay clean. A couple of years later, when I felt stronger, I found him and Clifford Woods, another childhood friend, working a gig together in Oakland. Dupree would rest in Clifford's car between sets. I think he was sick, needed to fix. His playing wasn't the same. Sadness seemed to shadow him. I followed him out to talk to him, but he just kept walking. I saw him one last time shortly before his death in 1993. We didn't have much to say to each other.

When I heard he had died, I felt my heart break. I often think how great it would be to have Dupree on the bandstand with me again. He always knew what I was trying to do with the music. That type of experience with bandmates doesn't happen very often. Because of the nature of what is called "jazz," each of us is listening to how we want to be heard, or how we hear where the tune is going. But the great players, such as Dupree, are always with me, and sometimes they open a rhythmic, harmonic pathway that perfectly fits my melodic intent as a singer. I have been fortunate to keep finding this kind of musician to work with.

After my military discharge in 1948, I worked as a truck driver in L.A. and filled my weekends with music and red devils (Seconal) and speed (from Benzedrine inhalers), which made a cheap but great high. I was hanging out with Robert, a cousin of my first wife-to-be, Mabel, and we'd get high and go listen to music. Mabel's sister Lil had a boyfriend, Reggie, who had a big black custom Cadillac, the coolest car in Watts. Lil told me if I got together with Mabel, who I'd known since grade school (and we didn't ever like each other), we could ride with her in Reggie's cool car. I wanted to be seen in that car, and so did Mabel who, at the time, was an 18-year-old Jehovah's Witness.

Mabel was tall, slender, attractive, and very intelligent. As she stood on the corner with her mother, aunts, and cousins with the Jehovah's Witness *Watchtower*, Mabel became fascinated by the fast life that "night" people were living. She was a hairdresser, clothing designer, and seamstress making men's shirts. Sometimes she would sneak off with the whores and addicts and pimps to drop a pill, or smoke a joint, and she loved what she thought was glamorous.

As for me, I had returned from my sojourn in the Army well dressed with what I hoped was a sophisticated air, even though as a

19-year-old I was still pretty much a social and sexual novice, with nothing to say to girls. But here was Dupree and other guys on the block asking me if I'd "gotten any" yet. The pressure was strong to get started sexing or be found out to be the same dumb innocent I had been before I left town two years earlier. So Mabel and I got together and rode in that cool car, but we hadn't even kissed yet. We eventually got together sexually in a monumental struggle against her morality.

Robert, who was Mabel and Lillian's cousin, was a weekend junkie too, and for $5 he and I could shoot heroin. Mabel didn't know why we seemed to be asleep but yet awake and I wouldn't tell her. I begged Robert not to tell her either, but he did and pretty soon she was on the drug too. When I found her at Robert's apartment, she was nodding. I wasn't interested in a relationship with a drug-using junkie and left her, but she was already pregnant with my daughter. I married her after much hassling with my mother who strongly disliked the Jehovah's Witness religion and felt that the relationship would be doomed. But it was clear that I must do the right thing. I married her, but we never lived together, and Mabel never expressed a desire to do so.

My daughter, Denyce, was born in March 1950. At the time, I felt very little of what I was told fathers are supposed to feel. Regrettably, like my father before me, I have been pretty much detached from that role. With both her mother and me addicted and often in jail, Denyce was mainly brought up by her maternal grandmother. My mother loved her granddaughter and spent as much time with her as she could. But I saw very little of Denyce as a child. Between my own erratic lifestyle—using drugs and being in and out of jail and prison—our relationship was hard to sustain. While she was growing up, I met her teachers, and took her for rides, to the movies, and to spend time with my mother and father. We wrote stories and painted pictures. She is talented, intelligent, and creative. As an adult, she has been successful in corporate sales and as a filmmaker. I wish I could have been a better father to Denyce. Over the years, we have spent time together, had some fun, and also some difficulties. We make amends and, most important, we keep trying.

One day in 1951, my childhood friend Gene got angry with me for driving his car when he left it unattended in my parents' garage. When my back was turned, he hit me, knocked me down, and kicked me in the face. I was badly injured, but for some reason, I continued to call him my friend. When Gene discovered that a local drug store kept Railway Express money orders in a large unprotected drawer in the rear of the store, Gene, Dupree, and I began to regularly steal them. We forged signatures on the money orders and cashed them at banks, posing as credentialed representatives working for a legitimate insurance business that Gene's brother-in-law had co-founded. Gene then went on a highly visible spending spree. The three of us were all apprehended at about the same time, and in 1951 we all ended up going to San Quentin.

My parents were humiliated and outraged. They came to Union Station in Los Angeles to see me off on the train to San Quentin. I was wearing leg irons and handcuffs, and was chained to all the other prisoners. I was filled with shame, fear, and guilt as I watched my parents trying to deal with the humiliation I had brought to them. They had suffered through my trial and had to deal with the difficulty of facing church members, family friends, and relatives, some of whom had angrily confronted me. Having been so closely involved in my life since childhood, they also felt betrayed. There at the train station, between the tears of her heartbreak and her anger, my mother blurted out, "Maybe now at least you can find out what's wrong with you!"

I had been in jail in both Los Angeles and in San Francisco when I had forged the stolen money orders that Kilroy had me sign in the Army. So, though I was familiar with jail, where people are waiting to be sentenced or who have short sentences, nothing had prepared me for the experience of prison, where people are incarcerated for much longer stays, even life, or death.

Going into San Quentin in 1951 was at first terrifying. The prison was ancient in structure. We were handcuffed and searched until it felt like they practically turned my asshole inside out. We got our prison uniforms and were sent to the cellblock called the Guidance Center. Here we were tested for intelligence and vision, and had a physical exam. That's also where they decide what level of security each inmate needs; I was given minimum security. After that, they decide which prison to send inmates to. For some reason, they kept me at San Quentin. I was taken to my cell and, at least for the time being, had no cell mate. Inside, I found a Bible, a toilet, a face bowl, and two bunks, one over the other, attached to the wall.

Though San Quentin was racist and segregated in management, if you understood the rules and walked between the white lines you could get by. The only thing I felt about myself was that, as my mother had said, there was something wrong with me. It seemed that since childhood, I always gravitated towards people who broke rules. And, of course, the adults in my life were always breaking the rules or lying and then pretending that everything was all right, like my parents stealing my bank and my father lying about the air races in Cleveland that he couldn't have taken me to anyway because of the racial restrictions in American culture at that time.

From San Quentin in 1951, I was sent to Chino, a minimum security facility, where I did time with saxophonists Dexter Gordon and Hadley Caliman, drummer Roy Porter, and other renowned jazz musicians. Mabel visited me and brought some heroin that I snorted as we talked. All along, I worried that the guards might suspect something. That night at bedtime, I was still very high, visibly not myself. Suddenly, the barracks were stormed by maybe 20 guards who came in screaming and yelling for everyone to get on the floor face down. They searched everywhere, and everybody, and then, without a word, they grabbed me and took me to solitary confinement. The prison guards suspected I had been using and their suspicion was enough to send me back to San Quentin two days later.

At San Quentin, I asked to be assigned to work in the library, thinking that would be the logical place to "find out what was wrong with me" as Mom had put it. At that time, many operations and activities were run by prisoners, overseen by guards or "freemen," employees who were in charge of all non-critical operations of the prison. These included services such as the library, education, food service, and laundry.

The "freeman" librarian was a crusty, standoffish guy named Hermann Spector. For some reason, he seemed to trust me and my thirst for self-knowledge and he allowed me to order books from libraries far and wide. Then, he chose me to be the "legal librarian." The legal library at San Quentin consisted of hundreds of law books—penal code, Superior Court cases, and Appellate Court cases. I kept a catalog of pamphlet opinions handed down on cases in federal and state courts, and I worked with and for inmates who were fighting their cases, including men in segregation who were fighting prison rules and others on death row who were challenging their sentences. I would catalog court briefs about various cases that inmates read to see if anything useful applied to their own cases. I assisted condemned prisoners like Caryl Chessman, Burton Abbott, and other high-profile inmates, like George Jackson, who was later killed in an escape attempt.

Ironically, here I was working in a law library, albeit in prison, not exactly fulfilling my mother's dream that I go to Stanford and become an attorney "so you can be somebody." But I did continue to work in the library off and on during the 16 years I was in and out of prison, except when I was away at camp fighting fires for the state in the forests and mountains.

Incarceration gave me the opportunity to study psychology, sociology, philosophy, world history, and everything else about the human condition. I took courses through U.C. Extension. Surprisingly, I found prison to be a place of enormous intellectual stimulation. Some of the brightest people I ever met were on the "Yard" at San Quentin.

My mother, who never stopped encouraging me to learn about addiction so that I might find a way out of it, sent articles and suggestions about what I might read or research about addiction, Twelve Step programs, human behavior, and psychology—a continuation of the habit of studying that we had always done together since my childhood.

I was also seeing a psychologist who was one of the nicest, most helpful people I've met. He helped me to understand some things about myself, especially how I was hurting myself. I wish I could recall his name and thank him today. He also nurtured my education so that I might better understand and overcome my drug problem. But the biggest help I got was from my mother's research and the collection of articles about addiction that she sent to me.

I stayed away from the Twelve Step program for alcoholics because I didn't think I was an alcoholic and found very little
that was helpful to me. I also stayed away because they were always
talking about God and I was pissed at my mother's God. She was
always preaching to me about how God was going to "strike me
down," or "God is going to make you pay." (She went on with it until
one day I got so pissed I ran outside and gave God the finger and
then, just in case, I covered my head and fell to the ground. I guess
God was laughing so hard that he forgot to strike me down.) So,
I wasn't ready to listen to what Twelve Step programs had to say.
A Twelve Step program for narcotics addicts had begun in 1953,
though it would be decades before heroin addicts were accepted into
mainstream thinking about recovery, before we understood that
addiction was addiction, no matter what the drug, whether legal or
illegal. The only thing that addicts, who used "illegal" substances,
had at that time was ordinary incarceration or commitment to the
federal Medical Center at Lexington, Kentucky. This was supposedly
a medical incarceration where inmates would learn about addiction
and be punished for what is now widely accepted to be a health issue
that is more effectively dealt with by treatment.

When I was paroled in October 1953, I started using again
right away and began an affair with Gene's ex-wife, Aurora. Gene
was the one I went to prison with for stealing and forging money
orders. Aurora and I lived together for two years and used drugs. I
was working at U.S. Rubber Co. and also at a liquor store in Watts.
We bought a new car. In the middle of a disagreement about who
should drive it at the moment, I inadvertently backed it into another
car and wrecked it.

Gene got out of prison and came back to L.A. expecting to
get back with Aurora. Before prison I had always been intimidated

by him. I had always been Robin to his Batman, but I had changed. I had lost my fear of other men. He never acknowledged what he did to get us busted in the first place, or that Aurora, his ex-wife whom he had physically abused, had turned her back on him. (Gene would later be shot to death by the father of his second wife. Gene had assaulted her and she had escaped to her parents' home. Gene followed her and when he banged on the door, her father killed him with a shotgun.)

When I got out of San Quentin and went back to L.A. in late 1953, my parents had just returned from the Mayo Clinic, where my mom had been diagnosed with terminal cancer of the maxillary sinus. My mother, Ruth Reed, was the matriarch of the Veal family's sisterhood and her three sisters were devastated. Since Dad was away working on the train so much, he bought a trailer to park in the front yard so that Aunt Ruby, Mom's twin sister, and her husband, Homer, could come to L.A. from Fresno frequently and be close by to help my mother. Lois and Alzena, her younger sisters, were also there much of the time. Between the shame of my having been to prison and the beliefs of my three aunts that my mother's terminal condition was due to her despair over me, it was very uncomfortable for all of us. Though I was living with Aurora, I began to spend a lot of time with my mother.

Mom was being treated at Los Angeles County General Hospital and the doctors convinced my father, who I think was completely numb by then, to allow them to do exploratory surgery. The surgeons removed the bone under her right eye, and this turned an attractive woman into a caricature of her former self. Her eye was supported only by flesh, and it hung down rakishly. When she saw herself in the mirror she couldn't stop screaming. Dementia quickly took over and she didn't recognize anyone but me, not even her twin sister or my father. She would walk through the house calling "Edward, Edward!" Even when Dad and her three sisters were there, they did not seem to exist for her.

My aunts, who were brought up to believe that children should do and be what their parents wanted, could hardly stand the sight of me. They felt that my struggles with my mother had broken her spirit. I wonder if my family's not-too-distant relationship with slavery had a role in this also. Under that system, slaves had to be the way the master wanted them to be. Their mother, my grandmother, was born into slavery.

I once heard a quote by Ritu Ghatourey, an Indian author, who wrote, "What you live you learn; what you learn you practice; what you practice you become; what you become has consequences."

Only now, as I write, have I dared to take a long, hard, honest look at what occurred between my mother and me. Recalling our struggles, the unkind things she would say to me about trivial errors, the persistent anger we both carried—it is almost understandable how she chose to blame herself for the path I took and what that might have cost her. A clue to that was the day she caught me injecting heroin on the back porch a few years before, just before I went to prison for the first time in 1951 at age 22.

She fell to her knees and uttered through her tears, "Where did I go wrong?"

I hated myself. It took many years to get over that experience.

The answer she might have found years later, had she lived, was where she had gone *right*. From the time I was a little boy she persisted in helping me to educate myself, up until her death, and even into this very moment, as I struggle with this memoir. My mother taught me to sing, to emote, and to question anything that was unclear to me.

"It's not enough to *know*, Edward, you must know the why and how about the process," she insisted.

When I sing in front of an audience, people have always admired my demeanor. She drilled that into me from the time I was a little boy when she made me perform for holiday celebrations and religious pageants, or the parts in plays she got me with other kids, or when I was doing recitations.

"Stand up there and sing and speak with excellent diction, pride, and dignity," she would say.

She is now ever present in my music performances and lectures about addiction and joyful living when I speak to addicts, their parents, spouses, and other loved ones who are involved with addicted people. I cannot recall a time that she has not been present and vocal in my mind. I talk about her all the time. My mother was very intense. She wanted prestige, honor, and dignified attention for me—well Mom, I've gotten a bit of all of it.

Her fear about losing another child after losing four children in childbirth probably explains why she was so intent on keeping me close by her side. Her illness was heartbreaking to all of us. But in her more lucid moments, she and I had some fantastic conversations and spent a lot of time forgiving each other for the struggles we'd had, the unkind things we had done and said to each other.

My mother died of cancer on April 23, 1955. I was at work at U.S. Rubber when news of her death reached me. I drove to my parents' home and saw my mom lying on what had been my bed, with her hands crossed over her breast. I saw her beautiful wedding and engagement rings. And then the power of my addiction kicked in.

I immediately thought, "Well she doesn't need them anymore and they can help me out. I sure need some help right now."

I touched her hand. It was still so sweetly warm that I knew, for certain, she wouldn't mind. So I took both rings and went to the pawn shop. Then I went to my dope-dealing, San Quentin bakery friend Tommy's house and almost overdosed. Almost too loaded to drive, I somehow made it to Aurora's grandma's house where I was living. I told Gramma, Aurora, and our friend Bennie, who was visiting, about my mom's passing. We all cried. When Gramma left to visit her sister in another town, we waved goodbye and retired to our bedroom. Aurora and Bennie shot some dope and Aurora and I started kissing and Bennie started kissing me and Aurora started kissing Bennie. We all took off our clothes and spent the next 24 hours fucking and shooting dope.

When I returned to my parents' house, Dad was there and everyone was in tears and enraged about the missing rings. I pled innocence, but of course nobody believed me. Nonetheless, I kept denying it vehemently and was indignant at their "callous distrust in my time of sorrow."

Now is the time to explain about heroin and what it did to my soul even, and especially, during the saddest, most painful moments of my life. It spun such a tangled web inside that it felt like I could never go back and be normal because the last thing I wanted was to feel anything so intense as the death of my mother. The despair, the worthlessness I felt about myself let me take her rings. I welcomed the numbness that heroin brought and the illusion that everything would be all right. The high would last four or five hours, depending on the strength of the drug, which varied from source to source. The need to escape what was chasing me, all the wreckage, shame, guilt, and fear I had accumulated, was so powerful that even after a couple of years in prison without heroin, the first thing I would do when I got out was "cop" some dope and shoot it. Once the high was over,

I felt anxious, angry, and desperate to get more to stop feeling the feelings I had, so I could stop hating myself. The low opinion I had of myself would stay with me and influence every aspect of my life for many years to come.

4

Für Elise

DIANE

I loved living in Stamford. It was everything the Bronx was not—92,000 people compared to the crush of 1.4 million, no high-rise buildings blocking the sun, endless trees and forests and grasses, long bike rides on country roads, a tiny pond a couple of blocks away where we went ice skating in the winter. My sister and I unleashed the tomboys we couldn't be in the city, climbing trees and chain link fences, playing softball. Just a short bus ride from the shores of Long Island Sound, we spent long summer days at Shippan Beach smeared with baby oil, toes scrunched in warm sand, listening to Patti Page, the Platters, Paul Anka, and Elvis on transistor radios, dreaming about romance, and coming home smelling like hot sea salt.

When we moved, I was allowed to decide if I wanted to start Hebrew school. As a child in the Bronx, I went to Sunday school where we read stories from the Old Testament and learned about Jewish holidays. That part was interesting, but going to services was not. My parents belonged to an Orthodox synagogue which, among other alienating traditions, enforces gender segregation that grants males the privilege of praying in the main sanctuary, while women and girls must sit in the "women's section" behind some sort of divider out of sight of the men. I remember being in a balcony with a sheer curtain that further divided us from the all-important men praying below, and I remember the women gossiping and showing off their furs and fashion during services. Even at a young age, I found the entire experience to be outrageously chauvinistic and demeaning. So, at 11 years old, I was grateful to be given a choice and not forced to continue in a religion that made me feel like a second-class person simply because of my gender.

I started 7th grade in junior high still socially shy, introverted, and becoming something of a loner. I was uncomfortable at parties, and dreaded proms and formal dresses that we couldn't afford and I never wore again. I was overwhelmed by the noise and crush of people, and never understood or learned the art of making small talk. The only way I could handle those situations was to shut down. My brain, literally, felt like it had turned off. For a long time, people assumed my silence meant I was a deep thinker when in fact my head was too overloaded to hold a thought.

My memories of junior high are a jumble—sitting against the walls in the basement of Burdick Junior High with all the other students during Cold War-era bomb drills, the awkwardness of going through ballroom dance lessons with equally uncomfortable boys in stiff jackets smelling of mothballs, taking French and Russian, and getting my first C ever—in algebra, which killed math for me.

What made me happiest and helped to make the transition from child to preteen to teen more bearable was riding my bike on country roads in North Stamford, finding solitary little wooded nooks within blocks of our apartment where I could get away from everyone, going to the beach, doing well in school, and the piano.

I had my first piano lesson when I was 9 years old at the Bronx YWCA in a large room with about five other beginning students sitting at five pianos, all of us playing at the same time. When my mother realized that I still wanted to learn after going through all that cacophony, she mentioned it to my grandparents and they gave us the beautiful upright piano my mother had played when she was a girl. All through the televised McCarthy hearings, I practiced scales and pieces like "Für Elise" that every beginner learns. When we moved to Stamford, my mother found a teacher with long thick jet-black hair that was twisted into two huge buns pinned at the base of her neck. She was stern, intimidating, humorless, and uninspiring.

In high school, we changed to Mr. Russo who was the jazz band director at Stamford High and also gave private piano lessons. Over the years, I developed a wild crush on him and practiced at least four hours a day after school, demanding silence from everyone who was in the house while I played. I don't know why my mother indulged that behavior and didn't put a stop to my tyranny, especially when Mimi got eczema from the stress of whispering to her friends on the phone with a pillow over her head in a closed-up bedroom.

5

Narrow Escapes

ED

In 1955, I was tried on a drug sale charge (which involved a tiny amount of heroin) and a parole violation. I was sentenced to five years to life on that charge and sent back to prison. The classification board at San Quentin that made decisions about where inmates would be incarcerated sent me to Folsom Prison because I had talked back to a guard who called me a "nigger." Sending me to Folsom, an unimaginably violent and ugly prison, was a way to punish me for that transgression.

Folsom is the second oldest prison in California (after San Quentin), built in 1880. It is smaller than San Quentin and has fewer inmates. Folsom is a very scary place where life is cheap since most of the population is defined as hopeless, worthless trash. When I was there, almost every day someone was stabbed to death by inmates or shot and killed by guards. During that stint I somehow was allowed to go to Forestry Camp with other minimum-security inmates. We lived in a nice barracks and fought fires, tended forests, and built hiking trails. I loved being out there in the woods. I had never been in the woods before, except for picnics or school outings.

After doing three years and going before the Parole Board every year, I was paroled in 1958. They knew I had been working at Forestry Camp and doing a good job.

I didn't think I could live in Los Angeles anymore where the police were hostile towards addicts, especially Black men with smart mouths like me. They used to warn me, "We're going to kill you, nigger." Plus, I was a petty thief and my dad didn't want me around anymore.

So, I went to live with my mother's twin sister Ruby in Fresno. Anything not locked up and watched was fair game, as my aunt would soon learn. She finally asked me to leave.

I stayed in Fresno. Down and out, I chopped cotton and pitched watermelon, lived in a fleabag hotel, and ate sardines and crackers. This was about as low as one could go, but I would find an even lower level. One day, cleaned up and feeling good, I went into a music store to pass some time listening to vinyl records in the private booths that record stores used to have for customers to sample albums before buying them. I was playing jazz piano trio ballads and singing along, recording it all on a tape recorder that was for sale, trying it out as if I was going to buy one.

The storeowner, who happened to be a sponsor of the Al Radka Show, a local live noontime TV variety show, heard me singing. She liked what she heard and got me an audition. I was hired to be on the show every weekday and sang two or three songs, accompanied by a live trio. The audience liked me and I got good reviews from the critics. I loved what I was doing and thought that I was on a path to success. Still, every day after I was paid $50, I went and bought dope.

It didn't take a month before I blew that opportunity. I was told that one of the owners of the station—who happened to be Frank Sinatra—wanted to meet me. It freaked me out, but I was intent on meeting him.

In the meantime, I went to shoot dope. The dealer needed money to buy drugs so I loaned it to him. He was late coming back and I was having withdrawal symptoms. There were a lot of "tricks" riding around and around the block looking for hookers. I stopped one of them and told him that the girls were dancing naked upstairs in this fleabag hotel on the corner. The trick came with me, and I took him upstairs. I told him to put his valuables in a bag and that I'd put it in the safe for him. Then I told him the "nurse" would be down to inspect him for any venereal diseases. I asked him to take his pants off and said I'd hang them up for him. Instead, I took all his valuables and his pants. I left him there and caught a cab.

I got loaded. Then I remembered Frank Sinatra was coming. But I couldn't go back on television. The trick might see me and get me busted.

So I caught a bus for Los Angeles.

I lived in a hotel in Skid Row on 5th Street in downtown L.A. run by the Parole Division. It was a dismal place filled with desperados like me and mental patients. I started washing cars in Van Nuys and ran into a friend of mine, George, from the joint. He had a job and a great place and said I could stay with him until I got on my feet. I got a job in Hollywood parking cars and busing dishes and that took care of me.

The second day I was in George's apartment, I met a childhood acquaintance in the hallway. Danny invited me to his room and showed me two brand-new sawed-off shotguns. Danny was a certified aircraft mechanic and pilot, and was working in an aircraft repair facility owned by his uncle at Compton Airport. He had made those weapons and they were beautifully crafted.

When I saw Danny I got a little nervous because in the past his thinking had been both brilliant and angry. This time he had an idea about robbing a supermarket he had been casing that cashed paychecks for shipyard workers every Friday.

Heavily trafficked streets bordered three sides of the store. Along the fourth side was an alley littered with trash, overgrown with weeds, and never used by vehicles, providing a perfect getaway path. It was so overgrown that nothing could impede our escape. Every Friday the armored car arrived at 2 p.m. Two large sacks of cash were deposited in the office staffed by the store manager.

We waited there one Friday. When the armored car left, I called the manager's office from a phone booth in the store. I asked him to hold on for a minute, giving Danny and me time to walk into the office. We stuck our shotguns in his face, taped his hands and mouth, took the money, and drove down our quiet escape route. We went to Danny's girlfriend's house and split what turned out to be $40,000. I left, caught a cab and went to my dad's house. A week later, Danny asked me if we could do another job because he was broke. Danny was always a fool about women—he'd give them anything they asked for, but going through $20,000 in a week? I declined and gave him $500.

For me, having that twenty grand was among my most unhappy life experiences, ever. I was able to move into a decent apartment, buy a car and some nice clothing. I was also able to keep the parole officer at bay by paying a guy who had a business to say I worked for him and was making a good salary. Still, I really had a dilemma. I had money but no place to keep it. I couldn't risk arousing the parole officer's suspicion by getting fancy. I didn't know what to do. I buried the money in my father's backyard, then got anxious and dug it up. I put it under the floorboards in my apartment, in the refrigerator, in a spare tire. But I couldn't sleep, I was so worried that one of my desperado parolee acquaintances would rob me or I'd be caught for armed robbery.

The money became a curse. I found myself handing out $5 or $10 bills to junkies on a street corner. The girl I was seeing, Betty, said very sarcastically: "I didn't know you was Jesus." I had bought a Cadillac to be cool, but I hated that car worse than I've ever disliked *anything* before or since.

One night I was sitting in the car at the top of La Brea Avenue at a stoplight, still feeling overwhelmed and burdened by the money. I looked at the oil well in the center of the avenue at the bottom of the hill and wondered if I drove as fast as I could into the oil well, would it be enough to vaporize the car and myself?

The next day I traded the Cadillac for a beautiful little two-door '55 Chevrolet 210. As I think about all of this in retrospect I now can see that I was being taught some very important lessons about money and possessions, relationships, and the futility of trying to impress others and not listening to one's self. Of course, the main problem was that I had never had any self-respect.

I got into a relationship with another pretty girl I met on the elevator in my apartment building. Frenchy was a hooker, but I didn't understand that for quite a while. Frenchy, her sister Jane, and their two daughters shared an apartment nearby and they sure did know a good thing when they found me. When the cash was gone and I was back to busing dishes and parking cars, Frenchy said, "So long, fool!" But I discovered that she had taken some of the last things I had of any value. So one night I saw her walking on Western Avenue, and she turned into the apartment of a guy from the impoverished 5th Ward in Dallas, Texas where she had also grown up. This guy, Moon, had been grinning at me like a friend and when I had asked him if he knew Frenchy, he said he never heard of her.

Now, lo and behold, Frenchy was going into Moon's building. I thought that was interesting and I decided I wanted to see her anyway. Coincidentally, I was back in my desperado act. Danny and I had taken a couple of gambling houses and I had acquired the biggest .45 caliber pistol I had ever seen. It was old and I kept thinking that if I had to shoot the gun it would blow my head off, but there I was standing outside Moon's door listening to Moon and Frenchy fucking. She was yelling and talking obscenely and grunting, sweet-talking and begging for more.

When I first heard them I thought to myself, "Shoot the lock off the door and make them beg for mercy."

Then I started laughing. I laughed so hard at myself I almost shot myself in the foot. I ran out to the sidewalk and started walking to my car, still laughing. Before I knew it, this guy walking past me starts laughing too. I looked at him. It was the pianist Les McCann going home from his gig at the Pico-Dilly club on Pico just off Western Avenue. Just then, we passed a building with a flat roof. I pulled the gun out and threw it onto the roof.

He asked, "What's going on? What are you laughing about?"

I told him about this fool with the gun I just threw away and we both cracked up all over again.

To this day, I've never owned another firearm. It was a good decision. Two days later my crime partner Danny and his girlfriend were shot to pieces by the L.A. police, like Bonnie and Clyde in blackface.

I still needed to hang out with "cool" people, be seen, be in the know. One day I was going to Watts to see my daughter who lived with her grandmother, her mother Mabel, her aunt Lillian, and cousin Janice. On the way, I ran into an old Latino friend that I had known since we were children. Oscar's family was big in the drug trade and I began getting my dope from him again. It was some of the best in town. So copping dope for others became a pretty good business for me.

Sometime in 1960, saxophonist Dexter Gordon called me to cop for him. My friends, trumpeter Dupree Bolton and pianist George Lewis, had told Dexter about me. So I copped for him, and he and I shot the dope at another parolee's house, but the police and the parole officer (that Dexter and I both happened to be assigned to) had been watching the house and kicked the door down. They took us to jail for violating the conditions of our parole and three weeks later we were on the bus going back to prison. On the way we stopped at Soledad overnight. When I got on the bus the next morning, Dexter was gone. The next I heard of him, he was in Europe, where he would be for many years to come, recording and performing.

This time I was sent back to Folsom Prison. They were trying to wake me up by punishing me for the next three years. I spent most of it at the California Department of Corrections Road Camp in Megalia in Northern California with a group of other inmates where we dug ditches, fought fires, cleaned out culverts, and got trash out of rivers and off highways.

6

College

DIANE

In 1960, the beginning of my senior year in high school, I was in the a cappella choir where I met Heidi, a German exchange student who also played piano and violin, and was in the orchestra. We became best friends and shared the agony of secret loves, she with Mr. Jordan, the high school orchestra conductor, and me with my piano teacher, Mr. Russo, who also conducted the high school jazz band.

My parents were outraged about my friendship with Heidi.

"How could you do this to us?" they lamented. "Her father is a lawyer. You don't know who he is or what he did in the war." And then they asked the dreaded question. "Was he a Nazi?"

Heidi and I never spoke of those things. Neither of us had been alive during the war which was ending as we were born. All we knew was the happiness of our friendship and the unrestrained sharing of secrets and dreams that is only possible once in a while, when the right two people meet.

Early in 1961, my high school got an invitation from a German public relations firm inviting the choir, orchestra, and jazz band on a five-week goodwill music tour of Europe during the summer. We would travel through eight countries. All expenses would be paid with the exception of our airfare. It was an exciting, heady time. The school accepted the offer, and put together a committee of city and business leaders to help raise $10,000 to cover airfare for 90 students and chaperones. We gave benefit concerts to raise some of the money, got corporate donations, rehearsed at 7 a.m. before school started, got our passports and shots, and prepared to graduate.

Heidi decided to forgo the usual U.S. tour that foreign exchange students take during the summer and return to Germany after graduation to arrange housing for everyone when we performed in her hometown of Hanover. She sailed to Germany about a month before we would leave for Europe. Her boyfriend Rod, a jazz pianist and saxophonist with the band, her exchange family "sister," Ellen, and I went with her to the ship. We all cried watching her sail away, even though we knew we would soon be reunited.

A couple of weeks before our departure, a special meeting was called for all the students going on the tour and our parents. It seems the public relations company sponsoring the tour was a fraud and bankrupt. The first hint of a problem was when the company tried to get $3,000 for the tour bus out of the funds we raised for airfare. It was only then, evidently, that the city officials and lawyers on the committee who should have done due diligence at the outset finally vetted the company, but it was too late. The trip was canceled. The largest donations were returned and the rest of the money was divided among the 90 of us as small scholarships.

I was crushed. I spent the summer grieving the loss of my best friend and wishing we could have at least been in Europe before finding out about the swindle. Heidi and I wrote and sometimes I saved enough from my summer job to go to a phone booth at a time we had pre-arranged through our letters. I would insert $10 worth of quarters into the coin box to call Germany for a couple minutes of conversation with Heidi. We managed to stay in touch for a while, but it would be 39 years before we would see each other again.

During that summer of sadness, I had a file clerk job at a bank as I prepared to go to college. From sophomore to senior year of high school, I had totally committed myself to piano, and had decided to major in music in college. One of my friends from the choir, who was a gifted multi-instrumentalist and president of the choir, also applied to some of the same East Coast music colleges that I had. When the results came in, I had been accepted, Howard had been rejected. My mother said it was probably because he was Black, and that if it had been just a few years earlier, when colleges and universities had quotas for Jews, I might not have gotten in either. I was filled with anger and shame and guilt. I had taken it for granted that he would be accepted because he was, without question, the better musician.

He hid his hurt, but wrote a bittersweet message in my yearbook: "Well, well, you've finally made it. I am glad you made it. Too bad I didn't. Good luck." Years later, I learned that he went to work for the post office.

I took my mother's advice (she wisely knew that my passion for piano might cool being away from Mr. Russo of my high school years). I turned down the music college and went to Boston University where, as a freshman, I majored in music.

My newfound freedom was exhilarating. I made myself learn to smoke and drink coffee and wasn't too bothered by the dorm-imposed dress codes, where girls couldn't wear slacks or jeans unless it was below 10 degrees, or the strict curfews that required freshmen to be in by 10 p.m. I lived a block from the Charles River in one of the multitude of brownstone houses on Bay State Road that BU had purchased and renovated as dorms. Each building housed about 25 girls, so it was a homey environment compared to the one high-rise dormitory BU had at the time.

I loved the cultural diversity of Boston with its many colleges and universities and students who came from all over the world. Even in the early 1960s, before all the real excitement and change began on university campuses, for me the stimulation of living in Boston was unmatched. I was drawn to the maturity of students, especially men, from other countries. One was a Nigerian student named Zak whom I met during my sophomore year in 1963. We spent a lot of time together, talking and walking along the Charles River. As the son of a village chief, he was often dressed in a long white flowing robe, a traditional garment that was worn throughout much of Nigeria by important men.

I excitedly told my mother about him on one of our weekly phone calls. After a long silence she said, "Aren't you ashamed to be seen walking down the street with him?"

Her reaction shocked me. This was the same mother who, in one of my earliest and most powerful memories, slapped me, hard, across my face when I came home from kindergarten one day and she heard me chanting, "Eeny, meeny, miny, moe, catch a nigger..." and said sharply, "Don't you *ever* let me hear you say that word again!" It was the only time in my life my mother hit me.

I couldn't believe this stunning hypocrisy had come from the same person who taught me to value tolerance and compassion. I felt betrayed and angry. From then on, I would have a lot of secrets.

7

Birth of a
Jazz Singer

ED

When I was paroled in 1963, I went to Chico. Three members of the Foursquare Church used to come to the nearby town of Megalia on Sundays to hold services, and they had encouraged me to come live in Chico when I was paroled. By then I'd really had it with L.A. So I paroled to Chico and was taken in by an elderly couple from the Foursquare group, a deacon, his pianist wife, and their daughter. I got a job with a cantankerous old guy replacing, repairing, and installing septic tanks. I joined the Presbyterian Church and sang in the choir, and met a couple of teachers who befriended me and took me under their wing. One of them taught a social science class where I spent a lot of time talking about the prison system and how it worked to keep people coming back. That got me into trouble with my parole agent who told me to shut up. But I couldn't shut up, I was too angry.

I lived in a basement apartment with two Africans who wore native garb and I started seeing a couple of young women, a wealthy Native American, MaryAnn, and Judy, a young white woman, who was also seeing Ace, another Black man. One day MaryAnn beat up Judy so badly that it got the police chief's attention. He had a talk with me and told the parole division about my dangerous involvement with these two women. Then MaryAnn injured a couple of men in a bar who had called me a stupid nigger. She broke out all the windows and turned the bar furniture over. Between these incidents and my continuing to talk negatively about the prison and parole system, my parole agent ordered me to leave Chico. I moved to Oroville where I had a friend, Freddie, who I knew from Watts and from prison. He had a janitorial business and I went to work for him.

About that time I started shooting dope again, and would go to Sacramento to cop drugs for myself and Freddie. On one of those trips, the dealer Bill and I went to the Music Inn, a jazz club across the street from the Sacramento County Fairgrounds, where Wes Montgomery was playing. We would go to the club on "open mic" nights. After the first tune I sang, Wes invited me to sing another and to come back. Whenever I was there, he asked me to sing with him. I was too shy to say much to Wes, but I did talk to his pianist, Ed Kelly, who was on the gig. (I got to talk to Ed Kelly again in 2005 just before he left the planet, and we reminisced about that time with Wes Montgomery.)

Back in Oroville, my parole agent gave me an ultimatum: first, to stop talking about the parole system in classes and second, to stay away from MaryAnn or he would violate my parole. I refused to obey either warning so in late1963 they violated my parole and sent me back to San Quentin.

Two important turning points happened during what would be my last time in prison. The first involved music, which somewhat helped to mitigate the pain of being back in San Quentin for the fourth time. I had the pleasure of doing time with some of the brightest, most talented musicians, artists, writers, and thinkers I ever knew and, particularly for me, the musicians. Though I had been singing all my life, I had never consciously thought of myself as a singer even though, as far back as I can remember, I always had a song in my mind. Or I'd be trying to imitate some singer, or practicing a particularly difficult tune or solo while imagining that I was singing with and leading the Duke Ellington or Tommy Dorsey bands, just as Billy Eckstine sang with and led his band.

But I never had the nerve to consciously claim I was a singer. That is, until I met Ralph Bravo. He was sitting on the bleachers in the Lower Yard playing guitar and a small crowd of fellow inmates were standing around listening to him. I was thunderstruck by the sound he was pulling from that instrument. Ralph was a guitar player unlike any other I'd ever heard. At the time, I avidly listened to jazz guitar players, always with an analytical and critical ear, and hoped they would play tunes in a key that allowed me to sing along. I could sing every note of a Wes Montgomery or a Grant Green solo, or the solos of Tal Farlow and Barney Kessel. I never got enough of Billy Bauer or Johnnie Smith. I knew it was Charlie Christian's sound after hearing the first note. As long as I can remember, I had a secret dream of making beautiful music with a great guitarist, but I had never openly claimed that I was a singer. I mention these great jazz guitarists because each of them had caught my attention as a "wannabe" singer. Some were very unusual rhythmically or harmonically, and each was dramatically different from other players.

The day I first heard him on the Yard, Ralph was playing "Embraceable You." I had been enthralled by what Charlie Parker had done with those changes, but here was Ralph playing chorus after stupefying chorus, and playing the changes harmonically, rhythmically, and lyrically in ways I'd never before heard or imagined. Arpeggios, no matter how rapid, featured each note as crystal clear as a string of beads held up to a window. The chords of each chorus were different, sometimes very subtly different, but new, unusual and each chorus would be a stirring and dramatic variation but still, unmistakably, "Embraceable You." Without thought, I started singing along, because I just knew where he was going and when he looked at me, a huge smile of encouragement spread across his face.

In retrospect, I think I took Ralph's smile as tentative permission to think of myself as a jazz singer.

It was much more complex, of course. But later on, as we talked, Ralph was open to listening to what I thought about his musical approach, what I heard, what I thought I might sing against his playing. I was astonished because I felt so ignorant musically that the only way I could really respond to him was by singing. This was the beginning of a two-year conversation between us about our music. I have always had a good ear and that seemed to make him very eager to keep playing, happy to have a musical foil, a partner to share what he was working at on the guitar.

Ralph Bravo was the most advanced player I think I will ever hear. He was so accurate, each note stood out. I have yet to hear anyone to whom I'd rather listen, or have as an accompanist. To me, he remains incomparable.

Not long after we met, Ralph and I were assigned to food service where we got to work a few hours and then make music and talk music the rest of the day. I was the student, though Ralph never treated me like I was less knowledgeable than he was. We would hang out with musicians in the band room listening to recordings or trying ideas. The "war on drugs" resulted in many great musicians going through or being incarcerated at San Quentin, musicians like saxophonists Dexter Gordon, Art Pepper, and Frank Morgan, drummer Frank Butler, pianist Jimmy Bunn, guitarist Frank Washington, and my old trumpeter friend Dupree Bolton. The more famous of them would get a pass to sit in with the Warden's jazz band while they were waiting in the Guidance Center to be assigned to the prison where they would do their time. That band had been a fixture at San Quentin since the 1940s when then-Warden Clinton T. Duffy, who believed that incarceration should be geared to rehabilitation rather than punishment, introduced a series of reforms. Among them was the formation of the Warden's Show which consisted of jazz concerts and talent shows, produced and performed by inmates.

I was asked to join the Warden's 17-piece jazz band as one of three vocalists. Ralph was asked to join as well, but he refused, saying he wouldn't work for "The Man" even though the band was full of exceptional and famous musicians.

The band performed monthly concerts for visiting law enforcement officials and other prominent guests who had been invited to see "prison life" at San Quentin. For performances, the musicians dressed in tuxedos cut from the blue denim cloth of the inmates' clothing and dyed black. The food manager was in charge of transforming the dining hall into an audience space and served steak dinners for the guests during the performance.

The band was filled with world-renowned jazz musicians who created musical arrangements to accommodate all instruments in the band. Three singers, accompanied by various combinations of

instrumentalists, would be spotlighted. I sang some of my favorite tunes—"Body and Soul," "Everything I Have Is Yours," and
"Blue Moon." The audiences were always fascinated by the quantity
and quality of the exceptional talent that the "war on drugs" had
scooped up.

I sang with the band from late 1964 to 1966, along with the
great alto saxophonist Art Pepper. Of the three singers in the band,
I was the only one Art soloed with. He played under me as well, getting inside the tune as much as I did. After two years with him, I felt
I could sing the way I wanted to. When someone like that wants to
be with you on your tunes, you know you're doing something right.
But racial barriers were so high that Art and I couldn't talk much,
though we sure made some music that we were proud of. We spoke
about those times years later when we happened to meet up at the
Great American Music Hall in San Francisco as free men.

The friendship that Ralph Bravo and I had that began one day
in 1964 sadly lasted only until I went home in 1966. I never saw or
heard of him again and, after he left prison, neither did his family.
As far as anyone knows, he never recorded. And I haven't, before
or since, felt the same about singing with a guitarist, or any other
musician. I keep listening for Ralph's guitar sound. I talk about him
a lot—as someone who not only inspired me, but disappeared from
my life before I had a chance to thank him. I have always wondered
what happened to him, especially much later when I seriously began
my own musical career.

The second important event was an epiphany I had after reading that the Warden's wife was going on a luxury cruise with their
children. I woke up in the middle of the night and sat straight up,
with a clear and unmistakable understanding that I had helped to
make it possible for the Warden's wife to take her children to Europe

while my daughter was growing up in jail visiting rooms. It was a modern-day slave system. I didn't yet understand that facet of the system, but right then I promised myself I would not return and that I would help other people understand how it worked, how that system was arbitrary, capricious, and toxic, and using us up. By the time I got out in 1966, I had spent nearly a decade behind bars on two sentences and two parole violations for crimes and incidents related to heroin addiction. I had done four stints in San Quentin and Folsom prisons because I wouldn't stop using drugs and because I talked about that system.

For me, incarceration was a two-edged sword. On the one hand, I didn't have to worry about paying rent or other bills and expenses, or where I'd live and what I'd eat. The time I spent working in the San Quentin library as the legal librarian gave me access to all the books of the world. The civilian head of the library came to trust me and allowed me to order just about anything. I read voraciously and continuously, including Freud, Jung, and Adler. I had a great therapist. I had conversations with inmates, some of whom were the smartest, nicest people and greatest thinkers I have ever known. I discovered that some people are in prison for extremely innocuous reasons. And of course there was also the music.

On the other hand, to survive prison you had to stuff your emotions and learn to step over convicts just shot dead by guards or stabbed to death by other inmates. You couldn't react or acknowledge that anything out of the ordinary had just occurred, even when you saw that it was your friend who was dying an excruciating death as they rolled him across the Yard on a gurney. You felt your insides churn, but your demeanor, your facial expression had to be stoic.

One day I was standing next to the mess hall when I saw these guys hurriedly pushing a gurney toward the entrance to the hospital in the rotunda of the South Block. As they passed me, I looked at the contorted body lying on the gurney and was struck by a pain I had never experienced before. It was my friend Billy lying there, dying horribly. The agony expressed in his twisted body and facial expression will always be with me. Billy had been due to go home in a month and we talked a lot about what he was going to do for work. He was a talented musical instrument repairman and had many job offers. He had big plans, but there was never any detail. That concerned me, but he always smiled and said that it was all going to be really cool.

About a week after Billy died, a guy that he worked with in the print shop came up to me and said he was having a really hard time dealing with Billy's death. It was not so much that he had died, but that he had seen him sneak a gallon of printer cleaner into the bathroom. Wondering what was going on, he followed Billy and just as he walked in, he saw Billy drink a large cupful of the fluid. Billy immediately began to scream and fell writhing to the floor with his tongue and eyes protruding. Since that day in 1965, I have carried questions. Why did he kill himself? Is there an answer? Did anyone know? Does anyone care? There were no repercussions.

8

A Ruinous Affair

DIANE

I left the East Coast in 1964 after my junior year at Boston University. I had initially majored in music—classical piano—until my love for the piano wasn't strong enough to overcome my fear of performing in public. Stage fright was a big topic that was always talked about in the School of Fine and Applied Arts. I envied the music and drama students who were able to work through their anxiety by losing themselves in the music or the role and forgetting everything outside of themselves. I will always remember the utter fearlessness of one drama student who was so committed to becoming an actor that even her uncontrollable stutter did not prevent her from taking on speaking roles. Every word she struggled to get through was deeply agonizing; you could feel the whole audience getting tense, waiting. I got so nervous for her I would stop breathing. I felt I could *never* do anything that courageous.

My one year as a music major had been a disappointing time. The warren of tiny practice rooms in the basement was a horrible environment. The rooms weren't soundproofed, making it very hard to screen out the cacophony of other pianos, trumpets, drums, and everything else people were playing in those little rooms. It became increasingly difficult to practice with the same commitment I had during high school and it was agonizing to play before the piano faculty for midterm and final exams. The last time, I was so nervous that I played the Beethoven piece faster and faster until my fingers flew off the keys and froze, lost, in midair. I was so paralyzed by fear that I had no idea where I was and had to start all over again.

By the end of freshman year, I knew I didn't want to go through another year like the last. The piano teacher who had motivated me to work so hard in high school was no longer in my life. I decided to switch to liberal arts. For the next two years, I took classes that interested me without much thought about how I would pull it all together into a major. No one paid attention as I fell through the cracks. When final exams ended in June 1964, my senior year loomed with no major or possibility of graduation in sight. Worried about not being prepared to do anything after three years in college and how I really didn't want to be a secretary or trapped in suburbia raising kids, I thought about California.

I'd been longing to return to Los Angeles since my first trip two summers earlier when my mother sent me across country to help her youngest sister recover from a hysterectomy. For all my life, this aunt had been a romantic, though remotely known person. To me, she was a heroic figure who, in her twenties, frustrated by the lack of available men at the end of World War II, had moved across the country by herself. She had eventually married and had two children.

On the weekends, my aunt, her husband Jim, my 4- and 9-year-old cousins, and I would pile into the station wagon and go sight-seeing. We went from Hollywood and Grauman's Chinese Theatre with its legendary courtyard of cement footprints and handprints of movie stars, to Knott's Berry Farm, to the pick-your own apple orchards in San Bernardino, to a bullfight in Tijuana. I loved the dry heat of California, the freeways that were so much cleaner and more orderly than the highways back east, the mountains surrounding the Los Angeles basin whose rugged spaciousness so dwarfed the rolling hills of Connecticut, the tropical flowers blooming in outrageously bold reds and oranges and yellows.

The most beautiful part to me was the beaches and the space on those beaches, in contrast to the crowded, noisy places we went to as children to escape the heat and humidity of Bronx summers. Everything about Southern California sparkled brighter, smelled fresher, and promised an openness of freedom and dreams I couldn't have begun to imagine on the East Coast.

So, as I tried to figure out what I would do next, the idea of starting over in a beautiful faraway place and reinventing my lost self was really appealing, even if only for the summer. My college room-mate, Joy, was happy to come along. We got on a Greyhound bus and traveled cross-country for four days and three nights, stopping along the way at dingy little bus stations in the middle of nowhere, eating greasy hot dogs, drinking soda, and not bathing. Though I was exhausted from not being able to sleep sitting up, hurtling across the country at night was a magical time as we passed clusters of dimly lit towns tucked into the distant flatness of middle America. Those hours in the darkness made me feel wildly free, unattached to heaven or earth.

During my first couple of months in L.A., I stayed with my aunt and her family. Joy got a job as a file clerk at the StarKist Tuna Cannery on Terminal Island and soon moved in with a young carpet layer she had met at my aunt's house.

In late summer, my aunt went to Hawaii for a week's vacation by herself, leaving me with Uncle Jim to help take care of my cousins. Sometimes, on days when the kids were at camp, he would come home in the afternoon from his job as a refrigeration/air-conditioning mechanic at Douglas Aircraft and take me with him to the local Tiki bar, before going home to drink beer and watch television. I liked the dark, quiet, cave-like place with its Polynesian lanterns and colorful lights creating a cheap tropical backdrop. At 20, I looked so young I couldn't even buy a pack of cigarettes without being ID'd. Even so, Uncle Jim got the bartender to add a little rum to those exotic tropical drinks with a tiny paper umbrella on a toothpick stuck in a floating slice of lime so popular in Southern California.

One night after the kids were in bed, I brought a bowl of popcorn into the living room and flopped down on the floor on my stomach to watch TV. Who remembers what a naïve, inexperienced 20-year-old virgin was like in those days? For one thing, I had no clue what effect I would have on the 35-year-old man sitting on the couch behind me. And, even if I had thought about it that way, I would likely still have been unconcerned. He was my aunt's husband.

So, it caught me completely by surprise when he seemed to literally jump on top of me. A lot that followed was a blur. At some point he asked if it was all right to go ahead. By then I was so curious about sex, I lost touch with myself, my sense of morality, and what would spin out of that room and into the world of family with unthinkable repercussions. I said yes. Then it was done, there on the living room floor, with my young cousins sleeping upstairs.

Like many other sexually inexperienced young women in the early '60s, I found myself in a situation that I was totally unprepared to handle. Growing up in the '50s, we watched white families on TV shows like *Father Knows Best*, *The Donna Reed Show*, and *Leave It to Beaver* involving one-dimensional, simplistic people who were either good or bad. The mistakes they made were always repaired and lessons were cheerfully learned in a half hour. The real-life problems they might have had were glossed over, minimized, or denied. Complex issues that real people struggle with weren't acknowledged, and it generally wasn't acceptable to talk about what was seen as embarrassing, shameful, or taboo in the culture. So there were no opportunities to learn about complicated human feelings and situations and what to do with them, and I had no one to talk to.

Nor did I have much practical advice about relationships. What my mother said was to wait for sex until I got married and to marry a man who loved me more than I loved him because then he would never leave me. I couldn't blame her. That might have been the only advice she got from her mother, who quickly declared them engaged when my dad gave my mom a wristwatch for her birthday.

I know I could have stopped after that first night. I know I did come to my senses and dreaded the inevitable and shocking discovery if we continued. But by then I was trapped: first, having finally experienced intercourse and the awakening of my sexual self; second, because I completely confused sex with love; and third, because one of the other things my mother told me was that men had no control over their impulses so whatever happened was the woman's responsibility. An absurdly one-sided view unacceptable by today's standards, but that's what my 20-year-old self had to work with.

I had my first orgasm with him, as innocently and unexpectedly as the first time I realized I had been watching whale spouts shoot up from the ocean surface and gently evaporate into a thin mist off the Mendocino headlands. It all happened so fast, I wondered if I might have just imagined it. I was so ignorant, I hadn't even known about orgasms. When it happened, it was so perfect and effortless, such a pure letting go, that later I thought it must be like the experience so many addicts describe about their first high that set a standard they could never again replicate.

The extraordinary thing about that summer was how ordinary it all looked on the surface. Years later, my mother sent me a box of old letters I had written to her. The ones from that summer were all about the great weather, good food, how bratty my 11-year-old cousin was acting, the little weekend sightseeing trips. That must have been a defining moment for me when I learned to split myself off from the secrets and lies I was living to appear quite normal. I was a shy young woman with no meaningful language to explain the complex emotions I was feeling.

When my aunt came back from Hawaii, I moved in with Joy who had left the carpet layer and was living alone in a small apartment. She helped me get a clerical job at StarKist Tuna where she worked. One day my uncle showed up with plane tickets to Las Vegas and said we'd go for the weekend.

The following week when I was at their house and helping my aunt fold laundry, she asked me outright, "Is something going on between the two of you?"

I was terrified. The lie fell out of my mouth. "No."

She tried another approach. "You were both away last weekend. Were you together?" I can't remember what I said because by then there was a roaring in my ears and I couldn't hear the story I told her.

Sometimes I wonder what would have happened if I could have hit pause and rewound a little ways back, and at least admit right then and there that I had lied. It would have been awful, but nothing like what was about to happen. Recalling the moment when I had the chance to do the hard but right thing makes me scratch around in the graveyard of memory to figure out when I decided that it was all right to do what was forbidden, that lying was something I would use as a first line of defense, that I would actually sacrifice my very integrity. Yes, it was about the shame of being caught doing something I knew was wrong, being backed into a corner and too afraid to tell the truth and face what would come next, but still, why didn't I take responsibility for what I had done?

One night not too long afterwards, and just three months after the affair had begun, my uncle came to our apartment. Expecting me to be delighted, he announced that he had told my aunt about our relationship and asked her for a divorce so he and I could get married. Too stunned to respond, my head started pounding. I can't remember what I said to him. "*What* did you do?? Are you *crazy? What were you thinking?*"

The family fallout was immediate and severe. My mother blamed her sister for having left me alone with him for a week. My aunt blamed me for seducing him and never forgave my mother for not supporting her. I blamed only myself. Remarkably, no one blamed him, the one who had jumped on me, the one who was 15 years older than me, the one who would live into his eighties and die without being held accountable.

I saw my aunt, at her request. We sat in her car outside Joy's apartment. "Which part of *no* do you not understand?" She spit it out, furiously. "What will you do when this one doesn't work out?

Go to Chicago or New York and become some other married man's whore?"

But her harshest words couldn't touch the burning humiliation and shame that I would carry inside for years.

And so my first sexual encounter was a ruinous affair with a 35-year-old married man who was heading into serious alcoholism. It was a mistake that wrecked my family, resulting in my mother and her youngest sister not speaking for 20 years. After that, they had occasional brief, tense conversations. But there was no road they could travel together out of that summer of so many decades before and the bitterness followed them from one century into the next. Long past the time I blamed myself alone for what happened, long since I fulfilled my aunt's curse with one married man after another, and long after my life became open and honest, and even joyful at times, my mother still blamed her sister for enabling the ruin of a young girl ...

Jim was a Missourian. The strains of racial bias lacing his conversation made him an unlikely person, on those grounds alone, for me to get involved with. Our interests in music, books, and politics were very different, but he was kind to me and introduced me to new experiences.

The first, of course, had been taking me into bars when I wasn't legally old enough to drink. He taught me to drive a stick shift (something my father could never accomplish without us getting into a fight). And, of course, there was the sex.

During the first year, when we lived together, Jim took me on a series of road trips. We drove to the Grand Canyon and meandered through enchanted landscapes of mesas, buttes, and badlands in New Mexico's stunning Painted Desert. We explored old Gold Rush towns, long since abandoned, in the Sierras during the spring when the wildflowers were in bloom. We drove across the baking Southern California Mojave Desert in 125-degree heat to Lake Mead in Nevada and stopped somewhere along the way to sit in the vast silence with the cacti. It was there that he took out a pistol I didn't know he had and stood behind me, steadying my hand so I could fire it. It would be my first and last experience with any type of firearm.

Then, driving up Highway 99 through the Central Valley at the beginning of a long road trip to Seattle, I lost control of his Renault Dauphine while trying to adjust the side view mirror. The seatbelt-less car rolled diagonally from the farthest left lane across the freeway and landed upright in the emergency lane on the right near a fence separating the freeway from a cow pasture. We survived. The worst that happened was the car was totaled and I had a swollen black eye. But the "honeymoon"—and our trips—were over.

Traveling had been a great distraction, creating distance from the family wreckage my uncle and I had caused. Being on the road was like the feeling I sometimes get flying at 35,000 feet, so far above the earthly world that problems are more distant, less pressing. I don't remember how I felt during those trips. Other than loving exploring the West and Northern California for the first time, I was emotionally numb. I don't remember a single conversation or place we stayed at, or what we ate, or how long we were gone. I was running to escape my shame, my family, myself.

I had started leaving my uncle emotionally from the moment he came to the door to tell me he had left my aunt. And while, after the first year with Jim, I moved in with Joy who by then lived in Redondo Beach, it would take me three long years to fully extricate myself from him. Marriage was out of the question. In the beginning, I stayed because I saw him as having risked everything for me and I felt I owed it to him. Unable to talk to anyone about who we really were, I couldn't get close to people and stopped writing to high school and college friends. Jim's drinking intensified. We were miserable.

When I was finally able to return home and face my family in late 1966, I agreed to let my mother make an appointment for me with a psychiatrist but the help or insight or relief I hoped I'd get didn't materialize. He listened, and then he waited for me to say something else, and when I didn't, we sat and looked at each other— well, I probably looked at the floor—for the rest of the session, which to me was further evidence about how hopeless I was that even a psychiatrist didn't know what to say.

I returned to California eight months later, got a job at UCLA typing and proofreading manuscripts for the graduate business school publication, and rented a tiny basement studio apartment in Beverly Hills. Jim had become an emotional war zone, increasingly using alcohol to dull the pain of losing his children and the disappointment that it wasn't working out between us. He'd often call me and threaten suicide and I would rush to Long Beach. I desperately wanted to move on, but couldn't bring myself to break it off for fear that it would be my fault if anything happened to him.

By December 1967, the only way I could think to extricate myself was to quit my job and return home to finish school, which made my mother happy. But by the next day I knew I loved living in California too much to be driven away because I didn't know how to leave an unhealthy relationship. Feeling defiant, I rented a one-room, furnished apartment in West L.A. Then I returned to the personnel office, interviewed and got a secretarial job at the Western Center for Community Education and Development through UCLA Extension that would start on January 2, 1968.

9

"Free Ed Reed!"

ED

Paroled to Sacramento in 1966, I lived in a little downtown hotel on J Street. I went to work washing dishes in a restaurant on O Street where many legislators had lunch. Needless to say, I was pretty unhappy. I was the chosen one in my family, supposed to do great things, and there I was washing dishes. So I began shooting heroin almost immediately after being paroled.

Then, still using periodically but not hooked, I tried to get my act together. I was promoted to "Banquet Captain" at the restaurant and took a sociology class at Sacramento City College. The class was taught by Larry Malmgren who was probably one of the most open-minded people I had ever met, especially for a Southerner. He wanted to understand about California's penitentiary system and how I got there. He thought I was a bright guy and wanted to know why I went to prison four times. He invited me to his home—a risky thing to do, but that's who he was. His wife Geri and I became friends as well. They kept inviting me to their house even when school was out. We'd sit and talk for hours. I began to think that I wasn't as bad as I had been led to believe. Maybe there were things I could do that would be valuable.

In Larry's class, I met some students who were involved with the farm labor movement. They invited me to move into their co-ed boardinghouse called Banyan House, run by the Presbyterian Church. It was full of women. I hadn't been sexual with a woman since 1963 and immediately had affairs with two of the women who lived there.

We were working on community organizing activities around racial parity, social welfare issues, the farm labor movement, and LBJ's War on Poverty. I became friends with Meredith, one of the activists in the farm labor movement, who introduced me to Freddy, a brilliant Latino working on his doctorate in sociology. Freddy connected me with the Catholic Welfare Bureau where I was hired as a community organizer to work on race relations and labor issues. Along with volunteers from Banyan House, we went into the fields to organize farm workers. We believed that teaching farm workers English would help them, and we convinced a farmer who had some space on his property in Sloughhouse (east of Sacramento) to loan us a building where we held English as a Second Language (ESL) classes and provided daycare for children of migrant farm workers.

The project attracted considerable media attention, resulting in Georgina Allen visiting Sloughhouse. Georgina was a public school educator and administrator concerned about the children of farmworkers. She liked that we had daycare for kids while their parents were in the fields and that we were teaching them English, reading, writing, and arithmetic. She was curious about my background, which had been mentioned in one of the newspaper articles. As we got to know each other, we became good friends. Little did I know how important her role would become in my life.

At Banyan House we had a lot of meetings about issues affecting poor people. We had food and clothing drives. At one of the meetings, someone suggested trying to organize telephone company workers, and we decided to take them on about wages and job discrimination. In the beginning, the phone company wouldn't talk to or acknowledge us in any way. So we organized a thousand people to send ten cents too much when they paid their telephone bills. This was before businesses computerized their billing systems and since most of their accounting was done by hand, the phone company had to write 1,000 checks in the amount of one dime each to refund the overpayments. After the first month, they'd had enough and agreed to talk to us. Those conversations ended with telephone workers negotiating better working conditions, and the phone company hiring people of color.

An organization called California Center for Community Development (CCCD), located in the central California town of Del Rey, was headed by Ed Dutton, brother of Fred Dutton, who was a UC Regent. Ed Dutton asked me if I wanted to come to Gilroy where they were training trainers and organizers. The faculty included people like Cesar Chavez, co-founder of the National Farm Workers Association (later changed to United Farm Workers) that was central in making the 1966 farm workers' march on Sacramento a success. After two months of training, I returned to Sacramento. Since we had been getting a lot of press for the migrant farm worker classes at Sloughhouse, a local Sacramento TV station, KCRA, sent reporter Spencer Michels (who continues to report on social justice issues for public television) to interview me about the work we were doing.

I was sporadically auditing classes at Sacramento City College where I talked to students about prison and parole and my organizing work. After the KCRA interview, as had happened before, the parole supervisor ordered me not to talk publicly anymore or be on television. When I told the class about this, the teacher invited the parole supervisor to the class where he and I could talk about prison and the parole system. The parole supervisor was so unconvincing in trying to defend the system that the students laughed at him. He came back to the class the next week with my file to show them what a criminal I was. The students objected and challenged the legality of sharing what was supposed to be a confidential file. Later that night, an older woman who was a student in the class told her son-in-law about how the parole officer had tried to warn the students about this "convict" in the class, and had brought my file to prove to everyone what a bad person I was.

The following morning, the parole supervisor had parole agents arrest me, claiming I had been using drugs. The fact was, I had been using heroin all along, but at the time I happened to have a prescription for morphine from a dentist—a fortunate bit of timing since heroin comes out in the urine as morphine.

With the one call I was allowed, I called the phone tree we had set up to turn out a crowd when needed for protests. I told them I had been locked up because of what happened in the class. Within two hours, hundreds of people came out to protest my arrest. They blocked all street access to the parole office and that got the media there. They chanted, "Free Ed Reed!" and tied up all the phone lines (it was possible to do that then) to the parole office.

Within a few hours, the parole supervisor was called by the Director of Corrections asking why I had been arrested. As fate would have it, the Director turned out to be the son-in-law who learned over dinner the night before that one of his supervisors had broken the law by publicly sharing a parolee's confidential file. The Director, believing that the parole supervisor had acted out of vengeance for the humiliation he suffered in the classroom, instructed the parole office to let me go that night and fired the parole supervisor the next day to turn off the unfavorable publicity.

The parole supervisor had been around the block many times. He knew a junkie when he saw one. Because the rules of parole had a phrase "with or without cause," he had been on firm legal ground to arrest me. But he had no business sharing confidential information from my file in public. That was against the law. By publicly accusing me of being a practicing addict, he had made me—the lying, thieving dope fiend—legitimate in the eyes of all onlookers.

Later, I used to see that parole supervisor on the street and he would smile and wave. He knew that I had beaten him. Sometimes he shook his finger at me. "Oh what a tangled web we weave!" he would laugh. I really had to shoot heroin then to celebrate that rare victory over oppression.

My friend Bill Dorn and I formed an organization we called the Sacramento Singlemen Self Help Group to organize homeless male migrant farm workers and alcoholics that we discovered sleeping in the weeds by the Sacramento River. We organized a march to City Hall where Singlemen demanded the right to food stamps, shelter, and access to health care and social services. Some of the men had family members accompanying them. The march received national media attention. But even though the reporter covering the march said migrant farm laborers were treated like slaves, those findings were quickly forgotten.

In late 1967, the UCLA-based Western Center for Community Education and Development, or WCCED (pronounced "wicked"), a federally funded anti-poverty program, came to Sacramento to train community organizers through the local Office of Economic Opportunity. I participated in that training and was invited to UCLA as part of a group of eight interns selected from several Western states. Beginning on January 2, 1968, we would spend six months being educated in methods of improving and practicing our community organizing and training skills.

Part Two:

After
the Summer
of Love

10

UCLA

ED

At the Los Angeles Airport (LAX), we were met by Diane, an attractive young woman who was the interns' secretary. When we got to the Western Center office in Westwood, MaryAnn, the interns' supervisor, whom I had met in Sacramento, was talking on the phone to one of the interns. We heard her say, "I'm sure you'll find a way to get here, my dear, we're depending on you." She was talking to Dale, who had not been able to scrape up enough money to get from her home in Arizona to Los Angeles. MaryAnn said, "Well, dear, we'll be waiting for you," and hung up. I was outraged that a program designed to train low-income community organizers had failed to think about giving us travel advances. I couldn't stop myself from asking her, "Do you even understand what poverty means?" The Western Center quickly provided Dale with a plane ticket and we were finally ready to start working. But that initial impression left a sour taste in my mouth.

One day I was having donuts and coffee at my desk when that cute secretary, Diane, walked up to me and asked if she could have one. She was a nice person and I was attracted to her. I was honored that she asked. We had a few more pleasant encounters and I asked her out. I had never been so impressed by anyone. She was open and kind, smiling, young, and beautiful. I told her when we were out on our first date that I was an ex-con and an ex-junkie, but she had no idea what that meant or what she had gotten herself into. Diane had a studio apartment on Gayley Avenue and I stayed there often. Before long, we were living together. People at the Western Center were alarmed. Diane was 24 and I was a 39-year-old ex-convict, "ex"-addict, as I had described myself to her, on parole.

But we persisted. I was fascinated by Diane—she was so present, attentive, accepting, and loving.

DIANE

Ed was like no one else. He treated me as an equal despite the difference in our ages. He was the first man who took me seriously, who saw my potential before I was aware of it, and from whom I learned so much. His ambitions and thinking were young and fresh and relevant to the times. He was creative, articulate, and radical. We made passionate love. We laughed endlessly, read Sartre, listened to Miles Davis, Wes Montgomery, and John Coltrane, went to foreign films, and explored Griffith Park on rented bikes.

Ed took me to Watts, three years after the devastating riots, to meet his beautiful, spirited, artistic 18-year-old daughter, who had grown up in a Jehovah's Witness home with her grandmother, aunt, and mother—the woman Ed had married 18 years ago but had never lived with. He showed me the Watts Towers, now a state and national landmark, that he had watched being built as a kid growing up in Watts. The 17 interconnected 90-foot-high sculptures of steel, glass, wire, and porcelain had been built by Italian immigrant Simon Rodia over a 30-year period. The community thought he was crazy and Ed said kids used to throw rocks at him. We went to Baldwin Hills where I met his father and stepmother who lived in a large house on beautiful sloping grounds with the last few of the many children they had fostered over the years since Ed's father had remarried.

Early on, with pride and a straight face, Ed told me he was an ex-junkie and an ex-con. "That's good," I said, "because I just got out of a relationship with a drunk and am not about to get involved with someone else with a drug problem."

A few days later, he left me in the car and disappeared into a dilapidated building in downtown Los Angeles. On the freeway driving back to Westwood, he started to nod, his eyes were very heavy. Though I had never before seen anyone on heroin, I knew something was very wrong. He admitted he was loaded. He says I punched him in the face, but since he was the one driving, I think it was probably more like I punched him in the arm to wake him up. He said it was a slip and promised it wouldn't happen again.

But it did happen again, and again, and again. By the second week of any month, he was borrowing money from me and anyone else who believed the outrageous stories he told about why he was short of funds because of this, that, or some other thing. We smoked a lot of marijuana together, but weed wasn't heroin. It was like he had a second job, working to get the money and transportation to buy, prepare, and shoot heroin into his arm.

I came to think of heroin as competition. The intelligent, funny, warm, loving person I was getting to know would withdraw and vanish into what became a human shell, drifting into himself, locking everyone out. I hated it. I fought it. I was angry because he kept saying he would stop and didn't. I couldn't square the person he was when he was straight—or at least just high on pot—with the person who was loaded and nodding and dropping lit cigarettes on the bed. Yet, I kept letting myself believe the elaborate stories he told about why he ran short of money and didn't press him to pay me back.

I felt betrayed over and over but couldn't bring myself to leave. Somewhere in the back of my mind I remembered the guy I had just left and his alcoholism and thought, right, that wasn't supposed to happen again—and then thought, but this is different. I wanted the eloquent creative strategist who was fighting to empower others and change the world. I really wanted to make it work, and that became my main job for many years to come.

ED

The Western Center was charged with monitoring programs that received federal poverty program funds through UCLA from the Office of Economic Opportunity (OEO). One of our projects as interns was to provide technical assistance to a major hospital in L.A. that had an OEO grant to build a mental health facility to serve poor people, which sounded great—except it was going to be built in Century City.

That was crazy. Century City is an upscale area where few poor people would ever be found. But we interns didn't have degrees, so neither the Western Center staff or hospital project staff could hear our argument about how useless and counterproductive it would be to build a facility to serve poor folks who could be arrested, in all likelihood, if they were caught in that part of L.A.

I wasn't prepared for the level of dishonesty and ignorance about poor people and people of color that many of the project staff displayed. The reality was that they knew nothing about the urban poor. They hadn't even talked to any poor people. So we interns decided the best strategy would be to develop a mixed media project as a way to educate staff about poverty and the population they wanted to serve to better understand what they were facing. We photographed and filmed street people who were homeless and hungry, addicted and injecting themselves on the sidewalk, drunk, aged, sick, and dying. I took pictures all the time, no matter where I was or what I was doing. Sometimes, when I was away from the office all day and had to come up with a plausible explanation to account for my time, I'd hand them the camera.

Our media project was a success. As the images of poverty were projected on the screen, we simultaneously played an audio recording of news programs, arguments and fights, and sights and sounds of the city. It was a powerful presentation and convinced the project to shift gears and get input from the community before they built anything. And then they also accepted us as partners.

Meanwhile, at the Western Center we were spending a lot of time in communication and organization management workshops with Jack and Lorraine Gibb who were humanist psychologists, and other experts. I went to La Jolla in Southern California and spent a week with Carl Rogers, one of the founders of the humanistic (or client-centered) approach to psychology. Rogers came to the Western Center and held a class for the interns about the group process he pioneered where participants tried to increase their sensitivity, responsiveness, and emotional expressiveness by freely verbalizing and responding to their emotions. The techniques Rogers taught were the foundation for the work I do today. I was amazed by his teachings, but it would be many years before I would be able to apply those teachings to myself and in the work I do with others.

One of the most difficult experiences I had at the Western Center was on April 5, 1968, the day after Dr. Martin Luther King's assassination, when I met Bob, the program director, in the office. He said, also pointedly looking at one of the Black secretaries, "I know you must feel awful because of Dr. King's death. You have my deepest sympathy."

This thoughtless, ignorant man, who had a position of power in a well-funded anti-poverty program, was stupid enough to convey the idea that the loss of Dr. King didn't affect him, a white person, at all. It was all I could do to keep from punching him in the face. I never spoke to him again. Good old self-righteous me. My anger was about a lifetime of injustice and disappointment aimed at Blackness.

Despite the mostly rich learning experiences I had at WCCED and the fact that many of the exceptional people I worked with supported and believed in me, I continued to use drugs and lie about myself to myself and to everyone I encountered. My unspoken quest was to find my true self and do good in the world. I didn't want to keep using drugs or go back to prison. But I had never acknowledged my true feelings of inferiority, fear, and ignorance to myself. Nor had I ever put into words that my only method of coping with those feelings was to keep shooting heroin, smoking weed, and challenging people. What I did was to ostentatiously drive a university car when I went to cop dope in Watts to show the street denizens how cool and successful I had become.

I had felt so fortunate to be chosen to work with this great group of Ph.D.s on the UCLA campus—the university of my dreams. My naiveté had me believing that these people had been anointed and guided by a God (that I didn't even believe in) and were thus honest, just, and fair. But I would soon be disappointed to learn that some were self-serving people working there who cared only about themselves.

One day, MaryAnn and her husband invited the interns to their home in Pasadena for lunch and to do some planning about our work. When we got there, we were all blown away. They lived in an enormous medieval-looking castle at the top of a mountain, like a place Dracula would have been proud to call home. Set into the majestic 20-foot-tall steel picket fence was a giant gatehouse and an immense and ornate gate like those in fairy tales. The gate was the entrance to a winding road that ended in a cobblestone cul-de-sac that in my imagination looked like Cinderella's kitchen door. We were all freaked out. None of us had imagined such a place existed in reality.

MaryAnn greeted us as we entered and climbed a couple of flights of stairs in near darkness to a long hallway that led to a large, bright, sunny room with walls covered with firearms and a huge window overlooking the winding road and the gate. The window had a large telescope attached to the stone sill. In the center of the room was a beautiful table with a soup tureen, a stack of small soup bowls, and a plate filled with crackers. There were chairs around the table for all eight of us. There was also a large pitcher of water and glasses.

MaryAnn smiled brightly and told us to sit as she ladled the soup into the bowls. We obediently began to eat soup and crackers, which were quickly consumed. MaryAnn then passed out cards imprinted with our daily $30 per diem and asked us to sign them over to her before getting on with our business of the day. I could not believe my ears. She was going to charge each of us our per diem for a cup of soup, crackers, and some water.

I was the first to speak. "Are you serious? Are you crazy? Do you think we're crazy?"

She looked at me as if I were insane, maybe even about to become violent. I think they had been pulling that swindle for quite a while and had never before been called on it. I went on a rant about "the war on poverty" and the collection of guns on the walls, mainly handguns of recent manufacture and only a few collectibles. Who were the weapons there to shoot?

I was really angry. We all went to the library to work. Someone picked up a stack of workbooks that we interns had spent a lot of time developing to give to the programs that we worked with. The workbooks had become so much in demand that they were in short supply. But as we looked closer, we saw stacks of our unused workbooks. It dawned on us that she was using those workbooks for her own private workshops. No one said another word. We just got up and left, feeling cheated.

Back at the Western Center there was a series of meetings with staff and interns, and closed-door meetings with senior staff to discuss the future of the program. OEO decided to close WCCED and created a new program under different management and in new quarters. The new program was called Western Community Action Training Inc. (WCATI) which, like WCCED, would work with community program staff in the OEO Western Region, assisting programs to make the best use of their resources by developing more effective methods of organizing community to fight poverty. All of the interns left, but I was asked to stay on. I traveled to Fresno once or twice a month to work with migrant laborers and their families, and I worked at WCATI. But life soon caught up with me once again.

In May, I learned that I had been indicted by the District Attorney of Sacramento County for writing a check with insufficient

funds in late 1967 before I left for L.A. At that time, I had been working for the Catholic Welfare Bureau, but I never had enough money
or heroin to keep me hidden from myself. So I had written a check
for $25 to buy drugs knowing I didn't have enough money in the
bank to cover it. That was a parole violation for a parolee who had
served time for writing bad checks.

When I got notice of the indictment, I told Dr. Roy Azarnoff, a
trainer at the Western Center, about it. He was one of the best people
I've known and one of the people who believed in me. Of course I
lied to him about the details, like the reason I wrote the check and
the fact that I was still a junkie. He accompanied me to court in
Sacramento and posted my bail.

DIANE

In early June, Ed returned to Sacramento and, naturally, I went
with him. On June 6, 1968, the night before his trial, we watched
television in stunned horror as Bobby Kennedy was shot and killed
after celebrating winning the California presidential primary. That
assassination was just two months following the murder of Dr.
Martin Luther King Jr., three years after Malcolm X, and five years
after JFK and Medgar Evers.

The next day, after a short trial, the judge found Ed guilty. It
mattered little that so many people, including myself as his former
secretary and a few other character witnesses, testified under oath
that he had a good job and was not using drugs. Of course I knew
better, but none of the others did; how could they? They only knew
what Ed told them.

He was immediately removed from the courthouse and taken
to county jail in handcuffs to await sentencing. It happened so fast, I

couldn't imagine driving back to L.A. without first seeing him. The next day I went to the jail, said I was his secretary and needed to talk to him about work-related things before leaving. It wasn't a visiting day, but the guard gave me special permission to see him.

In the few months I had known Ed, I had never seen him in such bad shape. He had shot a lot of heroin in the days leading up to the trial and was withdrawing. It scared me so much that I decided to stay over and go back to see him the following day during normal visiting hours. When I told Ed I'd be back, he said I should call his friend Georgina and see if she'd come with me.

Ed had talked a lot about Georgina, a recently retired public school administrator in her sixties, who had met and befriended Ed when he worked with migrant farmworker children. Her husband had died a few years earlier, leaving her to raise a 15-year-old daughter. Emblematic of her great generosity, Georgina had also opened her house to a soft-spoken, shy young man, Doug, who had been a Merchant Marine Officer, and she supported him financially while he studied to become a potter.

Georgina and I met at the jail and stood in line together waiting to sign in. The guard instantly remembered me—the white girl was here again to see the Black junkie.

"You were supposed to have left yesterday. What are you doing here?"

I tried to explain about work, but he said flatly, "No."

I sat with Georgina in the waiting room, and when they called Ed's name, she said, "Just come in with me. It'll be all right."

That was all the reassurance I needed to break into jail. I ran into the visiting area, which was laid out like a rat maze, rows of glass cubicles rounding into other rows, and I raced around looking for Ed.

When I found him, I sat down and quickly said, "I probably don't have much time." Then his eyes got very big, and I felt a hand come down on my shoulder.

"What are you doing in here?" the guard bellowed.

He escorted me out of the visiting area and I waited for Georgina.

Despite all that, I still couldn't drive 400 miles back to L.A. and leave without seeing him again, so I made an appointment with Sheriff Misterly. I wouldn't have had a chance if he had realized that the Ed Reed I was trying to visit was Black, or that he was the same person who had been getting a fair amount of media coverage as a community organizer in Sacramento—not to mention the same Ed Reed who had been the focus of a large noisy protest of supporters outside the Parole Office the year before when the parole supervisor had him locked up for failing a drug test. But when I told the sheriff how his deputy had manhandled me and not even given me the opportunity to explain why I had to stay over, he smiled in a grandfatherly way, picked up the phone and hit the speaker button.

"Deputy," he barked.

"Yes. Sheriff!"

"I have a young lady here who needs to see an inmate. Name's Ed Reed. I'm sending her down to see him. Don't give her any trouble."

There was a long silence.

Then, "Yes! Sheriff!"

He smiled and stood. We shook hands. I thanked him and went downstairs to see Ed.

Before he went to Sacramento for his trial, at the urging of colleagues from WCCED, Ed had applied and been accepted to UC Irvine through the Educational Opportunity Program (EOP). While he waited in the Sacramento jail to see whether he would be sent back to prison, a large group of his supporters started a campaign to get legislators and community people to write to the court and parole board on his behalf, asking for a short sentence so he could start fall quarter at Irvine. It was a partial success. Instead of sending him back to prison, the judge sentenced him to six months at what is euphemistically called the county "farm"—a minimum-security facility located outside of Elk Grove, south of Sacramento—and two years of probation. Ed's attorney and some of the other people who had helped get him that far then successfully petitioned the Probation Office to shorten his jail sentence to three months so Ed could start school in the fall.

Though we wrote to each other nearly every day, I couldn't bear the thought of being apart for so long. I applied for my first credit card and flew to Sacramento every weekend to see him during visiting hours. And so, for the first time since we met, I got to experience Ed off drugs.

His letters were full of social and political commentary, and dreams of all we would do once he was out. He was tender and loving in a wondrous way. His words melted me and gave me great hope that things could work out after all.

"Somehow I want you to know the value of life with you," he wrote, "to juxtapose the pain of non-trust pseudo-caring, of fear, of falsity, and most of all of aloneness, never being close, never relaxing with someone, of breathing a sigh only when alone. How different from having you near, needing you for who you are, what you are, for what you bring inside you. How long I looked for you, my darling."

It was completely out of the realm of my experience to understand what it was like to be locked up with so many people and have so much uncertainty about the future, but I liked knowing that my visits provided at least one constant he could hold onto.

He wrote: "There is, strangely, a relatively quiet spot here amid all of these wounded, striving egos. This quiet calm eye of the storm is inside me. True, it is deep inside and at times hard to find, but on [visiting] days like today my life has the gift of your solace, friendship and love ..."

One of the young men Ed met in jail drew psychedelic art on envelopes in exchange for cigarettes. It was the iconic art form of the 1960s, the abstract swirling of shapes and colors, the chunky calligraphy with political, spiritual, and social messages used ubiquitously on concert posters, album covers, murals, and in alternative newspapers. The highlight of my week was getting one of those envelopes that had made it past the jail censors—who sometimes didn't like the more political messages on some of the envelopes—with a letter from Ed inside.

One day in July my sister knocked on the door. She and her boyfriend had driven cross-country from Connecticut and decided to surprise me. I was floored. Thrilled to see my sister, but also a little fearful. She knew some things about Ed, but not that he was presently in jail. In the few days they were with me, we saw Janis Joplin at the Hollywood Bowl and then drove north through Central California in 100-degree heat in my non-air-conditioned VW bug to Sacramento to introduce Ed to my sister.

Although she said very little at the time, many years later Mimi would say, "I was shaking my head all the time wondering what you thought you were doing with this guy in jail!"

The day they left to drive back to the East Coast, I told my sister I would tell our parents about Ed so that she wouldn't have to make the choice of either telling them I was involved with an African

American man or not saying anything. I had put off telling my parents about him. I had no illusions about how the news would be received at home. This relationship would be as unwelcome as the one I had just ended. Even without knowing about prison and drugs, they wouldn't understand, much less approve. I finally wrote telling them I was seeing a very nice man who was sensitive, intelligent, caring—and Black. Because I was moving around a lot, having left my apartment in L.A. and staying in Sacramento at Georgina's house when it was close to the time for Ed's release, it was a while before my mother and I spoke.

In one of his last letters, Ed wrote about his reaction to reading Marshall McLuhan. "How many things occur in our immediate environment with us oblivious?" he asked. "I am more and more firmly coming to believe in the idea of multi-media experiments to broaden perception. I want to start with myself."

He was talking about continuing the mixed media work he had loved at WCCED when he simultaneously listened to music, read a book, watched television, and absorbed it all. He ended the letter with a thought that turned out to be eerily prophetic, "Darling, I hope you can get ready for a life in bedlam."

He was released in September, after three months at the county "farm." As we drove away from the jail, I fantasized happily celebrating his early release and the new life at U.C. Irvine that lay ahead for us. But Ed quickly dropped me off at Georgina's house and took my car. He returned loaded.

11

Irvine

ED

I was surprised when so many people—from my Western Center colleagues to legislators who had known me from my community organizing in Sacramento—came to my assistance to keep me out of prison and get my jail sentence reduced. Because I felt so bad about myself, a part of me had no idea why they would have cared enough to write letters and make phone calls to Probation. But their mobilization on my behalf worked.

I got out of jail in time to start the 1968 fall quarter at Irvine. I had such mixed feelings. The campus was like an island off the South Carolina coast. Living in Santa Ana and taking classes on that isolated, mostly white campus felt instantly unwelcoming, filled with people who, to me, observed me the way I might look at a Martian gorilla.

To cope with the hostile feelings inside me and what I felt was directed towards me from others, I would drive the 80-mile round trip to Watts in South Los Angeles, shoot heroin, and drive back in a near-unconscious state to attend my 1 p.m. criminal justice class. That was taught by one of the most ignorant people I had ever met. He expounded upon San Quentin State Prison as if he knew something about it. But I had been in and out of San Quentin four times and had left my cell there only two short years before. So to make myself look good, I argued with him a lot. Other than trying to be important, I had no idea what I was doing there.

DIANE

We found an apartment on Minnie Street, a low-end apartment ghetto in southeast Santa Ana which was on its way to becoming one of the city's poorest neighborhoods. The cheerless stucco, concrete, and asphalt that dominated Minnie Street reminded me of growing up on the streets of the Bronx. Our apartment was in one of those two-story buildings that look like motels with the long outside walkways on each floor. We were settled in time for Ed to start school and I got a secretarial job in the Student Activities Office on campus.

That's when my mother caught up with me and called on the phone. In the few weeks before Ed was released from jail, I had stayed with friends in L.A. and then in Sacramento with Georgina, so this was the first time we talked since I sent the letter telling her about Ed. I knew she would be upset. She was still traumatized about the affair with my uncle and I would have done anything to avoid telling her about something I knew she would be completely opposed to. I thought about how, when my grandmother really disapproved of something, like my teenage crush on Harry Belafonte, she'd say, "How can you put his picture on the wall. You'll give your mother a heart attack." I knew she didn't mean it literally, but it described a situation that to her was at the highest level of unacceptability.

Sadly, those were the same words I used when I told Ed how much I dreaded telling my mother about our relationship. Her reaction was much worse than I could have imagined. She was beside herself with anger. "I won't be able to look the rabbi in the eye again," she spat through the phone, and said things I would never have imagined she could direct towards one of her children.

I was shocked and deeply hurt. Even more heartbreaking, I would have felt deserving of her condemnation if she had said that when she learned about my uncle, rather than in reaction to someone she had never met solely because of the color of his skin.

Ed took classes. I worked. It felt like we were settling into a routine. But it wasn't long before he was driving to Watts nearly every day for heroin. Most of the grant money he received for fall quarter went right into his arm. When he ran out of money, he pawned my gold charm bracelet or earrings, and once in a while even forged one of my checks for $10 or $20. Our arguing began all over again. My hope that this new start would be enough for him to stop using evaporated.

We had a brief reprieve from our struggles when Georgina invited us for Thanksgiving to her cabin in the hills of Comptche, 14 miles inland from the beautiful former whaling town of Mendocino. Ed and I drove to her house in Sacramento on Highway 99 the night before Thanksgiving in a blindingly thick tule fog, and then to Mendocino the next morning with Georgina, her teenage daughter, and informally adopted adult son.

That marked the beginning of a lifelong love Ed and I would have for the Northern California coastline, a love that would survive no matter how rough our life together, or apart, became. For me, it was a place to reconnect with myself. Whether in sun or in storm, I spent hours sitting alone on the Mendocino headlands, waves crashing against the rocks, sometimes spotting migrating whales. Georgina, who had no idea Ed was still using, extended a standing invitation to spend time in Comptche whenever we wanted to, whether or not she was there. For many years, when we went to the cabin for a few days Ed would be kicking heroin. While I never saw his withdrawal to be as overdramatized as is often portrayed in films, it was bad enough. During the few days we would be there, his body craved the drug that would instantly relieve his discomfort. His aching muscles, sweating, insomnia, and involuntary kicking would force me to get out of his way and sleep in another bed.

The progression of disappointment and anger deepened. By the beginning of winter quarter 1969, I was so depressed and felt so defeated and hopeless, I just wanted to die.

ED

It didn't take too long for Diane to figure out that I was driving her car nearly every day from Irvine to Watts to cop some dope. At some point, she refused to give me the key, so I would hotwire the car. I swore that I was off heroin forever but she could always tell. She started keeping track of the mileage and pretty quickly knew I was still driving to Watts. So I disconnected the odometer. Then I needed the stuff more than ever to be able to go home and face her with the pain over the love in her eyes, with the shock, hurt, and humiliation in her voice, a woman who only knew how to love with her all, withholding nothing, whose whole world kept shattering.

One day in January 1969, at the beginning of winter quarter, I drove Diane to her job on campus at 8:30 a.m. and then decided to go to Watts. Interestingly the need to get loaded did not seem like a bad feeling. It was more a feeling of urgency and excitement, as if one is going to retrieve a sorely missed possession. I had to hurry because I might miss something by going to Watts, but the drug seemed like the only sane thing to do. I didn't think I was a no-good person, because I would right the wrong as soon as I copped and returned in time for my criminal justice class.

But I overdosed on that particular day. The dealer, a childhood acquaintance, spent a lot of time reviving me in a bathtub full of ice and injecting me with saline. I remember getting back into the car and driving away, almost running into a parked car and having to stop because my eyes wouldn't stay open. Then I drove some more and had to stop again. Somehow I got onto the 405 freeway to Santa Ana. All I remember is there was a driving rainstorm. I saw a house slide off a hill. I saw a giant spinning truck wheel in the wing window. Somehow I drove the 40 miles to the U.C. Irvine campus without mishap. I called Diane and asked her to meet me at the Student Health Center. She nearly fainted at the sight of me. It will always be a mystery how I managed to drive back to campus in that storm.

That overdose nearly cost my life. The next morning I was unable to get out of bed. The pain in my back was horrendous. I could barely move.

DIANE

The day Ed drove to Watts in a heavy winter rainstorm, shot dope, and overdosed was another lucky day for him. Once more he was with people who cared enough to revive him. He called me at work to say, in a thick, loaded voice, that he was driving straight to the U.C. Irvine Student Health Center to get help with his addiction problem and asked me to meet him there.

I couldn't imagine how that would go. It was 1969. Irvine was a wealthy white community in conservative Orange County where people had bumper stickers that said "America, love it or leave it." Except for a small number of students of color, this newest campus in the U.C. system was predominantly white with little experience interacting with African Americans, much less heroin addicts. There was a palpable sense of apprehension about the presence of the "underprivileged" EOP students of color on campus.

Only two years earlier, a group of 30 Black Panthers, men and women, had marched into the state capitol in Sacramento armed with rifles. When we first came to Irvine in the fall of 1968, Eldridge Cleaver, a parolee, author of *Soul on Ice*, Black Panther minister of information, and Peace and Freedom Party presidential candidate, came to campus and gave a speech. Shortly after that, Cleaver fled the U.S. and went into exile. A few months later, we learned from Ed's parole officer that the FBI had us under surveillance because Ed knew Eldridge from prison.

Ed arrived at the Student Health Center that afternoon looking terrible. He was put in an exam room, still very loaded and groggy, and he started to nod. A nurse came in, looked at him, and quickly backed out of the room. She returned with a psychiatrist who naturally knew nothing about heroin and thought Ed was minutes from death. I tried to explain that the danger was over, that Ed was just still very loaded from heroin. But the psychiatrist was freaked out and flatly said he was calling an ambulance to take Ed to the county hospital.

I panicked. If the county got involved, the parole office would find out Ed had violated parole by using drugs and he'd be sent back to prison. I ran out of the room and found Dr. Gerald Sinykin, the medical director of the health center. Quickly explaining what had happened, I begged him not to send Ed to the county where he would be arrested.

"He's an addict," I said, "not a criminal. Prison won't help him. I don't know what to do, but I know prison is not an answer."

Dr. Sinykin was a compassionate man. He agreed to cancel the ambulance on the condition that Ed and I promised to return in the morning and talk about what to do next. But by the next morning, Ed couldn't get out of bed. His back was in intense spasm and, despite a year of lies, I knew this was not an act.

By the second day, Ed managed to roll onto his side and agonizingly, slowly, stood up and walked down the stairs to the car. We thought that something must have happened during the time he was unconscious when he was being revived. Heroin is illegal. In 1969, when someone overdosed, they couldn't be taken to a hospital without risking arrest. People were often left to die, but some were fortunate enough to have someone around willing to help. Help took the form of slapping, hitting, and pulling arms and legs to increase heart rate and breathing, and injecting a saline solution to flush the drug out of the body. I once found Ed overdosed on the floor of the bathroom in our apartment—a possibility he had never warned me about, or told me what to do if it ever happened. I was so scared I instinctively did the right thing. I screamed, slapped, and pulled at him until thankfully he opened his eyes and, clearly annoyed, asked me what I was hollering about.

We assumed that the people who had revived Ed must have pulled a muscle or dislocated something to cause the pain he was having. Dr. Sinykin said we should give it a few days for the pain to subside and get X-rays taken at Orange County Medical Center, the teaching hospital for U.C. Irvine's School of Medicine.

We returned home where Ed spent a second, sleepless night in pain. Dr. Sinykin knew he couldn't prescribe anything containing narcotics, so he gave him sleeping pills, which were no help. By the third day, I couldn't take doing nothing any longer. At least I wanted Ed to have something for the pain. I told him if he thought heroin would help, I would help him get it. It was hard to watch him suffer knowing that, aside from its addictive qualities, the medicinal value of opiates for the relief of pain is unmatched. That was the first and only time I knowingly helped Ed get heroin, but it was worth it.

When we got to Watts, Ed pointed to a dealer standing by a building. He got out of the car and slowly made his way over to the man. Then we went home. Ed lay down on the carpeted living room floor, which he had discovered provided the best support, and prepared to inject the heroin with a homemade "outfit" or syringe. He dissolved the heroin in a spoon, dropped in a bit of cotton to filter out particles, drew the mixture up into a glass eye dropper with a needle attached to it using a thin wet strip cut from a dollar bill and wrapped around the tip of the dropper, and injected it into his arm. Then he slowly relaxed and was finally able to sleep.

The next morning Ed needed another fix but the eye dropper he used as the syringe part of his outfit had been damaged the night before. So I went to the store for eye drops. And because we were so short of money I decided to steal it.

I had never stolen anything. At the store I was so nervous I couldn't even find the section where the eye drops were and foolishly asked one of the employees for help. Then I walked around the store before going back to the eye drops and tried to surreptitiously remove the eye dropper from the package. I dropped it in my pocket and walked around a little more before starting to leave. As I walked through the door, the same employee stopped me, showed me the box and asked for the eye dropper.

I was busted, terrified and humiliated that I couldn't do a simple little thing like take an eye dropper without getting caught. They brought me to the manager who asked me why I did it. I blurted out I was a starving student and needed it for an art project. They let me go with a warning. We still needed the eye dropper, so I bought the eye drops and knew that, without a doubt, my fate would have been very different had I not been white.

Towards noon, Ed thought a hot bath would help soothe the pain as the drug started to wear off. I went a few doors down the hall to ask Willie, one of our neighbors, to help him into the bathtub. Willie was a big man and easily lifted Ed into the tub where he was soaking when the doorbell rang. It was Ed's parole agent and a narcotics officer.

Though the student health center had canceled the ambulance, Ed's name had been run through the system because it had been called in as a heroin overdose, and eventually the parole office was notified. They had come to collect a urine sample. We told them that Ed's back had gone out, but the narcotics officer was furious to see Ed in the bathtub and pulled his arm out of the hot water.

"So," he sneered, "you thought you'd be clever and get your skin all wrinkled to hide those fresh needle marks?"

He gave Ed a bottle and told him to pee in it. Ed said he had urinated before getting into the bath and would start drinking water as soon as he was helped out of the tub. The lack of space in the small bathroom forced the narcotics officer to step outside the door when Willie returned. As Willie bent down to pick him up, Ed urinated into the water that was draining out of the tub.

Then we all waited for about an hour while Ed drank glass after glass of water and told the officers what had happened to his back. Whatever he said, and he was a good storyteller, he never admitted to using heroin or overdosing, and the urine sample came back clean.

The next day we went to Orange County Medical Center. The X-ray showed nothing, but the doctor decided to hospitalize Ed for a while and run more tests. Over the course of the next seven weeks, the pain never lessened. The strongest drugs they prescribed were tranquilizers and muscle relaxers, a combination that caused hallucinations. The only time Ed had any pain relief was when he smoked the joints that a friend from U.C. Irvine brought to the hospital. I don't know how they managed to escape detection, but by then Ed had been moved from a crowded ward to a semi-private room in a temporary building, so they must have just lucked out that no one walked in or smelled anything.

By the time hospital staff finally managed to get Ed out of bed and weigh him, he had wasted away to 110 pounds, having lost over 40 pounds. At that point, the doctors decided to discharge him, telling Ed that all he needed to do was to be strong, "bite the bullet," get up every day and walk, and eat to gain back the weight he lost.

He came home and ate voraciously. He developed a painstakingly slow system of getting out of bed that took about 45 minutes and then walked shakily up and down the walkway outside the apartment.

During that time, I again saw him in a completely new light. He wasn't running away from life by using drugs, but working hard to withstand huge amounts of pain and do what he was told to do to get better.

Nonetheless, he didn't improve. Despite consuming large amounts of food, he continued to lose weight. When we went for a follow-up appointment at the county hospital outpatient clinic, they told him the pain he was having was gas.

Shortly after that, Willie's wife, Ruthie, came to see us and jolted us out of our inertia with the clear wisdom of one who, without more than a grade school education from a probably inferior public school in the South, was able to pinpoint the most obvious, commonsense thing to do. "If the first doctor don't help you," she said firmly, "then it's time to go see another one."

As a veteran, Ed was eligible to receive health care services from the Veterans Administration. We drove to the Long Beach VA emergency entrance in a neighbor's station wagon so that Ed could lie flat in the back. After one horrified look at his emaciated body, the ER workers rushed him inside on a gurney.

Later, when the doctor found me in the waiting room, he said Ed had a huge area of infection spread across his lower back. At first they thought it was tuberculosis of the spine, but after further tests, it was diagnosed as Pseudonomas, an opportunistic bacterial pathogen that can cause life threatening infections in compromised immune systems. Ed's was the second case of this type of spinal infection that the VA had in its records. The first person who had it ended up crippled, with a severely twisted spine. Fortunately for Ed, they knew which antibiotic to pump into him and he was put in a body cast from his chest to his hips.

Within the first week, he gained enough weight to necessitate cutting a large hole out of the cast to give his stomach more room. Ed's parole agent, who had been keeping track of Ed's progress, visited him at the VA. He left impressed by Ed's strength and resilience,

and successfully convinced the Parole Board to discharge Ed from
parole in August 1969.

The X-rays did not show a line from where Ed injected his
last fix to his lower back, so the VA doctors couldn't say for sure
that his injecting the drug caused the infection. Still, I couldn't have
been more certain that coming so perilously close to death after having gone through so much pain and suffering over those six months
would convince Ed not to risk using drugs. But again I was wrong.
After months of being bedridden, as soon as he was physically able
to get into a car and drive, he went straight to the dealer.

Ed had no intention to return to school. By late September,
he was back at work with the community organizing group that had
grown out of the Western Center at UCLA.

12

We Do?

ED

Being in the hospital for so long gave me a lot of time to think. When I wasn't hallucinating from the non-narcotic tranquilizer/ muscle relaxer drug combinations they gave me for the ever-present pain, I was surprised to discover my own prejudice and expressions of hatred and fear and how it fed my addiction. At UCLA, I had been trying to do things I wasn't confident about because I didn't know how to do them. With the exception of one Latino, all the trainers at the Western Center were white men with Ph.D.s. At Irvine, I didn't feel like I belonged or was wanted or that the experience I had lived was valued in the classroom. Discomfort can come from so many sources and become the kind of dynamic that is fed by stress, which in turn increases the need for the drug. I didn't understand how the discomfort of those situations and the stress from enormous self-doubt were driving my addiction.

So even after seven months in two hospitals, nothing had really changed. I still didn't know what to do with those feelings of inferiority. And I didn't know what to do about Georgina's insistence that I marry this young Jewish white woman who had to conceal the true nature about who and what I was from her family and our friends, and deal with their reaction to race on top of it.

Getting married wasn't our idea. It wasn't a good idea at all, but we passively went along with it because—as crazy as it sounds— we didn't know how to say no. The issue first came up when my new parole officer came to our apartment soon after we moved to Orange County in September 1968. He said that a condition of my parole was we'd have to get married if we wanted to live together. To do that, I had to divorce my first wife whom I married in 1950 when she was pregnant with our daughter. I started the necessary proceedings and when the petition was heard, the court found that since we had never actually lived together, the marriage could be annulled.

By the time the annulment was finalized, I had already been discharged from parole and the state could no longer dictate my private life. So, while we didn't have to get married, the idea had taken on a life of its own with Georgina. She had been accepting, supportive, and generous to both of us. She was also a generation older than me and felt very firmly that marriage was the next logical and right thing to do.

DIANE

When neither of us found a voice to take control and stop it, Georgina took on the work of planning the wedding at her house in Sacramento. We invited our families. My dad called to say that my mother and my sister would come, but he couldn't get away because of the store. Then he said what he always said during the awkward times when he didn't know what to say or how to say what he really wanted to. "You know we just want you to be happy."

It was remarkable that he was the one who called. I was always much closer to my mother, whereas my father and I had a hard time communicating. He and I struggled around his projected fears, but he wouldn't talk about himself or his feelings. I never knew what he really thought about Ed, but the undercurrent of his not talking about Ed then or ever—even after he and Ed met a few years later and got along quite well—was a clear message that the subject was off limits. Period.

We got married in November 1969. It was a small wedding. Ed's stepmother, brother James and daughter Denyce and her husband drove from Los Angeles (his father didn't come, either). My mother and sister flew in from Connecticut, and a few other friends were there. Ed and I were in a state of disbelief and paralysis the entire weekend, unable to do much more than be carried along by the momentum.

And here's the awesome power of denial. Even at that point, I hadn't really asked myself why I was marrying a heroin addict. If I said anything to myself about it at all it would have been something like: I love him, I know he can change, and I know I can help him. No one asked me that question because no one in my family knew about Ed's addiction, much less his criminal record (except my sister who had met him when he was in Sacramento County jail). Even Georgina believed that he wasn't using because, again to protect him and keep him out of prison, I told her he wasn't doing drugs during his trial in Sacramento and that's what she testified to on his behalf.

I wore a dark brown satin mini dress and a homemade waist-length hippie necklace that I copied from one I saw on display in a shop on Haight Street. It had long slender gold chains in a spider web design joined at the center by a large brooch and looped around so I could slip my arms through and wear it like a chain vest. We hadn't even thought about rings until the last minute, and then we scrambled around until I found a silver ring I had once bought from a street vendor in San Francisco.

We chose a track of slow, beautiful, wistful music from Miles Davis's *Sketches of Spain* to play softly in the background during the ceremony—but someone put the needle on the "Saeta" track by mistake, which brings to mind matadors strutting around the ring just before the bulls are let loose. Everyone tried to ignore the very loud and distracting music, which made an already tense situation even more bizarre. At some point, the whole scene felt so ridiculously funny I struggled not to start laughing uncontrollably.

Throughout the weekend, my mother was stoic and gracious. The thing about her is that she could always put on her dignity and function in practically any situation, no matter how hard it was for her. She loved being a mother and believed it was the best thing she had ever done, that it had given her life meaning. Throughout my life, no matter what choices I made that angered or disappointed her or that she clearly could not understand or condone, she always stood by me, and she always chose me, even when I didn't deserve it. Again and again, she demonstrated that she would not let anything jeopardize her relationship with her daughters.

I've often wished that Ed's mom (who died long before I met Ed) and my mom could have known each other. Together, I think Ruth and Simonne—such dignified and proper ladies of their time— would have figured things out and been great support to each other as Ed and I continued in our struggles.

Then the wedding weekend was over. Everyone had come and gone. We packed up the car and headed out of Sacramento to start married life together.

We were traveling with Frodo, our beautiful 5-month-old pure black Burmese-Siamese kitten, named for the hero hobbit in *Lord of the Rings* that I had been reading when we brought him home. Throughout his 18 years, Frodo was our hero cat. We picked him out of the litter because he, like his mother, would jump into the air to catch a rolled-up sock and bring it back to us. He grew up traveling in the car, back and forth from L.A. to Sacramento or Fresno, San Francisco, or Mendocino. When he was little, he rode on Ed's shoulder. If he got too rambunctious, we blew a little marijuana smoke in his face and he would curl up in a large green bowl in the back seat and go to sleep. He was so loving and smart and funny we couldn't get mad when he ate holes through Ed's wool sweaters and socks or brought garter snakes into the house and played with them under the couch.

Of all the cats that would follow him, Frodo was the one we needed most during those years. He put up with everything—our terrible fighting, cigarette smoke, steadily disruptive moving around from one place to another, and lots of other people and their animals. He was so mellow we never needed to put him in a carrier to go to the vet or anywhere else. He went for long walks with us in the city and in the hills of Comptche outside of Mendocino. He was at home wherever he was and charmed everyone. He was a constant and often the only brightness in our sad lives.

As we drove out of Sacramento and onto the causeway over the rice fields between Sacramento and Davis, the trunk (which in early VWs was in the front of the car) suddenly popped up, stopping just short of hitting the windshield. As it blew open, all of our wedding presents flew out, bumping and scattering across the freeway. A lot of stuff was shattered, blown away and ruined, including a beautiful red enamel cookware set that was badly dented and scraped from bouncing along on the road and the 18" tall sculpture of hands lovingly entwined like a double helix that broke into a dozen pieces. We were able to salvage very little—though we actually did glue the sculpture back together. In retrospect, that scene was a fitting metaphor that would describe our lives for a long while to come.

13

Stockton

ED

After recovering from the months I spent in county and VA hospitals with an infection that nearly killed me, I went back to work for Western Community Action Training, Inc. The work was based in Fresno in the Central Valley, so Diane and I moved there right after we got married.

It was the strangest time. Neither of us had had any notion about getting married. We were both struggling with my addiction. The lies it caused made us miserable. We didn't know how to be honest with friends, family, or ourselves about our lives, but we cared enough about each other to keep trying. Still, marriage felt crazy. Like, what was the point? What were we trying to accomplish? We never asked ourselves those questions.

Within about a month, WCATI sent me to provide technical assistance to the San Joaquin County Economic Opportunity office in Stockton. Among other things, they were being deluged with requests from Stockton's more upper-class residents, primarily from the president of the League of Women Voters, to do something about the county's drug problems. That was translated to mean the problem of white middle-class kids coming back from San Francisco's long Summer of Love, many of whom were burned out from psychedelics and addicted to harder stuff like heroin. After meeting with a lot of different people and groups, I developed a proposal for county officials about the steps I thought they should take. I recommended doing a needs assessment around the drug issue and providing assistance to an informal drug prevention group called "Friends," a group of mainly young people under 30.

As a result of that presentation, the county medical administrator hired me as a consultant to help his staff set up some drug prevention and treatment programs. In the eight months I worked on this project, I made $1000 a month and had an expense account. Through it all, I continued to masquerade as a "former addict" even as I was driving the 45 miles to Sacramento for heroin two or three times a week.

When we knew that I had been hired as a consultant in Stockton, I moved into a temporary apartment in an old Victorian house while I was looking for a permanent place. For those first few weeks, my wife of two months lived in a Fresno motel with our cat Frodo.

The morning after I moved in, it was raining buckets when there was a knock on the door. I couldn't imagine who it might be. I opened the door and was greeted by Kay, a gorgeous young woman I had met at one of the meetings while I was collecting some preliminary information for my proposal. I invited her in. She stepped into the room and opened her raincoat. As it dropped to the floor, she stood there wearing not a stitch of clothing.

This was late 1969. The sexual revolution was in full bloom and Kay was a beautiful flower child dying to be picked. I was so dumb that I thought she came because she thought I was wonderful. I had no second thoughts or questions about this naked stranger. Fortunately, I had scored some heroin the day before that would help me keep an erection for hours. I lived with the agonizing fear that my sexual shortcomings—having an orgasm too fast—would be discovered, and that would call my manliness into doubt. My ignorance told me that I was supposed to "make" women have orgasms, and the only way I knew how to do that was to use heroin which was, for me, Viagra before Viagra (and it was also another rationale to keep using). Well, women had orgasms because of my drugging and they loved it. Little did they know! But I knew and I hated myself.

I met another woman named Marilyn at the same time I met Kay. Marilyn had grown up in Stockton and was a major voice in the drug abatement chorus. Like Kay, Marilyn was affiliated with the group called Friends. When I had shown up at their meeting I was a novelty for two reasons. First, I was Black, and second, I represented the first "authority" about drugs they'd had access to. Afterwards, Marilyn invited me to her home for dinner and pretty soon we were going to bed.

This would be a continuation of the long line of women that came into my life before—as well as while—I was with Diane. Many of these women I never liked or respected. It would be a long process for me to acknowledge that, along with my drug addiction, I also had a sex addiction. And that it, like so many of my self-destructive choices, was related to my deep sense of inferiority.

My reason for having sex was not about the woman, but about enhancing my self-worth. Since I had unintentionally been taught by my mother's fearfully angry question, "What's wrong with you,"

I believed that if a woman voluntarily surrendered herself to me, I must be all right. If these women liked me, I appreciated it. I could tell myself I must not be so bad because they liked me and they were pretty good people. The more women there were, the less flawed I felt about myself in the moment. I had no conscious idea about the psychology driving this behavior or what I needed to do to feel worthwhile. The fact that I had just gotten married was irrelevant. I didn't think about how Diane might be feeling. I didn't know how to do that then. But I do know that of all the women who came and went, she is the only one who stayed in my heart.

From day to day, inside I was always freaking out. I was in a role where I had to present my task to the county medical administration, the Board of Supervisors, teachers and myriad community groups. I had to explain addiction to newspaper reporters, the League of Women Voters, and the Elks Club. I talked to them about an experience that I claimed was behind me while I was in the middle of it. So which way could I turn? Where could I go when I had chosen to put myself in the midst of that kind of dissonance? What did I do? I kept going and the self-consciousness and self-doubt continued to grow.

The only way I could continue with those overwhelming feelings was to keep shooting heroin. I was certain that my ignorance about what I had been hired to do would be exposed, and the people I worked with would find out how little I really knew and how inferior I really was. I had read and studied as much as anyone in the business, but I had no degree. I felt that the only accurate description of me was *liar, dope fiend, convict.* No matter what I accomplished, I only saw myself in the negative.

During those days in Stockton, music was the only place besides dope where I could find solace, to turn off the fear about my work, my marriage, my life. I couldn't even say "I don't know what to do" because I didn't know that I didn't know what to do. I knew very little about myself, except my fear and shame, and didn't really know much about *that* because all I did was try to escape it. Nothing gave me any peace except listening to everything Miles Davis recorded.

I thought Miles was at the peak of his excellence and I listened to him over and over. I could never get enough. To me, Miles was not just a great bandleader, but he gave everyone in the band a role in shaping the music. He encouraged his musicians to experiment and try new ideas, even if they didn't work out. Miles Davis's music, no matter the tune, tempo, or players in the band, always conveyed to me a sense of sad bravado. On top, everything was perfect, but underneath, to me, he always seemed to be seeking escape. Just like I was.

At UCLA, I was freaked out, scared, and angry. And I was angry again in Stockton because the thinking in those upper echelons (the boards, the medical staff meetings) was so ignorant about addiction and poverty, race and fairness. Justice seemed to be merely a word. They didn't know what they were doing. I would sit there and flip out on them, and that would shut them up, but I thought they shut up out of fear of not wanting to make the "nigger" mad, not because they understood. And that might not even be what they were thinking, but it's what I thought they were thinking. Madness! At some point, a guy in a gray suit sitting in the meeting called me "boy," so I believed they thought that I was inferior and felt the need to placate me.

Still, even without a degree, I developed programs that laid the groundwork for programs that exist today in San Joaquin County. To do something like that in spite of the anguish, the anxiety, fear, and shame was gratifying, unbelievable, and now, in retrospect, feels quite good to look back upon. I know we lost some lives but we saved lives, too.

DIANE

When I moved our things to Stockton in January 1970, Ed had already started working with parents and teachers, and with a group of young people called Friends. It was the ultimate irony to put a using heroin addict in charge of creating programs to help people with drug problems, but of course no one knew about Ed's active addiction. All they knew, and greatly admired, was that he was a former addict who was an articulate, charismatic, and inspiring leader.

From my first minute in Stockton I lived a double life. Married to a using addict, I salvaged as much of Ed's consulting check as I could for bills and rent, growing increasingly sad and angry about the seemingly endless hoping for change that did not come despite the opportunities he'd had in just the short time since I'd met him. Of course, I wouldn't know for a very long time how unprepared, inferior, and intimidated he felt pretending to be someone he wasn't.

As the wife of a consultant who was setting up new drug programs, I lived an isolated and secret existence. I couldn't talk to anyone about what was really going on without jeopardizing his job. And I lived each day in fear, worried about him overdosing and dying.

Then, the unthinkable happened. By the time I got to Stockton, just a few weeks after Ed, there was one, possibly two, and eventually three women connected with his work that he was having sex with.

I was devastated.

Even though Ed had told me during our UCLA days that he didn't believe in monogamy, there was no way I saw this coming, not just two months after getting married.

It's tempting to blame the sexual revolution. In 1970, it was working its way into mainstream culture, bringing new complications into relationships, including the illusion that we were free from old social constraints. But it was more than that, and would become as much a part of our lives as drugs for years to come.

Oddly, Ed lied a lot less about seeing other women than about using drugs. I could always tell when he was even a little loaded on heroin by the curl in his lower lip or the tiniest droop in his eyelid, yet he would repeatedly deny it until he hit some sort of mental wall when he was too exhausted to keep holding out. On the other hand, he was pretty open about his women friends.

My jealousy about Ed and the other women was so powerful I felt it was only a matter of time before I would explode. The loneliness and despair about the secret we shared and the seeming hopelessness of our situation—other women, drugs—became a boulder sitting on my heart.

Though neither one of us cared much about "being married" and would not have chosen that on our own, nothing had prepared me for this. We were living in a culture that suddenly offered choices never before thought of. Sexual liberation was great in theory, but not in my own personal life. Especially not after all we were already going through.

It was small consolation, and drove me a bit mad, that at least in the beginning many of the women Ed got involved with were people I would have chosen as friends. I actually did become friends with one or two. It was not only because of the special vibes you feel about someone that draws you to them, but also because we shared the experience of loving someone who was too consumed with his addiction and the work he had taken on to love us back —or more realistically, how he treated himself that made him virtually incapable of loving anyone. One of the women from our Stockton days, the irrepressible Marilyn, whose capacity for compassion was limitless, was someone who was there for me when I most needed support. In time, we would become lifelong friends.

Now I was not only carrying the secret about Ed's drug use, but also living with the humiliation that my husband was seeing other women—all of whom he was working with. It was more than I could bear. We fought a lot. I threatened to leave a lot.

One day, about four months after moving to Stockton, we both agreed that we should separate. He called the Salvation Army to come take our stuff—and for some insane reason I let him. As they were carting the few pieces of used furniture we had, including our fairly decent bed, down the steps, Frodo sat at the foot of the staircase looking back and forth, first at the movers, and then up at us, puzzled. At that moment, watching our cat, we came back to ourselves, sat on the floor and cried and, without bed or other furniture, we decided to try again.

We stumbled along. Once in a while we went to Mendocino for the weekend, and walked and talked, dreamed and made sand candles. We'd build a fire on the beach and melt part of a block of wax in an old pot. We dug holes in wet sand, and pressed some of the shells and beach glass and driftwood we had collected into the sides before pouring the wax, stirring in scent and color, and positioning the wick in the center. Then, warming ourselves by the fire in the inevitable fog or wind, we waited for the wax to harden before scooping out the candle. We still have one of those sand candles, and some of the wood carvings and collages Ed made using larger pieces of driftwood, wire, and beach glass.

But respite was always short-lived. Heroin was omnipresent no matter what we did. I begged him to let me try the drug that was destroying us because I needed to understand why it kept winning, but he absolutely refused. It was a line that, out of some sense of gallantry, he said he would never cross.

Why did I stay, and keep staying? Probably because I didn't know what would happen to me if I left. I was already losing myself into an abyss that was deeper and more terrifying than anything I had ever experienced. And perversely, while Ed *was* the abyss, he was also the focus that gave me purpose and kept me going.

ED

I was working all over the county, creating programs, and trying to help community people understand addiction. During this time one of the county hospital physicians and I were at war over what course to take about methadone. As always, I had been reading everything I could find about addiction, including articles about the recent use of the synthetic opiate, methadone, to help addicts withdraw from heroin, and the experiments to maintain addicts on a daily dose of methadone that blocks the effects of heroin. I championed the use of methadone to help people detox from heroin, but was opposed to the idea of using any drug to replace heroin—especially one like methadone whose laboratory purity made it so much more addicting than heroin and much harder to withdraw from. The county supervisors and medical administration approved my plan to establish methadone detox programs in the county, and also approved creating an outpatient methadone maintenance program at the county hospital.

I had also been talking about the need for community-based drug programs in Stockton. Someone mentioned the therapeutic community residential program modeled after Synanon for heroin

addicts at Mendocino State Hospital in Ukiah. I called and they
invited me to come see what they were doing and how it was working (although there was no real way to know how it was working
because no one was keeping track of client outcomes).

Diane and I drove to Ukiah to meet with them. From that
trip, I recommended that the county hire some of their counselors
and former clients to help with the methadone programs we were
working on developing at Stockton State and San Joaquin County
Hospitals. Eventually, these programs would prove to be one of the
great ironies of my time in Stockton.

On the way back to Stockton, we drove to the coast to spend
a couple of nights at Georgina's cabin in Comptche. As usual when
we traveled, we had our cat Frodo with us. By the time we got to the
road going up the mountain, it was nearly dark. We had only been
up to the cabin maybe three times, and we knew the eight-mile dirt
road winding through the mountains fairly well by day. But trying to
follow the road in the dark soon got us lost. We ended up with our
front wheels stuck in mud in what seemed to be a meadow, way off
the road. There was nothing to do but settle down in the car for the
night. We ate some of the food we brought for the weekend and fed
Frodo. Awake at first light, we collected small branches and twigs to
pack under the wheels, but our several attempts to get enough trac-
tion to drive out were unsuccessful.

Then we saw a jeep at the far end of the meadow coming our
way. A huge man in a plaid flannel shirt, canvas tool vest, and high
boots got out and walked towards us. We each had a private freak-
out, instantly imagining the worst. We were an interracial couple in
a rented red Mustang, stuck in a soggy meadow in a remote area, and
we worried about loggers, truckers, and local rednecks. Seeing this
large man coming towards us was discomfiting. As he approached,

he asked what was wrong. We walked as casually as we could to the front of the car and pointed to the wheels, explaining that we had driven off the road during the night trying to get to a friend's house. He followed us and stood for a minute, studying the car in the mud. Then he bent down and, effortlessly picking up the front of the car, he set it down on the hard ground. We later found out this gentle giant played Paul Bunyan in the annual Mendocino harvest festival.

DIANE

Ed had become an authority to the parents who wanted to save their children from drugs, and to the young people who had left home and thought drugs would give them the life they lacked but ended up hooked, lost, and back in Stockton. He had clarity and insight into people that resonated, gave them hope, and made them want to hear more.

Once or twice a month, a group of young people from Friends drove to Palo Alto for a two-hour training at the so-called and now long-defunct Human Institute. It was housed in an old, dark, drafty, windowless warehouse. The leader was a small man called Husain Chung who walked with a cane and thought himself a guru. Every week they held a Friday Night Psychodrama Theater where role playing was used for people to act out troubling events. This, along with encounter groups and other non-traditional methods, was meant to help people "get in touch with themselves" and work through problems. Young people were hungry to be real, open up, and break away from the strangling conformity that so defined the 1950s and early '60s. We were eager to explore who we were and who we could be without the baggage we dragged around behind us. I decided to go with the group from Friends to some of those Friday night trainings.

ED

The core group of young people involved with Friends was an assortment of dreamers and dopers.

Warren and Sally had just had their first baby. They lived in an old narrow Victorian where a lot of Friends meetings took place. Warren, who at 35 was older than most other members of the group, was the de facto patriarch. He was on parole after several years in prison on a 25-year sentence for possession of marijuana. Their house was a collage of psychedelic posters, tie-dyed velvet pieces thrown over chairs and sofas, blue light bulbs, a collection of poetry from unknown and anonymous Haight-Ashbury poets, Tolkien's *Lord of the Rings*, Shakespeare, assorted novels and magazines, and a scraggly Wandering Jew plant.

Mort and Mindy were newly returned to Stockton after a couple of years living in a commune in Humboldt County with other pot-growing vegetarian hippies.

Trisha and Carlin had left for San Francisco as flower children and came back hooked on heroin. They eventually got on methadone which blocked the effects of heroin but still left them with the feelings that led them to seek the oblivion they found using heroin in the first place. No longer able to get high on smack, they drank beer and became alcoholics.

And there was Kay and Greg. Kay was the beautiful, smart young woman who had knocked on my door wearing only a raincoat shortly after I moved to Stockton. She and her boyfriend Greg were student trainers at the Human Institute.

Lastly, there was Will, who lived with his parents and brother, Sam, in a modest home where the shades were drawn most of the time. Will was a partially-reformed speed freak while Sam was partly committed to kicking heroin. The tension created by two grown men, one speeding, one coasting, in an otherwise average household, must have been unbearable.

Will saw a shrink who worked at Stockton State Mental Hospital and periodically gave him a new diagnosis, like manic depressive, that Will tried on like new clothes. He spent hours poring over psychiatric journals and dictionaries, stylizing the new definitions into his identity and then, of course, he had to act them out. Sometimes, like when he was found walking naked down the middle of a street, he'd be arrested and institutionalized at the state hospital.

One day at a Friends' planning meeting that I was facilitating, Will became very agitated and paced around the room, talking to himself. This was typical Will behavior. People accepted him that way.

But I stopped talking and said, "Hey Will! We're trying to do some work here and you're being very distracting. So please, either sit down and participate or leave the meeting until you feel better."

Will stopped pacing, looked around, and said, "Okay, Ed." He sat down and was quiet and present for the rest of the meeting.

DIANE

At Human Institute trainings, one or two people would volunteer for a psychodrama session. Participants would play themselves and one of the student trainers would take the role of the person the participant had a problem with and needed to talk to. Then they switched roles, and the participant would play the "antagonist." Sometimes other "minor" characters would be added into the psychodrama. It was an interesting and sometimes eye-opening way to learn more about yourself by stepping into the shoes of the person with whom you were struggling.

The facilitators used music at key moments to awaken and intensify feelings of longing, sadness, closeness, loss, loneliness, and love as a provocative way to charge, change, and manipulate the collective emotional environment. Bob Dylan, Aretha Franklin, Gil Scott-Heron, Simon and Garfunkel, Richie Havens, Janis Joplin, and the Beatles singing about self-exploration and community, rebellion, and openness to life and love were lightning rods. There was a song for just about everything and music triggered feelings that helped people open up emotionally—at least in the moment. But even without the music, the process by itself was fascinating to watch and seemed to benefit those who took part. A lot was learned just by observing.

In late spring of 1970, Friends decided everyone should attend an upcoming 40-hour marathon at the Human Institute as staff training, and they wanted Ed and me to come as well.

Unlike the weekly sessions I had been to, this turned out to be 40 hours of intense confrontational attack-oriented encounter groups and sleep deprivation in a building without windows where there was no way to know whether it was night or day, how much time had passed, and how much time was left. It created enormous disorientation—a deliberate tactic used to wear out and tear people down until they were defenseless. Today it could be called a form of torture. There was a lot of emotional manipulation through the use of music and staff screaming at people to get real and get in touch with themselves. Many, especially women, were harshly criticized, mocked, and often reduced to tears. It was clearly not safe to be open, honest, or vulnerable in that environment. I was terrified and desperately wanted to leave, and I should have left, but I had no voice and still didn't know how to take care of myself.

Sometime close to the end of the marathon, we were divided by gender into groups that were told to assemble in separate corners of the building. I found a women's circle where I didn't know anyone and sat with them on the floor. Two of the women trainers went around checking in with us, one by one. By then, I was so numb with fear that I had no idea what to say. Even to say I was afraid didn't seem to be an option. Others who had said that they were scared had been mocked. My heart crashed around in my chest from the lack of sleep and dread of what was coming. Inevitably, one of the leaders turned and asked me how I was feeling. What a loaded question.

I grew up not knowing how to handle criticism or conflict. We didn't talk about feelings in my family, but that wasn't unusual. No one really talked about feelings when I was growing up and in all likelihood my parents' parents hadn't either. If you have no one to teach you, it's hard to learn. If you have no one to listen to your truth, you don't get validated. As a child, when I said something that made someone uncomfortable, I was told I shouldn't feel that way, that it was wrong or worst of all that I really *didn't* feel that way.

It never occurred to me, nor did I have the confidence to stand up for myself, like my sister did, and say, "But this *is* how I feel."

Instead of having the feeling and being able to talk through it, I became the feeling. With my family I would blow up and amazingly no one stopped me. Afterwards, I felt guilty and ashamed because exploding like that made me feel so out of control. Sometimes I thought I was born angry. For a long time, I believed I had a demon inside me that I couldn't do anything about, but I did know it wasn't appropriate to give free rein to that force with anyone outside my family. I hated conflict because it was a trigger for those dangerous reactions. With no language to explain to friends or lovers that I felt angry or hurt, I would shut down.

So when the trainer asked me how I was feeling, it was like trying to communicate in a foreign language that I didn't know. The only thing I could think to say was that I'd feel a lot better if Ed was doing better. The two trainers looked at each other. They got up. One walked away from the group, while the other walked over to me. Suddenly something was thrown over my head and they wrestled me down until I was lying flat on my stomach under a sleeping bag. One of the trainers sat on me, while the other hit me on my back.

"You're nothing but a doormat. This is what a doormat feels like," they yelled over and over.

I was suddenly furious and fought back from under the bag, screaming, until I managed to throw them off and uncover myself. The trainers smiled and clapped their hands.

"All right! You stood up for yourself. You got in touch with your anger."

Afterwards, I felt like I had been through some sort of initiation. Strange, unexpected, and violent though it was, it was somewhat empowering. No one had ever applauded when I acted out my anger before.

The 40 hours ended on an up note, with lots of music about loving community, but it was clear that many people were left feeling hurt, confused, and some were very raw and broken. Walking to the car with Ed, I wondered what does someone do who has been through that level of intense experience when they walk out alone into the light of day and have to resume ordinary life? What if they had left pieces of themselves on the floor of that drafty warehouse because no one had the sense or the decency to help them put themselves back together?

For a while after that, I became more assertive. Knowing Ed and his patterns, I instinctively knew when he lied to me about drugs, but had always let him. After the marathon, I took the risk of confronting him. He didn't like it. It made his life more complicated by backing him up against the wall when he already knew he was wrong. When it became too unbearable for this to be coming from the one person he relied on to enable him, his lies became more elaborate and he upped the ante. He'd say it wasn't what I said but how I said it. He managed to convince me that an effective person approaches another in a less hostile way and that trying to be his warden wouldn't get me anywhere; he didn't need a mother, and couldn't stand my suspicious attitude.

It seemed that no matter how I said anything, it was wrong. I got so caught up trying to find the right way to approach him, trying to please him and get a result, trying to remodel myself for him and still wanting his approval, I only succeeded in destroying another piece of me. Eventually I gave up and relapsed to my more passive self.

Ed once said that if he changed, I might be sorry and not like what he became, which made me think that if he did change, he might not like who I was, because he had already been asking me why I kept choosing to stay with him as crazy as he was acting. I thought that if both of us changed, maybe the relationship would intensify into something really beautiful and healthy. Or, maybe we would get bored with each other and be ready to go our separate ways. Whatever my fantasies, we didn't have the language to talk about how we felt, we could only act it out and that would end up in a struggle.

Ed's intention was always to clean up. When we went to Mendocino to escape our stressful life, he didn't bring anything but marijuana, but it hardly helped. After a weekend of withdrawing, he'd come home feeling miserable and needing to stop being sick.

"Got to go to the store; be right back," he'd say. When he returned, he was always loaded.

On one of those nights when we were just back from Mendocino, he brought a guy home with him. His name was John and he had been drinking beer. They settled in the living room and fixed. Within minutes, John swayed around and fell down, overdosing from the combination of alcohol and heroin.

For me, it was heartbreaking enough to come back from the ocean and have Ed immediately go out to shoot heroin, but having a stranger suddenly collapsed and dying in the living room took everything to a whole new level. Ed was so loaded he could barely keep his eyes open, but he told me to go wake up Wesley.

Now, one of the more incongruous things Ed did in Stockton was to convince guys that he shot heroin with in Sacramento to come to Stockton and clean up in our spare bedroom where we kept piles of driftwood we had collected on the beaches of Mendocino and Fort Bragg. The plan was that after they kicked, they could go to work helping Ed develop drug programs. Ed was always able to inspire others to do better, even if he couldn't do it for himself, and these guys really wanted to believe him and change their lives. So Wesley was the one who was not only with us that night, but thankfully he was also clean. He spent the entire night completely focused on the job of reviving the person on the floor, delaying his sense of betrayal now that he knew Ed was still using.

We spent all night packing John's armpits and groin with ice, pulling on his arms and legs to stimulate him, and injecting a water and salt solution to flush out his system. The only pleasure I had was not letting Ed enjoy his high. Every time he started to nod, I shook or

slapped or punched him to wake him up and make him keep pump-
ing the guy's arms. Occasionally John would holler out, which was of
great concern. If his unconscious shouting woke up neighbors who
then called the police, we could all have been arrested because heroin was involved. John didn't come to until 6 a.m., when he suddenly
sat straight up and asked what time it was. Then he jumped up and
headed out the door, worried to be late for work.

One of the strangest things about bringing someone back who
had nearly died from an overdose is their utter denial. John flatly
refused to believe he had overdosed until later that day when his
arms and legs ached from the pulling all night and he was unbearably dehydrated from the saline solution that Wesley had repeatedly injected.

Then, life went on as before and Wesley, feeling betrayed by
Ed, returned to Sacramento.

ED

At the same time I was planning and developing all those programs, I was also going to Sacramento three or four times a week to
buy drugs, sometimes every day. I didn't buy a large quantity. While
I hated myself for shooting dope, I pretended that I was not really
hooked because I only bought a little bit each time.

Then I would tell myself, "I'm not going to use anymore
because I don't want to get hooked."

One day I was on one of those excursions and as I was injecting myself in the dealer's house, one of the Stockton clients walked
in and saw the needle in my arm. The party was over. I knew that he,
who was using furtively, as I was, would go back and spill the beans.

When I got back to Stockton, I called the office. Everyone was ecstatic! News had come that the county had been awarded a large grant to work with the state mental hospital in Stockton on a methadone detox study that I had a leadership role in developing.

A party was planned for the next day. I was filled with dread because I knew that my secret would soon come out. Meanwhile, the phone was ringing nonstop and people started coming over to our house. I hid my car and pretended I wasn't home. I began to think of committing suicide, so I got very loaded and almost overdosed.

During the night, I decided that I had to go to the party the next day and face the music. And I did. There must have been over a hundred people gathered in Vicki's garden (she was the president of the League of Women Voters and had been a staunch supporter of my work). That day was a mixture of joy, anger, and heartbreak. I told them what I had done. I told them about my inability to do what I had done without heroin, and how phony I felt. There were tears, anger, pats on the back, and curses. One guy tried to punch me in the face. The next day I resigned.

The methadone detox program at Stockton State Hospital started two weeks after I lost my job. This was one of the first studies with methadone detox in California. The goal was for addicts to be detoxed from heroin and then get a job. Given what had just become known about me, I was shocked to be asked to talk to staff about the process and the expected outcomes for clients. It surprised me because I had expected to be tarred and feathered, run out of town on a rail. Instead, I was treated with a lot of respect. In reality, none of the medical people at the hospital knew much about using methadone to treat heroin addiction.

Methadone was still a controversial treatment. Drs. Dole and Nyswander had been pioneering its use in New York City, administering massive doses of the drug to heroin addicts. I had argued against using the highly addictive methadone as a maintenance therapy because it made so little sense to replace one drug addiction with another. Still, it seemed that using methadone to help detox addicts off heroin might be helpful since it not only blocked the effects of heroin but also alleviated the criminal issues associated with an illegal drug.

The program at Stockton State began as a one-month inpatient trial. Two weeks later I enrolled with the first group of patients in that program. I was #14. I was also asked to assist with writing and overseeing the dispensing protocol of the methadone. It was pretty crazy. I was one of the first patients in a program that I had designed and also had helped to get started.

I have always had a very low tolerance for drugs and found that the dosage of methadone that I received, even though it was considered safe, turned out to be well above my safe tolerance level. As a result, I got very loaded. When Diane came to see me, she thought I was shooting heroin again and I had a hard time getting her to believe the truth.

It wasn't long before the staff physicians decided that they wanted to better understand addiction. They wanted to see how much of the drug an addict could tolerate so they started a "token economy" where patients who made their beds neatly, shined their shoes, and ironed their clothing could receive an extra dose of methadone. Somewhere along the way, the doctors at Stockton State lost sight of the fact they were supposed to use methadone to taper people off heroin, not increase their addiction. As soon as I got word about what was happening, I called Dr. Jerome Jaffe, the head of the project funding source in Sacramento, and the state ended the project.

Needless to say, the abrupt closing of that program left a lot of folks back on the streets strung out on methadone which, because of its potency, makes it a wicked drug to kick and requires a very long withdrawal process. I didn't want to start using heroin again so I enrolled in the new county hospital methadone maintenance program. This was yet another irony since I had championed methadone detox, not maintenance, and that program was staffed by people I had recruited from the Mendocino State Hospital program we had visited when I was a consultant. As clients, we had to attend two weekly groups that were run according to the Synanon model used at the Mendocino State program, including brutal verbal confrontation for the purpose of "self-examination."

Even on a low dose, methadone was a hard drug to tolerate. Nearly everyone had terrible side effects. I had insomnia, constipation, and anxiety, and I felt loaded no matter how low the dose. I hated it. Methadone was effective at blocking heroin, but it did nothing to block the feelings that I used heroin to escape. A lot of people on methadone started drinking, and many became alcoholics. I stuck with methadone for a few months, but at some point in the fall of 1971, I couldn't take it anymore and left.

DIANE

After losing his consulting job when his drug use was exposed, Ed spent the next year in and out of methadone detox and maintenance programs. The Stockton State methadone program was a disaster and I was glad to see him leave it. The county's maintenance program was our last hope. We attended two weekly groups. Sometimes they put us in different groups, which we both liked, but many of the people in my group wouldn't even talk to me unless Ed was there. They saw me as an extension of him, but said he was the one who needed help, not me, because I was straight.

With the exception of my own unhappiness, I remember very few details from the methadone period. I nearly lost my VW bug which we had put up as collateral for an orange VW Squareback that Ed had bought when we first came to Stockton. When he couldn't make payments, the finance company came after both cars. I hid my car until I was able to borrow $500 from my parents to get it out of hock. That was when I had to tell them about Ed's drug use. I don't really remember how they reacted. They might have been in shock, saying very little, but the sadness and anguish they felt for themselves and for me were like a silent scream over the phone.

At some point I had a moment of clarity. I was confused about a lot, but did understand that I, too, was an addict. Put simply, Ed was addicted to drugs, and I was addicted to Ed. Despite his best efforts, he couldn't stop using. Despite my best efforts, I couldn't leave him. Even knowing that I was losing myself I persisted, hoping that the sheer act of wishing for change would make it happen.

I think Ed almost hated me at times for being there to clean up after him and keep things going. He encouraged me to do my own thing, with my own friends. He would say I couldn't keep following him through doors he opened because when he was gone, I'd have nothing of my own. But the times I did assert myself were threatening to him for he was dependent on me, too, and feared if I went out too far I'd discover something better and leave.

It was hard to accept that our relationship was based on reinforcing each other's unhealthy choices. I was initially attracted to him because he was exciting to be with, his work as an organizer and trainer in the poverty program was meaningful, and his imagination and creativity and eloquence were powerful and strong. I tried for

a long time to ignore the insecurity and fear within Ed the addict
that was so incompatible with the strong, charismatic change agent
he presented to others. Rather than accept the reality, I clung to the
image of the warm and compassionate person, helpful to everyone
except himself. I was loyal to him to the extent that I lied for him. I
was emotionally dependent on him to the extent that I felt I could
not live without him. And every time he fixed, I knew the possibility of overdosing existed and I lived in fear. Unasked, I served as
his punisher and mother because he didn't say no to himself and
needed someone who would. I became involved in his work because
I enjoyed it, but also because that made it easy for me, even at age 26,
to avoid thinking about what I wanted to do with my own life.

The repetition of being lied to, used, financially drained, and
manipulated undermined whatever strengths and self-worth I might
have had. At one point during our first few years together I felt so
insecure that I literally begged him to tell me that everything would
be all right—reassurance that of course he couldn't give to himself,
much less to me.

When Ed was in the methadone maintenance program, I
found unexpected support from one of the counselors, Luba, who
encouraged me to take a stand for myself. Luba was a recovering
alcoholic/addict. She had been married to a man who had her committed to a mental hospital in the late 1950s when she started using
alcohol and prescription pain medicine to cope with his rigid insistence that she obey his orders to keep house, stay home, and raise
the kids. She was eventually discharged from the mental hospital by
promising to be an obedient wife, but quickly filed for divorce, which
resulted in her losing custody of and contact with her children. At
some point, she went to AA. By the time I met her, she was clean and
sober, strong, confident, and accepting.

Luba talked a lot about letting go. She kept telling me I couldn't save Ed from himself, that no matter how much I loved him I couldn't control him. Once she asked me to imagine I was holding a little bird in my hand. If I closed my hand around it, the bird would struggle to fly away. But if I kept my hand wide open, the bird would feel less threatened and maybe even stay. Today, I believe that letting go has become my lifetime practice, but at the time it was so foreign to my belief system that I couldn't imagine loosening my grip even for a second.

By then, I barely knew who I was. If I was the responsible person I believed myself to be, then how did I let our finances get so horribly, impossibly out of hand? I was lost in some dim place where I couldn't think, speak, or act for myself without referencing him. Synanon coined the term "mother lover" for people who enable addicts as in "mother loves you no matter what you do" (and no matter the cost to herself).

Methadone took a huge toll on Ed. He was miserable not working and not being able to get high. Eventually he started using heroin again. By September 1971, I couldn't watch any longer. Despite investing everything I had emotionally, spiritually, and financially in him, nothing had changed. I packed some clothes, took Frodo, and went to stay at a friend's house. Ed called after a few weeks. He was in jail.

ED

Diane moved out when I started using again. I felt hopeless. No job, no money, no hope, no wife. It was then, in the fall of 1971, that I decided to kill myself. I wrote some bad checks and bought killer heroin that I took to a snitching dope dealer's house. I planned to overdose and get him in trouble but instead both he and his girl-friend overdosed and I ended up spending hours reviving them.

With my record of forgery, it wasn't long before I was arrested for the bad checks and back in jail, five years after getting out of San Quentin. Not being on parole helped and I had a progressive judge whose son had been helped by the work I had done in Stockton. The judge thought treatment might be better than jail. He sent me to "Our Family," a therapeutic community drug program at Napa State Hospital. This was the sister program to the one at Mendocino State Hospital that Diane and I had visited the year before, when I had been a big shot consultant to the county medical director.

Part Three:
The Long Slow Low Bottom

14

"Our Family"

ED

In 1972, the only alternative to incarceration for drug-related crime was the "therapeutic community." These programs followed rigid guidelines that originated in Synanon, one of the first drug rehabilitation programs, which had begun in 1958 in Santa Monica, California. Synanon believed that the way to help addicts was through strict discipline, mostly involving humiliation and punishment. Eventually, Synanon became known as one of the most violent and dangerous cults in America and was disbanded in 1991.

When I first got to Our Family at Napa State, I had to make a formal request for admittance to the program. I was asked about my history. As I proudly began to tell them about my accomplishments so they would know I was special, one of the committee members dragged a huge trashcan next to my chair and another person asked me to stand up and get into the trashcan where she said I belonged. I was shocked but managed to get into the can. Then I was told to step out of the can for a moment and take off my shirt and pants and get back into the trashcan where a piece of shit like me should stay forever. I nearly got up and left, but somehow I was able to keep it together and continue to answer their questions.

For the first 30 days, newcomers were allowed no contact with anyone outside the program, be it in person, by letter, or by phone. Every newcomer got the same treatment. Our heads were shaved and signs were hung around our necks saying things like "I'm an asshole." The slightest infringement of rules could mean sleeping in the bathroom on the floor for a week or cleaning the bathroom floor with a toothbrush (it was always clean!). Residents who had problems with each other were tied together with a rope around their waists until they resolved their disagreements. They'd walk around arguing and sometimes they would even begin to fight physically. Other times one of them would leave the program; sometimes they would both leave the program. But it was most interesting to see two supposed enemies begin talking and settling their differences. Most often they became friends.

The program used a form of group attack "therapy" called the "Game" that was developed by Synanon. A Game was made up of staff members and program residents. No one could refuse to participate, even newcomers who didn't yet know how it worked. Being new to the Game was terrifying. You had to figure it out on your own. For some people, the humiliation they experienced in their first Game caused them to leave the program. If you were asked a question, you either had to know what to say or be clever enough to pass the discussion to someone else who might or might not have the gift of gab needed in that moment. Anyone unable to answer questions posed to them would be subject to taunts from the 20 or so other participants. It felt a lot like being in prison, where I had to stuff my feelings and not react to whatever was going on around me. Out of self-preservation, I learned to be pretty good at the Game and soon I was one of those in the hierarchy.

While none of that gave me any insight into why I had been using drugs or what I could do to stop, it did keep me relatively safe emotionally.

The program had extremely strict rules about sexual relationships. You could get thrown out for what I was doing with women. I was having an affair with the program nurse, Betty, as well as with Marilyn from Stockton. And even though, by the third month I was in the program I had received papers that Diane had filed for divorce, she visited nearly every week and we were still lovers.

To top it off, as I got close to the end of my year in the program, I was also trying to have an affair with another client, Rosa. She was a lovely young woman who, like me, was getting ready to graduate. I got a pass to go to Fresno where I had worked as a community organizer after UCLA. I talked to Ward, who worked in the Fresno Office of Economic Opportunity, about getting my job back after graduation and hoped they would also hire Rosa. Ward said he needed secretarial help and if I thought she was good enough, he would hire her. Rosa saw what I was doing with the three other women and didn't want to go, but I persisted until she agreed.

We were both offered jobs. That evening, Ward and his wife Judy took us out to dinner. Rosa and I stayed at their house where we had a great night together. The next morning as we were backing out of Ward's driveway to head back to Napa, a drunk driver came swerving down the road and crashed into my car on the passenger side, killing Rosa.

As I write now, I am aware that this is the first time I have really told this whole story to myself, let alone to anyone else. Not that the Napa program staff didn't try to get me to talk about it. They had me in Games often after that, up until graduation, but I never owned the truth that my ulterior motive in getting Rosa to come with me was to have sex with her. Nor did I own that we had ever had sex. In the couple of months that remained until I graduated from the program, I could barely drag myself around.

I started to use again in part because of the guilt I felt about Rosa's death. What is amazing is how deeply I buried that story and never talked about it, not even during the many years of therapy I've had since. I think that Rosa was not that much into our affair, but she didn't know how to say no to me. She was in the program and saw that I was not only getting regular visits from both Diane and Marilyn, but that I was also involved with Betty. Rosa knew about all this, but she also needed a job when she agreed to go to Fresno with me.

I can understand why I felt I had to start using drugs again, starting with an overdose right after I graduated. I wouldn't talk about Rosa's death and needed to obliterate the terrible guilt I felt. I began by telling myself that "I need to have a drink." And since I could never have just one drink, I had six or seven. Then, when I was drunk, I told myself I needed to shoot heroin because it would make me feel better. And I argued with myself about the danger, but then convinced myself it would be okay because I would do it only once. Treatment had taught me that I can't keep using or I'd get hooked again, but I was sure that doing it just this one time wouldn't hurt.

My writing this story is the first time that I have allowed myself to face the fact that my sexing and drug use, my lying and cheating, my pretending to leap tall buildings in a single bound were intertwined with my thinking that I was flawed. I believed that collecting women as trophies and doing exceptional work that I actually knew little about would make me special, and would make people like me.

In the process, it killed someone who had trusted me. Only now, decades later, have I found the courage to face that fact.

DIANE

In January 1972, I moved to Davis and started working in the U.C. Davis School of Law admissions office. I began to feel relieved, free, and almost exhilarated to be alone, taking care of myself, not responsible for anyone else and enjoying it. But then I started getting bills for stereo equipment and televisions that Ed had charged to credit cards and then pawned—things and charges I never knew about. In California, my spouse's debts were my debts. On less than $400 a month income, I couldn't afford to stay married to him and filed for divorce.

I took women's studies classes at Sacramento City College and Sacramento State University, and joined a consciousness-raising group. While feminism provided a context for my experiences growing up female in the 1950s within the sexist confines of Orthodox Judaism, it didn't help me navigate into healthier relationships or resolve the inconsistencies between my politics and personal life. For many years to come, as Ed and I continued to struggle, I would lose friends whose patience, watching my ongoing difficulties with Ed, would eventually run out. "You're a smart woman. Why don't you just leave him?" was the argument I heard repeatedly from women friends and from therapists who knew next to nothing about addiction or codependency.

Napa was about an hour's drive from Davis and I often visited Ed on weekends. He would get a pass and we drove around the Napa hills smoking dope and making love in the back of the Bug. Seeing him in a treatment program, free of hard drugs during that year, gave both of us new hope that maybe this time it would be different—even though I knew he continued to see Marilyn from our Stockton days.

The little bit I knew about the approach used by therapeutic community programs appalled me. The research had not yet been done that would show that many addicts, as children, had been physically, mentally, emotionally, and/or sexually abused by their families, baby sitters, foster families, or others and that re-experiencing those familiar patterns of humiliation and abuse in a program that was supposed to help them might be counterproductive. The worst part, for me, was that while family members and significant others were tolerated on visiting days, the prevailing belief was that we were the cause of the addict's problems. So not only was there no help for people like me, but the sense of failure that I had not been able to "fix" my husband was constantly reinforced.

I occasionally hung out with some of the women clients whose stories were very different from the men. Women addicts were a largely ignored, misunderstood, and second-class group. Many got into drugs to please their already-addicted male partner, who was often also their pimp. They were heartbroken women, suffering from the rampant sexism in those early programs that openly called them whores and bitches. Nearly every one of them had been declared an unfit mother by the courts and many had lost their children to foster care when they were in mandated treatment or incarcerated. But while they dreamed about being with their kids again, their inability to envision a life without some man telling them what to do promised only more of the same.

After his "graduation" in late 1972, Ed and I continued to see each other and then at some point I knew he had relapsed and was using drugs again. Once he left the program, I discovered that my treasured months of being on my own and feeling relatively good about myself had been largely due to knowing that he was safe. This was a pattern that would repeat itself over and over—relaxing when he went into treatment, being on alert and worried when he came out. I wondered when I would be all right for *myself*, whether Ed was all right or not. It seemed that none of the major decisions in my life were made without some external pressure from someone I wanted to please. I wondered if and when I would ever stop trying to define myself in terms of others.

ED

One day, shortly after graduating from the Napa program, as I was nodding in a dealer's living room after shooting some heroin, I picked up an *Esquire* magazine with an article about the work of British psychiatrist R.D. Laing. The article was about his book, *The Politics of Experience*, which prompted me to ask myself, not for the first time, why was I using drugs. What was wrong with me?

I knew I was sad because my lover, Betty, the nurse at Our Family, was on vacation in Hawaii. After my graduation, I thought she and I would get together, but she up and left and it was all over between us. I didn't know what to do with myself, so I shot dope and then went back to the Napa program. But I still wouldn't talk and couldn't tell them about my involvement with Betty because I didn't want her to lose her job. They guessed, but I lied and said it wasn't true. And I still wouldn't admit that I had had sex with Rosa either. More lying. More secrets. That wasn't helping me. So I left the program.

I had taken the magazine from the dealer's house with me. The R.D. Laing article struck a chord and I read it again and again. I bought another Laing book, *Knots*, about the spirals of descent that we get into when we keep doing what we learned growing up. That's when I really started asking myself why I was doing what I was doing. It was just that there were no answers and none would be coming for quite a while.

In late 1972, I got a job with the Probation Department in Woodland, CA as the director of a halfway house for drug users on probation, and I actually stopped using heroin for a while. It was a project for men and we had a business detailing automobiles. The halfway house was a loony bin, but we did some good work there, both on ourselves and on the cars.

15

Vanishing Point

DIANE

In early 1972, when I started working at the U.C. Davis law school, the student body was 96% white male. By the fall of that year, due to newly implemented affirmative action policies to correct past discrimination that kept women and minorities out of professions dominated by white males, the entering class was 45% women and 33% people of color. As assistant to the Dean of Admissions, I read more than 3,000 applications and personal statements every year, and made the initial determination about whether an applicant should be automatically accepted, rejected, or sent to the Admissions Committee. I loved the work.

In January 1973, I met Jackson, a 25-year-old first-year law student who was four years younger than I. It was a meeting that would shake my life to its core and force me to face and live through my worst fears. The first time I saw him was when he was standing at the counter in the main office looking lost and upset. I walked over and asked if he was all right. We talked a bit, and then started going out.

At first, his love of nature, laughter, music, and writing poetry fooled me, and the fun and exhilaration of a new, sexually-charged relationship obscured his predominant self-destructive, dark self which, among other things, was having a major identity crisis. He was one-quarter Native American and that had helped get him into law school. That identity was something his closest friends later said they hadn't known about the tall, sandy-haired, part-jock, part-hippie undergraduate whom they had regularly bailed out of the Davis drunk tank. As a law student, he immersed himself in the Native American law student caucus and was active in the Rancherias (or reservations) in rural northern California. But in trying to be someone he wasn't, he lost himself.

When the red flags started going up—cocaine, alcohol, excessive drama, and his omnipresent underlying identity angst—it was hard to know how serious any of those issues were. There was also his jealousy of my then five-year history with Ed, whom Jackson had met one day when he showed up unannounced at my house while Ed happened to be there hanging out with my roommate.

Things were always happening to Jackson. In late April, he flew to Washington, DC for a national meeting of Native American law students. He called me one morning to say he had just come to sprawled on a sidewalk after being mugged and knocked unconscious. My stomach twisted into sickening knots, like it did when I knew Ed was lying about something. Maybe Jackson's story was true. I had no way to prove or disprove it. My instinct told me it felt like some of the more elaborate stories Ed told me that ended up being excuses for why he had no money or was stranded somewhere.

Jackson returned from DC a broken spirit. His drinking intensified and he insisted that I commit myself to him alone, something I wasn't prepared to do. My two attempts to break up with him were unsuccessful. Deeply disturbed, depressed, and rapidly alienating his friends, he saw himself as an anti-hero. He identified with Paul Newman in *Cool Hand Luke* and Jack Nicholson in *One Flew Over the Cuckoo's Nest*. Towards the end of the semester, he was Barry Newman in *Vanishing Point*, a story about a socially disconnected character trying to outrun mainstream society that was fast closing in on him.

One day in late May, Jackson called, shaken. He said he had been raped on campus, had stopped going to classes and didn't think he could take his finals. By then, I didn't know what to believe. All I could be certain of was that I was in a relationship with a 25-year-old version of Ed Reed.

In early June, I moved into a small apartment with orange walls that I planned to paint a more neutral color. Then I went to Connecticut to visit my family and celebrate with my mom who was recovering from a long-awaited hip replacement.

I returned to Davis with the familiar feeling of dread that comes when you still haven't figured out what to do about the unfinished business you left behind. On June 21, 1973 I was called into the Dean's office. He asked me to explain why my name was on a round-trip plane ticket to Connecticut that had been billed to the university credit card Jackson had been given for Native American law student-related business. I was speechless. Just before he left for Washington, DC in April, Jackson had given me a plane ticket to New York as a "gift" because he knew I was planning to visit my family in early June. I had given it right back to him, saying it wasn't his to give and insisted that he return it. I told the Dean I had never used the ticket, had returned it immediately, and would furnish proof that I paid my own airfare to Connecticut. I was scared and worried about losing my job.

Later, on that evening of the summer solstice, the longest day of the year, Ed came to help me clean up my new apartment. At about 11 p.m., the phone rang. I knew it had to be Jackson, but was too stressed about the credit card business to talk to him. It rang again. By the third time, Ed said, "What's happening? Answer the phone." Jackson wanted to see me. I said I was busy. He asked about the next day. I said I didn't want to see him.

Ed and I sat in awkward silence. Then Ed jumped up looking alarmed and said he had to go. He turned at the door. "Oh man. I had this vision of Jackson blowing up. I'm getting out of here, and you're coming with me," he insisted. "That fool has a shotgun and you're talking crazy to him."

I didn't think or question or hesitate. Ed has always had the ability to "see" into people. At some deep level, I knew that the tragedy he described could well be more than just a bad feeling.

We went to Ed's place in Woodland and talked through the night. I told him everything—about Jackson's increasingly troubling behavior, his drinking and drug use, and about my being called into the Dean's office. That's when Ed told me some of what he'd learned from the Probation Department in Woodland (where he was working) about the trouble Jackson was in. By morning, Ed had convinced me to talk to Jackson right away and insist that he tell the Dean I was not involved in whatever he was doing.

It was a cloudy, muggy June morning. I went home, took a shower, and drove to the trailer park where Jackson lived. And then everything went into slow motion. I felt as if I was slowly floating around the trailer, calling his name. I knocked on the door. For a moment, I thought I heard footsteps and felt a slight tremor from inside. I got the extra key from under the step and unlocked the door, pushed it open, and stood on the steps, looking up and down the narrow hallway.

To the right was his bedroom. Jackson was lying on the bed, fully dressed, with a long shotgun cradled under his right arm. I thought he'd had too much to drink and, when he sat down on the bed to clean his gun, he must have passed out and fallen back. Then I noticed a spattering of red spots, bright and sticky looking, on the floor coming from the bedroom. His head was leaning to the right on the bed. Though I was still sure he was just asleep, my heart was pounding and I couldn't even say his name. I moved into the bedroom, inching around the bed, not taking my eyes off him, looking for the rise and fall of his chest. He was so still.

At some point I passed the invisible boundary that permitted me to see him as whole. The right side of his head that had been bent away from me was gone. Too shocked to scream, I stood trembling, trying to breathe, unable to stop looking at the horror of his blown-apart, bloody head. I didn't see the gaping hole in the roof, or the blood-splattered walls and furniture. I didn't smell the flesh that had been rotting for several hours that dim, humid morning. I forgot about the striped kitten he had just brought home that we had played with together a few days earlier that the police later found locked in a room.

I just stood there.

Then, after a little while, I felt very calm and thought, okay, I'll just leave now and get ready for work.

I got as far as the nearest phone booth and called Ed. My voice shook so hard he barely understood what I was saying. He was there in 20 minutes and called the police to report a suicide. We later learned that they found a note. Jackson had written simply, "*I have reached my vanishing point.*"

ED

Diane was working at the U.C. Davis law school and I continued my sex addiction with her and two other women. I met Jackson at her house one day in early 1973 when I was there getting stoned with Diane's roommate. Jackson had stopped by unexpectedly. As we all talked, he took out a bag of cocaine and shared it with us. When he found out I worked for the Yolo County Probation Department, he asked if I would help him find someone there to talk to about his case. Jackson was in trouble for misusing a university credit card he had been given for business related to the Native American law students' caucus. He was facing a conviction and probable expulsion from law school, and wanted to talk to someone in the Probation Department to clarify what, if any, options he might have. I got him an appointment with the chief probation officer in Woodland who told Jackson there was nothing they could do to assist him. From then on, it would be up to the court.

A few months later, Diane had moved into her own apartment. One night I brought brooms and mops over to help her clean it. At about 11 p.m. the phone started to ring. So unlike herself, Diane didn't answer it. When I asked her what was going on, she finally picked up the phone. She said very little. First she said she was busy. Then she said she didn't want to see him and hung up. I wondered what that was about. I had a hunch it was Jackson and started feeling nervous about the way Diane talked to him.

I knew he had a shotgun that he had purchased with the university credit card. I was sitting on the couch and suddenly saw his face appear before me. Then his face exploded. I jumped up in terror, went to the door and told Diane that I "saw" his face blow up, that we had to leave.

"I'm getting out of here, and you're coming with me," I said. "That fool has a shotgun and you're talking crazy to him."

She followed me to the car without a moment's hesitation. That night, when we talked nonstop until morning, was the beginning of Diane's own devastating ordeal. At least I was able to be there for her when she really needed me.

DIANE

That first day, the day I found Jackson, was the NO. Please don't make me have to know what I know. Please don't make me have to see this, remember this forever. And when it's only been an hour or two, you think about the hours and days, stretching into weeks and years and wonder how or if you could even make it past right now. The pain is too big for your body, every cell hurts. You fight the knowing, yet ache to let out that first anguished scream and don't succeed at either. And you make your first deal: I'll do *anything* if you just make it not be true. You fall to the ground and someone is there stroking your hair, rubbing your back, holding you. They give you a pill and you fall into a deep, black sleep and awake with a powerful ache even before you remember. And then you're amazed (when you think of it) about how the second day seems so normal and how much you hate its newness and anyone who doesn't know, and how much you hate anyone who laughs and anyone who doesn't agree that it was your fault.

School was out for the summer and hardly anyone besides staff was around. The building was eerily quiet and empty. Not having much work was a blessing because I couldn't concentrate or focus. I was too obsessed thinking about what the shock of instantly breaking the thread to this life would be like.

During those first few weeks, I found the counselor from the student health center that Jackson had been seeing. He asked me to sit in the leather chair and get comfortable. Then he had me close my eyes and relive out loud every detail of what I had seen. I cried throughout, and it helped relieve some of the anguish, just a little, in that moment.

I made an appointment with a woman therapist, but she went right into anger, assuming that Jackson had expected me to find him, and said I should pin his picture to the wall and throw darts at him. It was a horrifying thought.

One of his law student friends who had seen him that last night at a bar in Davis came by to tell me about a dream he had of Jackson. At the end of the dream he saw the numbers 5 and 12 and asked if I knew what their significance was. I had no idea, but remembered how Jackson always marked time. "Today is the third day of the sixth week we've been seeing each other," he would say. When I finally figured out the date we first went out up to the day I found him, it turned out to be exactly five months and 12 days. Sometimes in my better moments I wanted to believe it was a message from Jackson telling me to go on, to keep living.

I moved out of the apartment with the orange walls and stayed with a friend who was leaving Davis at the end of the summer. I was too fragmented to find a place of my own and I liked feeling unanchored, weightless. For a few weeks, I housesat for a faculty member and took care of his dog. When I wasn't walking or feeding that beautiful pure white 110-pound Great Pyrenees, I spent long hours baking in the sun by the pool.

Ed was always close by. In between my raging and bargaining and guilt and the horror of remembering, Ed helped me start to wake up a little, to remind me I was still alive. He was the only grounding, the only closeness I could tolerate. I doubt I would have made it without his support. At the same time, I was frightened to let myself get too close to him again, not knowing how quickly I'd be able to extricate myself when his next bout of self-destructiveness resurfaced.

I drifted around campus in the quiet, hot, dry heat of summer, the time of year when trucks pulling huge uncovered bins filled to the brim with tons of ripening tomatoes would caravan down Interstate 80 to processing plants. The air was always full of the smell of hot smashed tomatoes that had bounced out of overfull trucks onto the road.

One day I found a small enclosed grassy area behind some of the greenhouses that dotted the campus. It was a cool, green place and I often took Frodo with me. Sometimes the air exploded with wonderful flying buzzing things, hummingbirds and bees, butterflies and dragonflies. I felt Jackson's spirit there in the natural world he had so loved. During the spring we had roamed the Vacaville hills where pink and white flowers blooming on fruit and nut trees blanketed the sky and earth. He had taken me into pastures to meet cows and sheep and their newborn. We had watched nature come alive and reproduce, felt power in the wind and energy from the sun. It was in that grassy place on campus where, maybe for the first time, I started falling in love with life, loving its beauty, and having brief flashes of guilt-ridden gratitude that I was still part of it.

The comfort of that solitude ended with the start of fall semester in late September when the students returned. Then it became surreal, beginning what Joan Didion so perfectly called the time of magical thinking. I looked for Jackson everywhere, expecting him, knowing that once he came back the nightmare would end. Sometimes I thought I saw him, walking ahead of me in the hallway, on the street, a glimpsed profile in a passing car. I kept expecting someone would call and tell me where I could find him. I dreamed that my mother told me our friend Georgina had seen Jackson and I woke up running to the telephone to call her. Sometimes I yelled at the universe that I had been patient and accepting for long enough already and it was time for him to come back.

From students and faculty there were questions like "Did he know you were coming?" "Did he know you would find him?" Or there was awkward silence, as if this person who had been part of their community and left so suddenly had never even existed. Most of them wanted to know what was wrong with Jackson so they would feel reassured that he took his life because he was somehow defective or sick or weird. With rare exceptions, like the criminal law professor who was known to weep in class whenever he talked about a particular death penalty case, and less than a handful of others, the seeming indifference especially among faculty was enraging. They would have preferred to sweep the whole incident away.

I moved into a small garden apartment on L Street. Two units were on either side of mine, with a similar configuration on the other side of a park-like swath of grass and tall trees. Every apartment had a swamp cooler on the roof. When it was turned on, it made the air so unbearably thick and wet and humid inside that many of us slept outside on the grass when the summer nights never really cooled down. Lying on patches of shaded grass during those hot, still days when time slows to a lethargic crawl, Frodo would suffer the heat with me, stretched out to his fullest length. He watched closely, following me in and out of my abyss, ever trusting, sleek and black, with his crazy, loving green eyes.

Later in the fall, Lilia, a law student and psychic, offered me a reading. She said that in his last weeks, Jackson's aura had been nearly nonexistent, that he had been preparing himself to die and no one could have affected his life or death one way or the other. Though of little comfort to me, she said the relationship had been for my benefit, to expand my growth, and to toughen me.

I surrounded myself with women friends, first- and second-year law students. Most were in their late twenties and incredibly excited to have broken through the barrier of male-dominated professional schools. We wore long skirts and dresses, took off our bras, stopped shaving our legs and underarms, became vegetarians, bought waterbeds, and practiced yoga. One day I took my best friend, ever wise and loving Katy, to the grassy place where she held my hand and listened, and then quietly told me about being a teenager helplessly watching a barn burn to the ground with her 5-year-old twin brothers inside.

Exactly seven months from his death, Jackson came in the middle of the night when I was somewhere between awake and asleep. His face appeared in the dark, alive and whole. He receded, came back, and then was gone. Frodo was sleeping wrapped around my head. When he moved and woke me, I sat straight up, relieved, crying, trying to crawl back inside the dream.

Ed and I were together a lot. Sometimes he stayed with me, mostly not. He worked at different jobs and tried a semester at Sacramento State taking drama classes. On weekends, we would go to Keystone Korner in San Francisco or the Bach Dancing & Dynamite Society in Half Moon Bay to hear live jazz. Occasionally we drove to Mendocino and sometimes to L.A. to visit his brother and daughter. I knew the love relationship with Ed was one I would not have again with anyone else. But even after seven years he would say he didn't know me, though he really did, so very completely. "You aren't in touch with yourself," he rightly observed. "You give more importance to what I want than what you want, if you even tell yourself what that is."

Then he was using again and the old familiar fear was back. I started to panic. I told Ed if he overdosed and died, I wouldn't give myself any time to feel pain. I couldn't imagine where I'd get the will to live.

One day in late spring of 1975, four years before his 50th birthday, Ed said, "I get scared of being old and alone." I felt his oldness and aloneness. I could get in touch with Ed's pain so easily—or maybe it was my own feelings imagining what his pain must be like. I still hadn't learned how not to drown in him.

Then he was forceful, taking an enormous risk. "I give myself three years," he said. "I want a partner. We either work towards a common goal or nothing." Then he suggested that we use his VA benefits to buy a house together.

"How could that ever happen," I wondered out loud, "with you shooting every penny into your arm?"

The next thing I knew, he was calling to tell me he had met a woman with whom he went to Reno and married.

16

Wife #3

ED

E ventually I left the job in Woodland and briefly rented a room from a woman named Sunny. There, I met her friend Ann who worked for the Sacramento Area Economic Opportunity Commission, the county agency for the War on Poverty. When Ann saw me, she grinned and sang, "Oooh!" Ann was a good person who was just looking, like so many of us, for someone to make her happy I didn't go out with Ann at that point because I wasn't attracted to her.

I enrolled at Sacramento State University, living in the dorm and taking classes in dramatic arts and American history. The kids in the dorm drove me crazy. I was the oldest person living there and at the end of the semester, I left school.

I was hunting and pecking everywhere trying to figure out how to make myself happy and figure out what to do next. I wandered around and worked for a mental health facility in West Sacramento. Then I went back to work for the Sacramento Singlemen Self Help program that I had helped to start in the late 1960s.

At some point in 1975, I ran into Sunny again and Ann reappeared. She was still taken by what she thought she saw in me, the man of her dreams. Poor woman. What an unpleasant surprise was in store for her.

I was still seeing Diane, and had tried to convince her we should buy a house together, but she wouldn't agree. I knew that she and I depended on each other in the sickest of ways. While I didn't feel that I never wanted to see her again, I knew it had to change and I was the one who had to make the change because I was the one who was shooting dope.

I think now I understand that while my relationship with Diane held great attraction, it also had elements of poison. Much of my pain and feelings of inferiority came from how I felt with Diane. I would think about her with anger because I envied what I saw as her being so much more capable of conducting her own life than I could be for my own. Every time I fucked up she was there to pick up the pieces, and that was a superior place as I perceived it. I really had rage in my heart. There had been so many times that I went and fixed just to show her that she wasn't running my life.

Not only that. Diane and Marilyn, from my Stockton days, had become friends and started ganging up on me about my using, took me to task about my lies. I cussed them out, went out and got drunk, shot heroin, overdosed and nearly died.

When I came to, I just wanted to get even with them. That was my one thought when I went to see Ann and ended up going to Reno with her where we got married. Just like that. Sadly, I had a fit of laughter at the artificiality of the ceremony and the chapel, the wedding, and the marriage. I was still in love with Diane. What Ann wanted disgusted me—someone to "be her man," she said. But she had some money from a settlement and that would make it easier to get the heroin I wanted to escape the dread I felt listening to Diane and Marilyn telling me the truth about myself. It felt like they had been throwing rocks at me, and it hurt like nothing I had ever experienced.

Ann dressed me up in her very expensive style, which I hated. She said she wanted me to write and rented a room in Mendocino for me. I sat on the beach all day, kicked drugs, and wrote an article about the Chinese opium drug wars of the turn of the last century, which was eventually published. Ann would come up to Mendocino on weekends and I'd get blind drunk. When I returned to Sacramento, I started shooting heroin again with her money. I felt like I had to get loaded when I was with her.

In 1976, I was employed by the California Department of Corrections at their headquarters in Sacramento. I worked in the Division of Adult Parole Operations with a college intern. We wrote a proposal to the Department to help parolees successfully complete their sentences. We wanted to educate parolees to focus on getting jobs and having better relationships with their families and in the workplace. I was there about a year.

Ann and I bought a house in South Sacramento. We were married for three years, during which time my addiction went out of control. In 1978, I went to the drug program at the VA in Martinez. They gave me Valium combined with another drug to ease the withdrawal and I started hallucinating frightfully. When I refused to take more of it, they discharged me. Ann (bless her heart) took me to the VA in Palo Alto. When they said they couldn't take me, I climbed the fence around the facility and threatened to jump onto the freeway. They talked me down and ended up letting me in. I stayed a couple of months and when I went home, I hit the ground shooting dope.

Shooting dope sent me back to the VA, this time to the one in Menlo Park. The director of that program believed that most addicts had never been to any place where they could have fun and enjoy themselves. He took us to many of the nicest hot springs in Northern California—Wilbur, Harbin, Esalen, and Tassajara. Despite it all—and they were indeed wonderful places—not one of us stopped using. Though it didn't help my drug addiction, I did love and still do love going to the hot springs.

DIANE

Ed's sudden marriage was a stunning turn of events though as time passed it did give me some breathing room. On the surface not much had changed. He continued to call and periodically visit me. In an impressively ironic and wickedly amusing turn of events, I became not only the ex-wife, but also the other woman. Gradually we saw less of each other, and it was a relief of sorts that someone else was taking care of him—or trying to—and I would have a rest.

A month or so later, in late summer 1975, I drove up the coast to Anchor Bay with Frodo in my lap for a long weekend. I rented one of several tiny cabins scattered across a wide windblown, sun-drenched meadow of tall dried golden grasses on a high bluff overlooking the Pacific Ocean. Alone and having occasional moments of inner calm that I can usually find inside the sound of a thundering ocean, I roamed the headlands and contemplated the loss of something I wasn't sure I ever had. The truth was that Ed and I really didn't know each other very well.

With his unfailing cat wisdom, Frodo seemed to understand it was time to jolt me out of my sad stupor. One afternoon, sitting in a rocking chair in front of the window overlooking the ocean, smoking a joint, and lost in no particular thought, I was vaguely aware that Frodo had come in through the front door and dove under the daybed. He scuffled around for a bit before crawling out with something … yes, he had a small snake in his mouth which he very gently deposited in the middle of the room. The terrified creature froze on the spot while I, another terrified creature, and acting the perfect stereotype, screamed and leaped across the room, grabbed a long wooden spoon from the kitchen sink and jumped onto a chair. Frodo calmly ignored my screams to take that thing out of the house. He sat perfectly still, watching. At its slightest movement, he would leap on the snake or bat it or pick it up, and it would freeze again. As this drama played out, I finally understood that no one was coming to save me and came down off the chair. Crouching as far away from the creature as I could, I used the spoon handle to nudge it towards the door and keep Frodo from recapturing it. When it finally crossed the threshold and disappeared into tall dry grass, I slammed the door, cat still inside.

I would have liked to stay in a permanent state of escape, but had to go back to work. Before starting home, I foolishly smoked a joint and ended up driving in a perpetual state of panic. Going south on the coast highway means being in the right-hand lane, the one closest to the edge, where it would have been so easy to slide off the side of the mountain into the ocean.

Back in Davis, I swung wildly in and out of extremes. Sometimes I just wanted to get lost in sex, but felt a great terror about the vulnerability that would bring being intimate again with someone. I didn't trust myself not to find another Ed or Jackson, and then I would panic and decide to renounce any further closeness with anyone ever again. Ed had tried to pry my heart open. "Give yourself to somebody once in a while," he said. "You'll get yourself back." But it never seemed to happen.

In 1976, I was promoted to Director of Admissions at the law school. With increased responsibility and workload, work became an emotionally lifesaving, mood-altering remedy. I loved what I was doing. It was easy plunging myself into work to escape discomfort, something that would become a long-lasting practice. It was a deceptively clever way to replace one addiction (the one I suspected years ago about my relationship with Ed that had yet to be confirmed by anyone) with another—although, in reality, I was merely adding a second one. Work made me feel better about myself. I was more in control, and it was so very easy to lose myself in it.

I eventually started dating and had affairs with men and with women. At some level, I was opening up to new experiences but, in keeping with my history, they were generally people in unhappy relationships. While I wasn't intentionally looking for them, they weren't hard to find. So many relationships got wrecked by the pressures of law school. And then, the few people I did like who were unattached would move on once they understood that, because of how I talked about Ed, I really *wasn't* unattached.

I was in my early thirties with enough failed relationships behind me to question why I kept seeking out and re-creating secrets and drama. In truth, all it took was feeling a strong physical attraction to someone who needed me and who, often, like my father, was emotionally unavailable. That's how it had worked with my uncle, with Ed, and with Jackson. To a young woman with low self-esteem and no boundaries, the combination of attraction and being needed was hard to resist. I didn't yet know that those were just feelings, and that feelings do not have to be acted on.

Aside from the suffering I inevitably caused myself, it was terribly shocking that I called myself a feminist yet kept betraying other women by having affairs with their husbands, boyfriends, fiancés.

The shame of what I was doing kept me from talking to anyone about it. So by keeping myself in the solitary confinement of my own dangerous mind, I had no way to learn about how un-unique I really was.

ED

My long slow low bottom was speeding up and reaching new depths, even for me. Every time it seemed I had reached as low a place as I could go, I'd enroll in a treatment program, bounce back, be a model client, and be discharged, only to start using again.

Through the late 1970s and early 1980s, I had completed, been thrown out, or walked out of many VA and other drug programs. By then, my third wife Ann had divorced me. When she moved out of our house with the delinquent mortgage that was eventually fore-closed, she took the cushioned toilet seats. That was so funny to me. I laughed a lot about how the removal of those toilet seats signified the end of our marriage.

I was working as an employment specialist in San Mateo and lived in a motel room off the 101 freeway. I met and got involved with two more women. I was so miserable.

17

Making a Difference

DIANE

I left the law school in 1977 to take a job as Executive Officer (EO) with the board that licenses psychologists in California. I had applied only because a friend who was chief deputy director in the Department of Consumer Affairs asked me to. (The Department is the umbrella agency for state licensing and regulatory boards.) With no academic degree, I didn't expect to get the job and was unnerved when I did, certain it was only a matter of time before people realized someone had made a mistake. I was to administer all phases of four annual licensure examinations, respond to consumer complaints of alleged misconduct by psychologists, work with the investigations unit and the state attorney general's office, recommend policy to the board, respond to requests for information from the governor's office and legislators, prepare the annual budget and more—though none of *any* of that had I done before.

During the first weeks, the only way I could breathe was to find a niche that motivated me to feel brave and jump in. That niche turned out to be enforcement, a piece that the previous EO had all but ignored. I found a huge backlog of unopened consumer complaints in boxes piled on top of file cabinets. Many were from women who had been sexually victimized by their licensed therapist, and each one involved potential and serious psychological harm. The outrage I felt for women who had been abused and then found courage to report it, only to be disregarded by the board that was supposed to protect them, gave me a starting place. Perhaps I felt a shared bond with those women who reminded me of my own shame and lack of healing in the relationship with my uncle that had also involved a power imbalance.

I went to Los Angeles to observe an administrative hearing against one licensed psychologist, John Dresser, charged with sexual abuse of two women clients. The hearing was a horrifying process, similar to rape trials, where victims were treated like perpetrators, accused of seducing the therapist. The obvious power imbalance in these types of "relationships" should not even be up for question. It was clear that these two women, subjected to harsh cross-examination by the defense attorney, were broken, their trust violated, victims of, as Masters and Johnson put it, "emotional rape." Dresser didn't deny having sex with them, but he did blame them for initiating what he called "consensual" acts. Since there was no law that explicitly prohibited sexual abuse or misconduct with patients, the only severe disciplinary action that could be taken was to revoke his license on the grounds of gross negligence. And that was done.

Back in Sacramento, I told the board about the hearing. It was not difficult to convince them that this was a high enforcement priority, especially because half of all consumer complaints filed with the psychology board during the course of the year involved sexual misconduct or abuse of a client. We found a legislator, Assemblymember Herschel Rosenthal, who understood that this was likely a widespread problem, going beyond just psychologists. He introduced legislation, AB 1072, that passed and was signed into law in September 1979. The bill provided specific authority to all of California's healing arts licensing and regulatory boards to suspend or revoke the license of a person who has committed an act of sexual abuse, misconduct, or sexual relations with a patient in the course of his or her professional duties. Those boards included physicians, psychiatrists, nurses, acupuncturists, psychologists, dentists, social workers, marriage family therapists, veterinarians, and others.

I often worked into the night in my little windowless office, until the janitors came to empty the trash and vacuum. I felt so much more in control and happy about my work than my relationships, not to mention how good it felt to work on issues that so personally resonated with me— in this case, holding offenders accountable and stripping them of their license. It didn't take long for work to become a daily fix, even when there was nothing to escape. Eventually, I reached a point where I felt all right missing my own birthday party to work on something that could have waited until the next day.

In the two years I was with the psychology board, between licensing exams, board meetings, and administrative hearings, I traveled all over the state. Whenever I drove into the Bay Area, coming over the hills on I-80 and catching a first glimpse of the Bay and the magnificent San Francisco skyline, I dreamed about living there.

In June 1980, I moved to Oakland and decided, *finally*, to return to school and complete my B.A. I was 36. To support myself, I worked as a legal secretary, though with no formal training I felt like an imposter. I got temp jobs at various law firms all over the

Bay Area, and enrolled at San Francisco State University, majoring in Women's Studies.

One of the classes I took, "The Politics of Reproduction," was taught by Angela Davis. It was a heady experience to sit in the same classroom with her just feet away. Her intense dignity, brilliance, and beauty had practically every young woman in the class swooning after her. One day, she mentioned some events linked to the Civil Rights movement when suddenly she stopped. "Who knows what I'm talking about?" she asked the mostly blank faces in the class. "What do you know about the civil rights movement?" It was distressing to realize that in just 20 short years—the span of most of these young women's lives—so much of what was part of our most vital and recent history was disappearing.

Angela spent the rest of the class educating young feminists about the civil rights movement from which so many other new social justice movements had sprung. At the end, she cautioned, "We have to be vigilant and protect every hard-won right we have gained, because no sooner than it's granted will it be in jeopardy of being lost."

18

Meeting
"God"

ED

After Ann divorced me in 1979, I was doing pretty well in my job and had a nice little apartment in Menlo Park. But I started shooting dope again. I knew that wasn't okay so I thought if I went to the mental health facility in Redwood City maybe they could tell me what was wrong with me. You see, I thought I had to be nuts to buy something to inject into my body from those "Scabby Willy" drug dealers. To endow Scabby Willy with license to dispense my medication seemed a little backward.

I was given a 72-hour examination. As I was walking around getting familiar with my surroundings I kept feeling that I was being observed by someone. Finally I spun around and saw this tiny, very attractive woman looking my way. She shyly approached me, apologized for staring, and explained that I looked a lot like someone from her past that she had been very close to. She was articulate and quite alluring in a well-bred manner. I was amazed. What was she even doing there?

Her name was Sue. As we got to know each other, she confided in a whisper that she was God in partnership—that is, she was co-God with Stevie Wonder. She said this with such candor that I actually wanted to believe her. I thought, "Wow, this could be a new pathway to salvation away from Scabby Willy."

I had not had any belief in the idea of God since that day many years ago when, in response to my mother's ongoing, angry admonition that God was going to strike me down, I had run outside in anger, gave the finger to GOD and ducked, expecting to be struck down. When nothing happened, I began to question my mom's attempts to control me, to "make something out of me," as she put it. So far, none of the drug programs I had been in seemed to be helping, and I couldn't bring myself to join AA because of all the references to God in their Twelve Steps.

But now here was this pretty person telling me that she was "God." Well, since I had never run into God before and people all over the planet were raving about God, and I had trusted Scabby Willy, I thought, "What have I got to lose?" I might even learn something and be blessed for eternity. The idea of "co-Gods" did strike me as a little strange. But what the hell, she sure was cute and by then I did not have a lot at stake.

Sue and I decided to leave the nuthouse and move into my apartment. We couldn't stay there long because Sue had to smoke weed and play Stevie Wonder at maximum volume day and night— that's how she and Stevie stayed in touch doing their God work—and the landlord threatened to call the cops. So we moved into a tiny room in a dilapidated three-story dump in Redwood City that was run by meth heads.

It was perfect.

Everyone just wanted to be left alone, talking to themselves, doing methamphetamine. Meth heads have this strange communication that sounds like perhaps a Martian or maybe Neptunian or even a Plutonian tongue.

One of the guys there, Doug, had bought one of the earliest computers from Radio Shack. He also had three shortwave radios, a drum set, three chairs, a public address system, and a desk—on the roof. (I had watched him when he laboriously transported all of this equipment up a ladder to the roof. It took two days.) He came to our door to explain that he was in communication with 39 planets and since he realized that it might be a little noisy, he needed our consent to "work" three nights a week for six years. We, of course, agreed and wished him success. He began yelling to Mars that very night. He was apologetic when I saw him the next morning, but he was also excited because the Martians had offered him an all-expense paid visit.

One morning I woke up hearing the noise of a racing car engine accompanied by yelling coming through our window. Doors opened and slammed closed, bang, bump, and I heard the hurried, urgent, unintelligible voices of speed freaks outside our roach-infested room. There in the driveway was Doug, who had been yelling at the top of his lungs nonstop for nine days and was now in angry mourning because Radio Shack had come to repossess the computer and the stereo radio that had all fallen off the roof—well, not exactly off the roof, but fell from just underneath the roof.

According to Doug, all this was the fault of the guy from Radio Shack. We all knew that Doug climbed out of the third-story window with his one free arm (and the stereo tucked under his other arm) to get up to the roof. His duffle bag was on his back, and he always put on his black motorcycle helmet and his silver space coveralls to keep the spatial atmospheric radiation off of him. He'd get up on the roof, turn on the stereo, boogie by himself, talk to Martians, and then go back to his room without ever dropping anything. That is, until this uptight asshole came to repossess the $4000 worth of equipment Doug had paid for with a bad check. Doug was just at the most critical part of his climb up to the roof to his latest "git down." Can't blame him if the equipment fell when the fool screamed and nearly fainted, watching his top-of-the-line computer and stereo swinging from a line attached to this silver-clad black-visaged apparition from a comic strip nightmare. A spider-thin man crawling up a wall!

As the Radio Shack guy was leaving we heard him muttering to himself that he was sure to be fired. How would he ever explain to his boss how he came to do business with Doug?

One day I saw that Stevie Wonder was going to perform in the Bay Area and I bought tickets for Sue and me. She was very excited at first but as the date of Stevie's show approached she became very calm, very still, and on the night of the show she was almost catatonic. As the show reached break time. I suggested that we go backstage. Sue refused to speak to me. She then got up and left. Our relationship was never the same. Soon after the concert we moved to an apartment in Berkeley, but by then Sue had emotionally shut down, angry that her fantasy about Stevie Wonder had been shattered. We were unhappy, and would soon separate.

DIANE

As his relationship with Sue ended, Ed started to bounce in and out of my life once again. I let him stay with me during many of the times he was out of treatment programs and didn't have a place to go to.

When he was in various VA programs, I sometimes went to the weekly so-called "family group" for wives and significant others; there the unspoken motto was "stand by your man." The game at the VA was to keep the lid on anger, despite lies, cheating, and betrayal. Women were not encouraged to question how they had sacrificed themselves, placing their "man's" needs before their own. Jeanie, who led the group, actually had the consciousness to understand what was happening to those women, yet encouraged the pacifism that contributed to and reinforced the craziness in their lives. She was the cruelest sort of enemy women have: a woman who worked to keep other women from finding their voice and standing up for themselves.

Without a doubt, the sickest part of that program was the requirement that a significant other attend those family meetings for clients to get a weekend pass. How crazy was that? Even I who had been an enabler for so long without really understanding what to do about it, even *I* knew that making me responsible for whether or not Ed got a weekend pass not only fed my own dysfunction, but continued to fuel Ed's resentment over his dependence on me.

As I began my second semester at San Francisco State in the spring of 1981, I took a consulting job with the Department of Consumer Affairs. It was a women's health project exploring the perinatal health care system and its reliance on intervention to solve problems of low birthweight and infant morbidity and mortality that could have been prevented with prenatal care. Covering the Bay Area, I worked with consultants from L.A. and the Central Valley to organize public hearings on the issue. One of my most thrilling moments was getting Angela Davis to agree to testify at my Bay Area hearing and, at her request, writing the testimony that she read. After the hearings, we analyzed the transcripts, along with further interviews and an extensive review of the literature, and wrote a 400-page report of findings and recommendations.

State Assemblymember Tom Bates decided to use our recommendations for legislation that would require the State Department of Health Services to provide more Medicaid-funded comprehensive primary care services for low-income pregnant women at risk for poor outcomes. Bates asked the Department of Consumer Affairs to keep me on the payroll to help write the bill and organize statewide consumer support through the network we had developed that ultimately got the legislation passed. It was signed into law in September 1982 by Governor Jerry Brown, despite opposition from the California Medical Association and the American College of Ob-Gyns, along with the California Department of Health Services, all of which resented a non-health entity telling them how to provide health care. Once more, I felt passionate about the work I was doing. It gave me purpose and made me feel like I had a place in the world.

Late in 1981, Ed was living with me again and working for a recycling center in the Oakland hills. He joined a gospel and jazz choir called Traveling Voices at Merritt College and started singing publicly for the first time since I had met him. For years, I'd heard Ed sing or scat complex solos recorded by dozens of jazz greats, but hadn't realized the extent of his amazing voice and talent. He was given a role in a musical production the group was working on and, along with being in the chorus, was chosen to be the soloist on "Sophisticated Lady." Sitting in the audience during his performance, I understood that he had yet one more very special gift. When he left the Traveling Voices in early 1982, a light went out of him. It was like he lost his spiritual peripheral vision, despairing of ever being worthwhile. He was increasingly vocal about his resented dependency on me and the obligations that living in someone else's space created.

I wished I could stop taking his life so personally when there was clearly not much I had ever been able to do to fix it. It was an unsettling place to be, rising in my professional life while my personal life was such a mess. There seemed to be no amount of success, reward, or recognition I had achieved that could lessen the sense of failure I carried inside. Still, had it not been for my own work that helped to anchor me, Ed's descent into darkness would have once again dragged me down with him.

ED

In 1982, I was living in Oakland, mostly staying at Diane's, and got a job working at a federal halfway house as a counselor. The day I first saw Jenny at the program, she was sitting and nodding, obviously under the influence of an opiate or some equally powerful pharmaceutical. She was a lovely young woman of 19. During that morning's staff meeting, there was talk about sending her back to prison for violating her parole. The federal inmate transport system made the rounds of the community facilities once a month to drop off new parolees or pick up people who were going to be transferred somewhere else. Typically, the parolee didn't know they were going anywhere until they were ordered to get on the bus.

On that day, Jenny had no notion of what was in store for her, a sheep being led to slaughter, dumb as grass. She had initially been sent to federal prison because she was caught in possession of some drugs she brought from Mexico for her "man," who had also been paroled to the same facility. Jenny and her man were not on speaking terms because he felt that she was not smart enough to be of any further use to him. At that point, Jenny was hooking to get dope and salve a broken heart. (And I was still shooting heroin because I told myself that it was the only way I could stand to work in that environment, even though the job paid well.)

Because Jenny was newly arrived at that halfway house, I thought it was too soon to send her back to prison without working with her first. They put her on my caseload, and after the staff meeting, I went out to talk to Jenny. She had grown up in El Paso, Texas with two brothers and her mother. Her father had run off with another woman when Jenny was an infant. He lived in New Mexico and she had only seen him once or twice that she could remember though he was in regular contact with her two brothers. She said that she understood, and it was okay. I asked her what it was that she understood. She said he was very busy. He had some important job at Los Alamos National Laboratory.

I began to think about Jenny a lot, and eventually we became lovers. I told myself I was getting involved with her not only to protect her because she was so physically gorgeous that she stopped traffic, but she was also vulnerable. We started hanging out during the day. It didn't take too long before we were shooting dope together. We used to sit on the side of the hill at the Oakland Rose Garden, get loaded, and make love before she had to go back to the halfway house. When Diane went back East on a trip, we spent a lot of time at her place while Jenny was supposed to be looking for a job.

Eventually, I went to her parole officer in my "counselor" role and made the case that she should be sent home to her mother in El Paso, not returned to prison. We went through her file and really found no good reason to send her back to prison. I talked to her mother in Texas and we got Jenny sent home in late 1982 to finish her parole.

She was home for about two weeks when she began calling and begging me to come to Texas to live with her. I asked her if she was crazy. The very thought of living with a white woman in Texas was the most insane idea I could imagine. It gave me the creeps. Especially with a showstopper like Jenny who looked the way Ava Gardner wished she could look and attracted male attention every place she went.

She kept after me. What bothered me was the fear I felt about the whole national race thing, the hatred by whites that I had been brought up under. Even so, I had always crossed boundaries and now here I was enamored of this woman that I really liked. I cannot call it love. Diane was still in my life and we had been sharing an apartment, but I talked to her about Jenny all the time. I finally decided that I wanted to go to Texas, let them lynch me if they had to. I had to take that chance because I felt that if I didn't, I would never forgive myself for my cowardice.

So, in January 1983, I quit my job and flew to El Paso. Jenny, her mother, and her stepfather met me at the airport. They were very kind and grateful to me for helping Jenny stay out of prison. Jenny's stepfather had a one-room cabin at the corner of Roundup and Cowboy Streets in the middle of a huge wooded preserve in Lake Hills, Texas, a tiny town of 700 in the Texas hill country northwest of San Antonio. Jenny and I moved into that cabin. There was no running water on the property, no indoor toilet, and the outdoor toilet was unusable, so we kept a shovel by the door. We had a wood stove and Jenny was a great camping cook. We always ate well. And we didn't use drugs.

When I first got there, I decided not to show my face and get lynched. We lived about two miles from the nearest store, so Jenny put two one-gallon jugs in a backpack and walked to get water for us to drink, cook, and wash with. I hid for two weeks until I finally found the nerve to come out.

I bought a pickup and Jenny and I started to build and repair fences for the community. We went bathing in Lake Medina every day and, in spite of my fears, I began to make friends with what turned out to be some very kind people. We got a beautiful German shepherd puppy and one day when Jenny was walking in the woods, she came back with a rabbit that followed her home and told us his name was "Bunny Bunny."

Later that year, when we started to smoke weed, it began to come apart. We had to go into San Antonio and other towns to cop marijuana. Once, we were stopped by a Texas Ranger, who somehow knew my name, which made me very uncomfortable. Then we discovered that the uncle of an acquaintance of ours was a drug dealer, Popeye, who had been a former sheriff. He talked Jenny into going to Mexico to buy heroin because she could speak Spanish like a native. It was a successful trip. As they were planning their next one, all I could think of was the Texas penitentiary.

Diane came to visit for a couple of days in July on her way back to Oakland from Connecticut, after visiting her family. She had been freaking out about my going to Texas to live with a white woman and, in typical Diane fashion, needed to see for herself that I was okay. Towards the end of the summer, Jenny and I began to understand that we were finished. We both knew that I was still in love with my ex-wife. It was all a little sad but full of lessons learned, like I really didn't know what I was doing. Why was I in Texas, one of the worst places in the world to end up in prison? I didn't really know what love was, or why I followed Jenny to Texas. She asked me to, but I don't know why I agreed when I knew how dangerous it could be for me living with a white woman. I don't know why the universe let me get away with that. It wasn't long before I returned to California on the Greyhound bus and back to Diane's house. Through the years, Jenny and I have remained friends and are still in contact with each other.

19

Before It's Too Late

DIANE

By 1983, I had my B.A. The statewide women's health project—the most perfect of all consulting jobs I would ever have—had ended and I was trying to figure out what to do next. But complicating everything were questions that started coming up about things I thought had been resolved years before.

When I was in my twenties, I had decided that I didn't want to have children. But that was before I had become immersed in a project about pregnancy and childbirth at the precise moment when suddenly, everything was about babies. Women in their late thirties were panicking about their biological clocks ticking away, and that made me aware of my own. Almost at once, pregnant women were everywhere, including my sister, friends, colleagues, even the editor of our perinatal report. If they weren't pregnant, they were trying. I was not only swept into that tidal wave, but found myself wanting to have the experience of childbirth, and that completely unnerved me.

I hadn't been with anyone for a couple of years. I was lonely. I missed my family and my newly married social worker sister working with her husband in their apple orchard in Connecticut. But burdening a newborn with the job of filling the empty space inside me was a terrible reason to have a child. Anyway, how could I even consider bringing new life into a world that cared so little for people and for life? Still, the feelings persisted.

One thing I knew was that if I did get pregnant, I would have to stop smoking a pack and a half of Marlboros every day, something I had failed to do after countless attempts in the past 21 years. This time, I made it through the initial emotional basket case phase, crying all day and riding out alarming surges of anger. It was unnerving that my brain seemed to have stopped working and that I couldn't concentrate long enough to hold a thought or write a lucid sentence. An acupuncturist friend put needles in my ears and that helped relieve the craving pressure in my lungs. As a last resort, I tried smoking a joint every time I wanted a cigarette, but all that did was get me high and hungry. I went several days without a single conscious minute when I wasn't obsessed about smoking, always on the verge of going to the store to buy a pack.

Then I did the classic addict thing. I told myself I could handle one or two cigarettes every now and then, just to relieve the stress of withdrawal. I bought a pack of Marlboros, smoked 10 over three days, crushed the rest and threw them in the trash. The next morning I fished them out and smoked what I could salvage. Other times, I put whatever was left in the pack under water and threw them away, but by morning was ready to smoke whatever had dried out. It was disgusting.

All that dumpster diving clearly proved no amount of will-power was strong enough to defeat this addiction, no matter how hard I tried. Almost as bad as letting my own self down was admitting failure to everyone who knew I had quit and was cheering me on. I talked about the first slip when I went and bought a pack. But the humiliation of buying, destroying, and resurrecting the second and then the third and fourth packs was too humiliating, so I stopped talking about it at all.

That's when I really understood what Ed went through during his countless tries to stop using heroin: the initial intention, the first slip, the illusion he could control his using, then the renewed promises, inevitable using again, and the final dive back into shame-driven secrecy and lying. That's when I got it that I was also a substance addict even though the "real" drug addicts and alcoholics, all of whom still smoked and many of whom would die from tobacco-related diseases, ridiculed the notion that a smoker was as authentic an addict as they were. For the first time, I felt compassion for Ed's struggle and could empathize about how hard it was, and especially how bad one can feel about oneself.

By then, Ed had returned from his adventures with 20-year-old Jenny in Texas. He came back to Oakland with no money or job and started shooting dope again, which began a new cycle of treatment programs.

Jenny was special to me. I had complicated feelings about the many women Ed was involved with. I knew some better than others, and liked some better than others. I was always relieved to have a break when he was with someone who seemed strong and self-sufficient, but over time, as Ed wore down, so were most of the women he found. Jenny was young, strong, beautiful, and smart, a fantastic cook, storyteller, and animal whisperer. Despite her time in federal prison, her optimism about people and life was like a light. I worried about her being with Ed who was so much older and who was bottoming out. As troubling as all that was, there was nothing I could do to change any of it.

I told Ed I was going to try to get pregnant and thought that, even though I really wanted a girl, maybe it wouldn't be so bad to have a boy that I would raise as a male feminist. "Well," he said, "if it's a boy, he'll never have to leave home." While I think he meant it as a bit of a joke, it perfectly described the enmeshment and dependency between us that exposed one of my biggest reservations about having a child. Then he apologized for having had a vasectomy a couple of years before without telling me first, though he had known full well I had never talked about wanting to have children.

Going back to school seemed to be a good place to land for a while. I had learned a lot about public health during my work with the perinatal project. Graduate school felt like the right direction to go, and I'd leave with a piece of paper giving me credibility. The more I tried to talk myself out of the baby idea, however, the firmer its hold became. I called an adoption referral clearinghouse and found out that there was a five-year wait for an infant, couples had first priority, and interracial adoptions were not allowed unless one person in the couple was the same race as the baby. Lots of older kids were available, but it felt like I would probably need to grow along with a baby. Then I talked to someone at a local sperm bank about their donor insemination program and felt encouraged, or reassured, or at least more optimistic that this was a good option.

One night I dreamed about a very old woman. She had sharply chiseled features and gazed into the far-off distance. She wore a flowing black cape. Wisps of her long gray hair escaping from the corners of her hood blew around her waist. "Oh honey," she said as her image faded, "it's just a midlife crisis."

20

Sparks of Hope

ED

In the fall of 1983 when I came back to Oakland from Texas, I stayed with Diane, on and off. Since we both loved going to Wilbur Hot Springs, in the coastal range mountains northwest of Sacramento, it wasn't hard to convince her that we should go to the Tassajara Zen Buddhist Monastery and Mountain Center for a few days. The long drive to that beautiful isolated retreat twisted through the Carmel Valley on a steep 16-mile one-lane dirt road in the Ventana Wilderness area of the Los Padres National Forest. Life was simpler for us during those few days at Tassajara when we feasted on wonderful vegetarian meals, soaked in hot tubs, read, and hiked. We walked along the creek and through the woods until we came to a long slide down a series of large, marble-smooth, moss-covered boulders that ended with a drop into a deep pool below. But no matter how wonderful it was, of course I always had to take myself with me.

One day after lunch, when I was once again planning how I would commit suicide and end my misery, I met a Buddhist monk on the path. He stopped to talk when he saw the suffering on my face. After listening to how badly I felt about myself, he said that, to him, I was perfect and had never made a mistake. I almost fainted when he uttered those words. It felt like my head was literally spinning as I walked down the path to the bookstore. When I walked through the door, the first book I saw was *There's Nothing Wrong With You* by Zen teacher Cherie Huber.

I was struck by the improbable coincidence of getting these two messages within minutes of each other and what that meant to me. When I was four and had been caught under the bed trying to understand how matches worked, my terrified mother screamed, "What's wrong with you?" And I, in my little boy's overly literal mind, believed—and acted out—from that scolding until I walked into the bookstore in Tassajara that if my mother, as smart as she was, didn't know what was wrong with me, then it must be something really bad. Her question, what's wrong with you, from so long ago, had haunted me all my life.

In that moment at Tassajara, it was hard to know what to do with the monk's statement and the book title that so perfectly fit together, but it did start a new trajectory for me. It was an idea, like a whisper, something that stayed with me and waited for me until I was ready to do something different about myself.

DIANE

The recession of the early 1980s made it a lot harder to find a job. Having to resort to temporary work in law offices and traveling all over the Bay Area was paying the bills, but I was doing a sort of middle-class version of factory work. Commuting on BART, I watched people's faces—dead in the morning, dead at night, avoiding eye contact, buried in books, newspapers, and headphones. Silent, distant people moving like sleepwalkers on and off trains, through stations, up escalators into the streets to join other sleepwalkers. Seriously, was this what I had to look forward to?

I started having a recurring dream about being on a space age rapid transit train. The tracks followed a stomach-churning roller coaster path, sometimes lurching to the side and running along the perilously narrow edge of what could only be a bottomless void. As the train approached the summit where there was an unbelievably steep plunge that didn't seem survivable, I panicked, unable to see what happened to the forward cars that disappeared as they hurtled over the top.

The closer I got to my 40th birthday in February 1984, the more intensely I felt that I was bottoming out emotionally. Then, a few days before his 55th birthday on February 2, Ed started to melt down, confessing to having lied about a job that never existed and paychecks that he had claimed were lost or stolen. He was exhausted and broken. He stood in the middle of the room, coming unraveled.

"I have lied, stolen, and cheated everyone who has been my friend or lover. I am empty. I am always afraid and then I run towards what I fear—rejection, failure, loneliness, poverty. I find them. And I become them." Then he was crying. "I don't want to live on the edge like they do on the streets in East Oakland. But why should I get help to feel better only to do the same thing over again?"

By Valentine's Day, the day before my birthday, he was in the VA again and we would not be allowed any contact for 45 days. It would be a hard program. Since he had been there before, they were punishing him for relapsing by making him sleep in the bathroom for the first two weeks. That must have been really therapeutic.

I was again withdrawing from Ed, in a now-quiet house full of piles of his things that had become co-mingled with my own. I was about to turn 40 and all I could think of was hiding under the covers and sleeping until I could wake up whole and healthy from this bad dream. Instead, there was the old stabbing feeling of loss, the readjusting, and trying not to dwell on him sleeping in the shitter for two weeks. He had to do his work, and I had to do mine.

One day I found an Al-Anon pamphlet that I had picked up the year before in one of the VA programs and stuck in a drawer. Even that recently I had denied I was *that* bad. But now, seriously thinking about the 20 questions in the pamphlet to help families and friends of addicts/alcoholics identify whether they could benefit from Al-Anon, I was shocked to see so much of myself in it. The resistance I had towards Twelve Step programs had weakened to nearly nothing. I was 40 and no longer felt that I would live forever. I was not inclined to keep freely giving up chunks of my life. I was willing to try anything. I was ready to listen.

I chose Nar-Anon over Al-Anon for the simple reason that it focuses on narcotics addiction which, by its very illegality, makes being involved with a heroin addict more complicated than being with someone abusing alcohol or any other legal drug. At least I would be around people who I assumed had been through what I had.

I went to my first Nar-Anon meeting at Merritt Hospital in Oakland. Meetings always began with the reading of the Twelve Steps.

Step One: We admitted we were powerless over the addict— that our lives had become unmanageable.

That stopped me. After 16 years of failing to change or save Ed, I could without hesitation admit I was powerless over him. And about my own life being unmanageable? I could certainly keep it together outwardly, but inside I didn't know where I ended and he began. There's a funny little saying about that: "I'm not myself today. Maybe I'm you."

I listened to one person after another who, in telling their stories, told my own. People spoke of their successes—refusing to give their addict money, setting and maintaining personal boundaries—and relapses into enabling behavior. One woman shared the latest encounter she'd had with her heroin-addicted son. During the past week, she had refused to let him inside the house when he showed up hungry, dirty, and homeless. Instead, she gave him a blanket and walked him to the garage. Everyone in the room applauded. I felt like crying.

There were those concepts again that my friend Luba from the methadone program in Stockton had tried to tell me about: detaching, letting go, staying centered in the midst of chaos. I wanted to learn how to do that. I was so tired. I wanted to stop presuming that I had to hold up the world.

But it was when someone recited towards the end of the meeting what's known as the "3 C's" for codependents that finally brought tears of relief:

You didn't cause it.

You can't control it.

You can't cure it.

Ed was still in that 45-day black hole of no communication with the outside world, so I wrote a mental letter to both of us.

"Dear Ed. Well, you better believe it. After all these years, I've got myself a program. Wonder why it took so long to get that it's not my job to fix you. It's yours. Nine little words I wish I'd been able to say to you years ago: I know you can handle it. I love you."

It was a beginning. Something was breaking loose, nudging me forward. I applied to graduate school at U.C. Berkeley with no assurance that I could support myself through a two-year full-time program and not knowing how I would manage the distractions Ed would bring. I also decided either to get pregnant or look into adoption. It was a familiar process, like the other times in my life when I would just close my eyes, jump, and see what would happen.

ED

I had no idea what to do with myself when I left Texas and returned to Oakland. Diane allowed me to move in with her again, temporarily, and I answered that by lying, cheating, and stealing checks from the back of her checkbook and pawning her jewelry again. I had never given myself permission to use drugs, but I started using again right away even though I hadn't shot dope in the nine months I spent in the resort town of Lake Hills, TX at the corner of "Roundup and Cowboy" dirt roads. I was about to learn that the real problem with drugs was the illusion they offered about living your life, the lies the drug allowed you to believe about yourself, and your choices in each moment. I had started using 36 years before and had made some very big mistakes. Now it seemed that I would again go down that path.

I went to work at a busy, old-fashioned 1930s grocery store in Berkeley that was being managed by the grandson of the original owners. The young man hired me to assist him in running the store. I soon discovered that we had a lot in common, mainly drug use and thievery. I noticed that he did not keep a record of the cash he took from the register. In the afternoon he would announce that he had to run an errand and he'd be gone for a short while. Then he would return and announce that he had a lot of back ordering to do and didn't want to be disturbed. If anyone asked for him, I was to say he was out shopping. He would very politely ask if I needed anything and then he'd leave and be gone for most of the afternoon. Soon I got it that he was not keeping any record of sales. I was so happy! This was a busy store that took in a lot of money, especially from sales of beer and wine, meat products, vegetables, and breakfast food. I learned that he had not been running the store for very long. So I began to help myself to money, slowly at first. But when nothing was said, I became greedier. Lucky for me the store went out of business before I probably would have been arrested, again, for theft.

DIANE

In April 1984, my sister gave birth to a baby boy and I flew to Connecticut to meet my newborn nephew and help Miriam. I stayed with my parents for part of the visit. One night, my cousin Jake, the youngest son of my mother's middle sister (not the youngest sister in California), knocked on the door. I hadn't seen him in over 20 years since I'd left for college.

It was hard to make the leap from the wild little boy I remembered when we were all growing up in Stamford to the now 32-year-old tall, dark, handsome young man with longish hair and a diamond stud in one ear that my mother couldn't help but laugh about and pull on a little.

We walked out into the cold Stamford spring night and went to the movies. Afterwards, we stood outside the door of my parents' apartment and made plans to talk some more. We said goodnight and had a little cousin hug. He kissed me on my lips and quickly put his tongue in my mouth. I pulled away, half shocked that such an unlikely move had come from such an unlikely source. I don't think he planned it. I think he surprised himself. We never spoke of it.

I knew only fragments about him. He was 13 when I left college and moved to California. Around the time I was struggling to get out of the disastrous affair with my uncle, Jake was starting to use drugs. After high school and a year of college, he married and had two children. Within a few years, he had destroyed the marriage, got involved in some level of drug running and drug deals, and made money that he gambled or drank away.

He always seemed to talk in riddles, probably because he was high a lot, which would explain why so much of the time I had no idea what he was talking about. Yet, at some unspoken level, we recognized ourselves to be the two black sheep of the family prone to danger and complications, and that in itself was a strong pull.

Jake kept saying he was falling in love with me. At the time, I'd been going to Twelve Step meetings for only a few months. Working hard to resist the formidable magnets of attraction and rescuing that I felt so strongly with him, I had to laugh at the joke the universe seemed to be playing on me. He was precisely the sort of man I would be drawn to—needy, reckless, and irresponsible, but perceptive and sensitive.

He was irresistible for a long time, but at least I knew I could choose not to act on the feelings that sometimes overwhelmed me when we were together. And I never did. Instead I tried something entirely new. I went to meetings and talked about my fear of getting involved with yet another inappropriate person. I talked about it like my life depended on it, and it did. There's a saying in Twelve Step programs that we are as sick as our secrets. I know that to be true because I lived it. Making the choice to spit out rather than swallow a secret that would ultimately poison me freed me.

While it took some distance, years in fact, to get far enough away from that tumultuous time, I finally understood that the uncle who started it and the cousin who ended it were bookends to my 20 years of restless wandering in a personal wilderness.

ED

Since the first drug detox and treatment programs I had been in, from Stockton State and the San Joaquin County Medical Center to Napa State Hospital, I had been in and out of countless programs all over Northern California: in Sacramento, Vallejo, Oakland, Hayward, San Mateo, and Redwood City. I had been in VA drug treatment programs in Martinez, Palo Alto, Menlo Park, and San Francisco, at times for 24 hours or less. Or I stayed a month or two or three. Sometimes I had a bed, other times I had to sleep on the floor in the bathroom and clean the floor with a toothbrush as punishment for having relapsed or broken a rule. Those programs were like a revolving door. They gave me respite, whether for a week, a month, or a year, but then, sometimes, I'd "graduate." Programs loved throwing big parties for the "graduates" before they flung us back into the community with no more structure, rules, punishment or, most importantly, any real support.

And then there were the county mental health programs. One of the first I checked into to find out what was wrong with me gently showed me the door after 72 hours, saying they couldn't find anything. The last one was at the county hospital in Oakland when I had Diane take me to the psych emergency room because I was afraid I would hurt myself and couldn't find a program that would take me right away. That was the night before my 55th birthday in February 1984 when I slept on the floor of the waiting room and ate peanut butter sandwiches, waiting for a bed to become available. In the morning they told me to call Diane to come pick me up—I had been too well behaved to get a bed in the county psychiatric ward. Within weeks, I was back at the VA in Menlo Park, my fifth time there for drug treatment.

In reality, all of those programs were only a "shelter in a storm." We were treated like wayward children. While they knew very little about addiction, they knew a lot about psychological punishment. They kept saying the most important thing was not to use, but to me it seemed to be much more complicated than that. Like, why did I have to use in the first place, especially because I hated it so much? The death rate of client overdoses was horrendous. We knew about that horror because staff was continuously telling us about the death of some former client. It seemed their intention was to frighten us with gory details about how it happened. I kept asking the program, why are we using drugs? Why do we overdose so often? Why do we get clean only to use again? They couldn't answer, but would tell me I was no longer welcome at that program. You weren't supposed to ask questions, just follow instructions.

As I spent more and more time feeling deeply depressed, our cat Frodo was about the only one I could talk to. Whenever I stayed with Diane, Frodo was always close by. Like a concerned caregiver, he would sometimes sit next to me all day, listening intently while I talked to him. Who knows what I said to him? All I know is, he was always by my side and I told him things that I couldn't say to anyone else.

In May 1984, I started working at a rubber plant in Oakland. When I walked in I was struck dumb. The machine they assigned me to operate was the same model rubber mill I had operated at U.S. Rubber Co. in L.A., the one I had been using in 1955 when I got the news that my mother had just died. I had to go get loaded, remembering what I did that day 30 years before when I had gone to see her—stealing the rings off her fingers and pawning them to buy heroin.

The job at the rubber company paid decently and came with health insurance. Working there should have allowed me to stop stealing from Diane and pay my way. But it was only a short time before I was shooting up all of my money and lying, cheating, and stealing once again.

With the health benefits from my job, I was able to get into a private 28-day inpatient treatment program. Merritt Peralta Institute, or MPI, was run by people who had actually studied addiction and how it affected individuals and family systems. The program director, the late Barbara Stern, herself a recovering addict, had been through Synanon and had acquired an advanced degree in psychology. Her understanding of addiction and her leadership made MPI a state-of-the-art program.

We learned about the process of addiction and worked on our recovery through the Twelve Steps of Alcoholics Anonymous. We spent a lot of time on the 4th Step, the one about taking a personal inventory, the necessity of honesty and, in particular, how we had become our emotional selves. This allowed me, for the first time, to let go of my fear, shame, and dishonesty. As I began to speak my truth, it was a shocking and enlightening experience because I had never looked at my true self. I began to understand how I had become who I was and possibly a way out of the hole I had jumped into because of my negative beliefs about myself. I also heard that no one was to blame but me. I couldn't believe it when I heard a counselor say, "Your life is a consequence of your choices" even though, at the time, I didn't understand what that meant. I had never seriously considered the concept of "my choices." I didn't even know I had a choice about how I could respond to the beliefs, behavior, and demands of others whose company I so desperately felt that I needed.

For the first time I was willing to "listen." I had been deaf to the punitive model used in the other treatment programs that blamed, shamed, and punished clients. At MPI, everyone was treated with respect, something not on the agenda of many programs of that time, and that made me hungry for the lessons I was getting from the very knowledgeable teachers there.

As they learned more about me, the program director and my counselor were impressed by the work I had done in Stockton. When my 28 days at MPI ended, they thought I might not be ready to go back into the community. Even though MPI offered a comprehensive aftercare program, they thought that because of my long addiction history I would benefit from more time in treatment. They urged me to enroll in Walden House in San Francisco. I trusted their judgment although, at the time, none of us were aware of the damage done by the ignorance and arrogance of those early treatment programs. The only reason I thought this might be different was that people I respected at MPI thought I should go to Walden House. Unfortunately for me, it would turn out to be just more of the same old approach.

DIANE

I was accepted to graduate school in public health at U.C. Berkeley for fall 1984. In June, I started fertility classes and kept records of my cycle, temperature, and the changes in mucus that signify ovulation is occurring. To get my body strong and ready, I stopped drinking alcohol and fumbled through another couple of failed attempts to quit smoking.

In July 1984, after 12 years of therapeutic communities and useless family groups, Ed was finally not only in a cutting-edge treatment program, but one with an intensive family component that offered educational classes, groups, and counseling. I attended them all. I learned the emotional mechanics of how relationships change to adapt to the stress, craziness, and unpredictability of living with an addict or alcoholic, how enablers interact with that, and what I could do to break a lifelong pattern of putting the needs and feelings of others before my own.

I had been worried about how I'd get through graduate school with Ed in and out of my life. So, still very much the codependent, I was relieved when he decided to go into a 12-month program at Walden House with an additional six months living in their satellite housing. If he stayed until the end, I could make it through school.

When fall semester started, I managed to squeeze law office temp work into the days or half days when I didn't have classes, and settled into a manageable routine. Sometime after my first midterms, I had what would be the last time I would dream of Jackson. He was on death row, but very calm. We sat quietly together, holding hands. There was a contraption above us with two lights. He said that when the one on the left blinked he would have to leave and wouldn't be back. I wanted to talk, but he smiled and softly said there was no need. And then he was gone.

I saw how much of what I had done over the last 11 years, particularly where Ed was concerned, had been directly related to or exacerbated by Jackson's suicide. After I found Jackson, my fear that Ed could die by his own hand injecting a drug into himself became ever more real. But because I didn't believe or understand that I had no control over what Ed did, letting him go seemed impossible. From the Twelve Step work I was doing, I was finally able to stop blaming myself for Jackson's death and accept that ultimately I could not have prevented it.

Back in Connecticut for Thanksgiving, I asked my mother if she would come to California to help me if I had a baby. At first, even though she said she would rather see a husband in the picture, she was happy and excited, loving the idea of having another grand-child. But after thinking it over for a couple of days, she said while she understood how I would want a child, she disagreed with the method and thought adoption would be preferable.

"Insemination is unnatural," she said. "The child will suffer because it won't know its father. Plus, it's irresponsible to get preg-nant when you have no job or means to support yourself, much less a baby."

Once more I would disappoint my mother's idea of what my life should be, compounding the guilt I carried since the affair with my uncle tore our family apart. Unable to bear the thought of giving up my own vision of what I wanted, I pressed on, as I usually had in the face of her disapproval.

I chose a sperm donor from a binder of anonymous donors and had my first insemination in late January 1985. They sampled my mucus to be sure it was at the height of its fertility and showed me what it looked like under a microscope. The sheer beauty of those delicate, lacy, spider web-like shapes and patterns that lived inside me announcing my body's readiness was a magical, almost psyche-delic sight. I felt good and hopeful.

I couldn't have imagined the devastation that followed when I got my period, and again when nothing happened after the second time. During the third insemination at the end of May, I closed my eyes, visualizing sperm swimming to meet my egg. I saw a dance, and a baby turning over and over, moving out of me, through its internal universe into the world. Then I had a dream about being with my sister. She was holding her year-old son and wouldn't let go of him, even for a moment. I was holding a computer.

During the summer I had more time to take advantage of the couples counseling at Walden House. Astrid, a rarity among therapists, understood addiction and codependency, and was a skilled and compassionate advocate for us both. She worked at peeling the layers off 17 years of our unaddressed issues. During one session, Ed and I had a telling exchange.

"What will it take for me to pay my debt to you?" he asked.

I thought about it a few minutes. "Well, I'd love you to return all the money you took from me, but that's not realistic. Anyway, I never kept track." I paused. "What I really want is for you to be honest with me."

Kaiser finally scheduled an endo biopsy to evaluate my fertility. All this waiting reinforced my feeling that I had waited too long, made foolish decisions, had no foresight and now, at nearly 42, was too old. But when I traveled back in time to figure out at what point I should have stopped what I was doing, I couldn't decide what I would have given up to have started this process earlier, and kept validating rather than regretting what I had chosen.

By the end of December, after about a year of trying, I was slowly giving up the idea of getting pregnant. As that reality was sinking in, I sometimes felt a terrifying rage when I saw a very pregnant woman. To me, there was nothing quite as beautiful, sensuous, or intimate as an eight-months pregnant woman who is instinctively, unconsciously, lovingly stroking her vulnerable belly with its perfect roundness. It was disquieting how I fantasized murderous things, like running over the pregnant women crossing in front of my car or tripping the one passing me in the laundromat. I don't remember that fantasy lasting very long. But I felt so alone and sad after a yearlong emotional roller coaster of hope and disappointment that I ended up distancing myself from a lot of my women friends whose successful pregnancies had left me feeling so much loss. I couldn't talk about it, especially to them. How could I? Sorrowfully, some of those friendships never recovered.

In early February 1986, a little over a year since I had started inseminating, the fertility test results showed that both of my tubes were blocked. So the egg leaving the ovary could never have entered a fallopian tube where it would have waited for just a single sperm to fertilize it before moving on to the uterus. All that record keeping, temperature taking, my beautiful lacy stretchy mucus—and the egg had no way to get into the tube. Kaiser said the next step was tubal surgery with a 50% chance of getting pregnant and a high risk of ectopic pregnancy. That's when I started to look into adoption.

ED

By February 1986, I had been clean for 18 months. Six months earlier, I had moved from the program's residential facility to satellite housing. When a resident moves to satellite housing, Walden House requires the person to get a job so I went back to working for temporary agencies. Walden House also expects satellite housing residents to be positive role models and support clients in the residential program. Right around that time, I was having sex with the mother of a client and had already talked to the assistant director about how the woman was coming on to me. He and I just joked about how she was behaving. But someone else mentioned it one day when I was in the assistant director's office, and he came down on me as if he didn't know anything about it. He made an example of me and my behavior to the whole community. I was so ashamed and angry that I started shooting dope at the satellite house. I hoped the assistant director would catch me so I could talk about how his joking encouraged my behavior with the woman. But when neither he nor any other staff seemed to notice my drug use, I thought they didn't care, that they had just been using me. So I decided to leave.

I packed my belongings, shot cocaine in the bathroom, went to a phone booth, and called the program to tell them how stupid they were. When I stepped out of the phone booth and looked down, there was blood on my pants cuff from when I injected the cocaine. I started to cry and couldn't stop for what seemed like hours. I was 57 years old and I had just done it to myself again! And now I was homeless.

Then this brainy "me" thing decided I needed some alcohol. My true self said, "That's stupid." But my addict self said, "Aw shut up and get a drink, you'll feel better." I had never liked alcohol but would always drink it in the absence of narcotics. The "one" drink I was going to have led to four or five and of course I got drunk. My brilliant mind then suggested (since I hated being drunk) that I should shoot some heroin. That made me start tripping about shooting dope. My true self kept saying, "You can't do that. It might kill you." But restless, angry, discontented "me" said, "See how stupid you are? You need some 'smack' to calm yourself. It'll be cool. Shut up and shoot some dope."

There I was, homeless in the San Francisco Tenderloin with quite a bit of cash in my pocket from my last temporary job. So I found "Scabby Willie," shot dope and overdosed. For some reason, he spent hours trying to bring me back. He didn't rob me either.

I couldn't get over that. Only now, years later, am I beginning to understand that he must have thought I was a good guy.

I was in and out of nasty Tenderloin hotel rooms that made me prefer the street, but at some point I'd get paid from the temp work I continued to do. Then I'd go shoot drugs and walk. I had a BART pass and rode the trains until they stopped running. Sometimes I slept in hospital emergency rooms until it was time to go to work the next day.

DIANE

Ed called on my birthday to tell me he was using again. At least this time he still had money from his job, and hadn't yet burned all his bridges, as was his habit. He asked me to come to San Francisco to meet him and gave me flowers and a card. We talked a little. He was sad, said he felt hopeless about his life.

Only six weeks before, Ed got a five-day pass and we went to Mendocino, marking the 18 years since we met. It was a homecoming in a place we both loved. But something seemed off that weekend. His behavior had changed. Then I got angry at myself because I really didn't want to know if he had relapsed. What I needed was enough time to get through the next three months and graduate from school.

Still, sitting in the car with him, I felt my codependent default setting kick in, something that was prone to happen under this kind of stress. It was my birthday but someone else's life was flashing before my eyes. In Al-Anon they talk about how well the program works—as long as the addict isn't using. The hard work is when the using is happening.

Three days later, Ed left satellite housing. He came to my house when I was at school, took two pairs of his work boots from the closet and threw away a big plastic bag full of his clothes and books that he had left at my house before he went to Walden House two years before. Later, I found the bag of clothes in the dumpster. No note. No call in the week that followed. As the days went by, the self-torture began and I got scared, reliving how Jackson had alienated everyone before he killed himself. By now, Ed might have crossed the line where he wasn't at all concerned with life, anything, or anyone.

I finally reached Astrid, our Walden House therapist.

"Remind yourself you're powerless over Ed," she said. "Allow him to mess up his own life. Don't give him more to feel guilty about. Now is when your own recovery program gets put to the test. Now. Today. When your disease is trying to take over."

And so when he finally called from a motel in Oakland to say that his money had run out and he had no place to stay, this time I didn't use a proverbial pillow to soften the blow of his proverbial fist smashing into the proverbial wall he was about to hit.

This time, I didn't stand between him and the consequences of his choices.

This time, I could say those words to him. "I love you and care about what's happening with you. But only you can decide what to do to make your life better."

The hardest part for me was knowing that he was living on the streets. At first, he said it was an adventure riding BART all day. He had a bright courage in his voice and didn't ask if he could stay with me. Nor did I offer. For a while, he rode BART during the day, and went to the San Francisco bus terminal or county hospital to sleep in the emergency room at night. It wasn't long before he had no money and then he sounded scared.

I couldn't sleep. I was stressed between getting ready for finals, graduation, and working. I wasn't sure how long I could stay detached, and didn't know how to trust my feelings or differentiate between enabling and being a friend.

One of my closest Al-Anon friends said it might help to talk to her husband who had a couple of years clean and sober from cocaine and alcohol.

"Ed needs to stop feeling ashamed of who he is," said Louis. "If he's judging himself, he's not helping himself. If he has no money, it's a direct result of what he's been doing. He has a lot to come to terms with, and he'll never be too old to do that. Hopelessness is what happens when you get back into the compulsion again. He needs to get his ass up and get going."

Louis said that as long as I set boundaries and enforced them, it would be okay to be flexible. I could let Ed stay for a night, or give him a meal now and then.

21

Goodbye Scabby Willie

ED

One day I gave most of my money to somebody in the Tenderloin to get what they said was the "best dope" in town. He returned with some baking powder or something. I started to get angry. Then the anger went away and I just felt very sad, really heartbroken.

I was sitting on a bus stop bench trying to figure out what was going on with me and what to do next when I became aware of a horrendous odor. It smelled like a dead animal. I looked around and to my right I saw this gigantic man. He was over 6 feet tall, grotesquely fat, and had a terrible-looking injury hanging from his abdomen. The odor was from him, and he was about to sit next to me on the bus bench.

I yelled, "You can't sit here! This is my bench!"

A shock ran through me. I was actually claiming a bus bench as my own! I stood up.

I wanted to walk past the giant, smelly man, who was to my right, but he stood in my way. I thought later on that I should have called an ambulance for him, but I didn't because everything was about me.

Then I heard the voice of one of my teachers from a drug program, a couple of years before. He had given me enigmatic but great advice. He said, "When you don't know which way to go, turn left." So I turned left and walked until I got to 90 - 9th Street, just below Market Street where the homeless and dispossessed congregated. It was there that I found an AA meeting.

I was still not that much into Twelve Step programs. I was mad at my mother's God and to me there was too much God in that program. But I went in anyway and stayed, even though this meeting turned out to be the bottom of the barrel. There was vomit on the floor and everyone looked like zombies to me. But the guy running the meeting was talking with confidence and before I knew it, I was participating.

When it was over, I took BART to Oakland where I went to another meeting at 40th and Howe Street. As I entered the room, a woman sitting by the door looked up at me. She stood, took my hand and led me to a seat in the front row. She whispered that I should raise my hand when they asked if anyone wanted to talk. So I did. I think I talked about how sick and tired I was of being sick and tired and how glad I was to be sitting there, listening and starting to get it.

I was feeling that this might lead me to where I wanted to go. After all the years I spent resisting Twelve Step meetings, this one got my attention, and the feeling stayed with me during the final death throes of my bottoming out.

I called Diane and explained about the meetings I had been to and my new efforts to stop using drugs. Then I got a job in downtown Oakland at BASS Tickets. I was doing a little better, not using every day. But when I did use, I was shooting cocaine. Diane didn't know about the cocaine and, unlike when I was loaded on heroin, couldn't tell when I used it. She let me move back in with her.

Probably the last feeble attempt I made at feeding my addiction began when I saw a pistol in a dealer's house and asked him to loan it to me. When I took that huge .45 automatic pistol, the thought was that I would rob somebody so I could buy a lot of dope or else kill myself. So I walked around looking for someone who seemed, to me, "weak" enough to let me rob them. It never occurred to me to say "stick 'em up" or shoot the gun. I never did find anyone who fit my picture of a robbery victim. So I returned the gun and borrowed some dope until payday.

Then on July 8, 1986, after staying at Diane's for about a month, I woke up and felt I couldn't go any further. I didn't want to keep lying and stealing, hanging out with all of the "Scabby Willies," doing what I was doing. I didn't want to be discontented anymore, constantly trying to reject the discomfort that was always with me. I wanted to be present. I had come as far as I could and knew there was a lot of learning to do. I told Diane that I had decided to go to 90 AA meetings in 90 days, a standard suggestion for newcomers.

DIANE

Sometimes, the funny thing about what turns out to have been a life-changing day is how you can't really know it was until enough time has gone by. So it was with July 8, 1986. After all the broken promises and false starts, there was no way to know, when Ed handed me a pawn slip and said, "This is for your gold bracelet. I can't do this anymore. I'm going to 90 meetings in 90 days," that it really *would* be the first day of his clean and sober recovery.

I took his announcement with a grain of salt, and expected very little, except the worst. It wasn't until a few weeks later, after he actually had gone to meetings every day, when we were talking about my upcoming trip to Connecticut that he said, with unexpected vulnerability, "I think I'm scared to be alone. I'm scared I won't get to meetings. I'm scared I'm going to use. I'm scared I'm not going to eat right. I'm scared I'm going to isolate."

My automatic reaction, even after two years of Al-Anon, was: he needs me, I will stay.

But what came out of my mouth unnerved me because I had not consciously thought it and didn't know where it came from.

"I've been here and you've isolated, you haven't eaten, you've overdosed in the bathroom. Ed, this is not about me. It's about you."

He considered that for a minute. And he agreed.

Right then I felt something shift in me that might well have been a gentle tidal wave. I had let go. I went to Connecticut with an easy heart, at peace, not needing to try to be in control.

ED

I did go to 90 meetings in 90 days, and I kept going, sometimes every day, for a year or so. I tried to practice what they said about taking the cotton out of my ears, putting it in my mouth, and learning to listen. My old ways of thinking had taken me to the penitentiary four times, the crazy house eight times, and 25 drug programs. I used to wonder why it took all of that. I think I now understand that anger is a great way to close your ears and I had been very pissed at myself since I was 4 or 5 years old. Why? When I was a kid, adults were always asking children, "What's wrong with you?" And even though that question was so common, I was an overly literal child.

I believed that adults knew everything and I assumed that whatever "it" was that was wrong with me must be really awful if the grown-ups didn't understand it.

And, of course, all that I had experienced simply growing up as an African American in America certainly helped to solidify the idea that I was flawed. I spent the next 50 years trying to reject all the discomfort those ideas and experiences kept bringing to me.

One of the first things I heard at AA was "what other people think of you is none of your business." That hit home. It immediately took me back to how I had always tried to please people and would drag myself through the mud because someone else thought I should do what they wanted or because I didn't have the college degrees "you're supposed to have," or the car, or the suit of clothing.

I thought about my hanging out with the great trumpet player, Dupree Bolton, during the 1950s. In those days, I knew I needed to go to work. I was young then. I hadn't yet become as desperate and miserable as I would be later on. I still had consciousness enough to say no to Dupree when he pressured me to buy heroin for both of us, even though, in the end, I usually gave in.

I had lost that consciousness and my principles when I thought nothing I was doing was worthwhile, even when other people thought I was doing a good job. Even when I actually had been doing good work and not using, I was always too afraid they would find out that there was something wrong with me. I would be so worried that I couldn't stand it and eventually would have to get loaded.

Until I really looked at the ideas I carried I didn't understand how much I needed to please other people. There's a saying in Twelve Step rooms: "Scratch an addict and you'll find a codependent."

I think that's how it begins, being other- rather than inner-directed. So other-directed that there is a saying in Al-Anon: "When a codependent dies someone else's life flashes before their eyes."

I got drunk as a 12-year-old to please other kids. I shot heroin the first time on Labor Day 1947 to please my Army buddies. Being a stranger in a new town, I might join up with anyone. I just didn't want to be alone. And I wanted to be liked. I had been an only child for ten years with an overprotective mother who had lost four children in childbirth and my dad, who worked cross-country on trains, was often gone. I had always felt so needy, so alone.

It's very easy to think that others see us as we see ourselves. I had an enormous amount of self-consciousness that caused me such discomfort I could hardly stand it without the drug, which took that feeling away. Twelve Step programs say that you have to find out who you are. You have to work on getting clear about how you became yourself, about your purpose and what you want. You have to think about and choose the kind of people you want and don't want in your life. I needed to be clear about what I was doing and stop worrying about what other people might be thinking. I needed to ask myself what was really bothering *me*? What kept *me* stuck? What did *I* think?

Since the day in 1947 when I first shot heroin, nothing but prison, drug treatment programs, and nuthouses had ever stopped me from using or wanting to use drugs. Before AA, I had never confronted myself and admitted that I was powerless over drugs, alcohol, sex, material things, and other people, and as a result my life had become unmanageable.

It took me 40 years to understand that wherever I was going, I would always need help to get there. That, I would learn, is the reality of living.

AA says: "Keep coming back, it works if you work it."

22

Frodo

DIANE

We were at a turning point. We had a chance to make a new beginning. What lay ahead would challenge us in ways we could not have imagined.

It was also an ending. About a year after Ed got into recovery, our beautiful pure black cat Frodo fell gravely ill. We had just moved upstairs to the larger apartment. Until then, he had been holding his own, but the move completely destabilized him and he surrendered to an untreatable cancer growing inside him that we hadn't known about.

He gave us a month to get used to the idea. Time to get used to his not sleeping on the bed with us, walking on our heads in the morning, patting our cheeks with his paw after the alarm went off. He was there, but he wasn't.

We ached during that last month, watching the life flow out of this dearest of friends who had been with us through the worst of times and had stayed so close to Ed in the terrible last years before he began his recovery. We tried homeopathic remedies, appetite stimulants, fluid therapy, but the vet said to forget about those things. Just focus on making him happy and comfortable.

Frodo made no attempt to explore the new apartment. He found comfort curled up in a chest drawer stuffed with sweaters that had been left on the floor as we unpacked. One evening, we helped him into his drawer and sat on the bed. We cried, watching him so helpless and weak. But even then, as always, Frodo noticed. He stood up, climbed weakly out of the drawer and walked towards us, looking concerned as he always did when he knew one of us was upset. He was coming to comfort us. It was devastating to see him in that act of selfless love and for a moment we cried harder. We helped him up onto the bed, held him between us, and knew we couldn't continue to weep, for he wouldn't go until we let go of him.

Eighteen years with this beautiful old soul with the green eyes came and went so fast. There was no more time to hold onto. He had lived long enough to see us in recovery and he knew we had each other, at last. Frodo had given us time to feel what it would be like without him while he was still here. Once he knew we would be okay, his work was finished.

Ed in Cleveland, circa 1933

"A morose little boy with heavy-lidded brown eyes looks out from the cover of Ed Reed's revelatory new album *Born to Be Blue,* and with every song Reed tells the story of how that 5-year-old went out into the world with a raw wound in his soul." (Andrew Gilbert)

Ruth Reed, circa 1927

My beautiful mother, who prepared me for my joyful life
onstage today, both in music and my lecture series.

John Reed, 1948

Ed's father, who worked as a dining car waiter on the Southern Pacific Railroad
where he was active in the Brotherhood of Sleeping Car Porters.

Simonne Frum, 1950

Diane, Miriam (on lap), and Simonne, who loved being a mother
and believed it was the best thing she had ever done.

Irving Frum, 1944

Diane's dad, with 5-month-old Diane and some of
the four-leaf clovers he loved to collect.

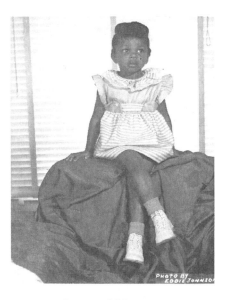

3-year old Denyce

Ed's talented, intelligent, and creative daughter, born in 1950.

First marriage, Sacramento, 1969

Getting married the first time wasn't our idea.
It wasn't a good idea, but we passively went along with it because—
as crazy as it sounds—we didn't know how to say no.

At the wedding

Ed's brother James, daughter Denyce, and her husband John.

Frodo, 1969-1987

A constant and often the only brightness in our sad lives...ever trusting,
sleek and black, with his crazy, loving green eyes.

Stockton, CA 1970

Ed as drug prevention/treatment consultant to the county medical director.

U.C. Berkeley, May 1986

Graduating from the School of Public Health.
This was two months before Ed got into recovery.

Oakland, 1988

With Ed's daughter Denyce.

Oakland Rose Garden, June 2, 1989

Marriage #2. We asked the judge if he would officiate on his lunch hour, and invited all of our friends. Ed called it a "brown bag lunch" wedding.

Oakland, 1989

At home—after the wedding, before the earthquake, and before we
stopped smoking. Ed's T-shirt says "Caution: inner child at play."

The "Love Bench"—Mendocino headlands, early 1990

The fabled massive 5' high, 7' wide redwood bench, decorated with carvings
of love symbols, peace signs, and personal messages enclosed with hearts,
sits on a rugged cliff above Portuguese Beach where the river meets the ocean.

Jenner, mid-1990s

A weekend on the coast with friends in recovery.

Mendocino, 1996

Sisters! Diane and Miriam.

Sea Ranch, 1997

Rollerblading on the Northern California coast.

Reunion, 2000

After 39 years, Heidi, who lives in Germany, found Diane through the internet.
A bicycle ride over the Golden Gate Bridge was a highlight
during Heidi's first visit to the Bay Area.

Ed and Simonne, 2004

While some people close down in old age and shrink their world,
Diane's mother opened her heart. During visits to Connecticut,
they sat together at the kitchen table and Ed sang to her.

Part Four:
It's Not a
Fairy Tale

23

Recovery

ED

On July 8, 1986 I committed myself to working the Twelve Steps of Alcoholics Anonymous. I talked to Barbara Stern, the director at Merritt Peralta Institute (MPI), and got permission to go to aftercare groups, even though it had been two years since I had left MPI. I found an AA meeting at Merritt Hospital on "Pill Hill" in Oakland. There would be 75 or more people at any of those meetings. Everyone shared their joy and pain as we all worked on practicing the Twelve Steps. We openly shared our addict/alcoholic lives and learned to let go of shame, heartbreak, and fear.

We also worked the Steps in my aftercare group and for that we needed a sponsor. I was quite fortunate that Diane, who never really went too far away, was still in my life. We were living together again. She was going to Al-Anon meetings, also at Merritt Hospital, and had met a woman whose husband, Louis, had gotten sober two years before. Louis gave me an understanding about recovery that

taught me how talking and telling the truth are the main keys to the
process of being and staying in recovery.

I went to meetings every day and looked for a sponsor.
Eventually, I connected with someone who was much younger than
I was. I liked his style and the things he talked about when he shared
at meetings. When I asked him to be my sponsor, at first he said
he was worried it wouldn't work because of the age difference, but
I thought it would be fine. There was something about Wayne that
had an intention for sobriety written all over him. I knew he would
teach me a lot. When Wayne spoke, his subject matter was about
sobriety and Twelve Step recovery. When he became my sponsor in
Alcoholics Anonymous, he immediately put me to work on my 4th
Step and got me to talk about myself. Honesty was his key. He was
not only a great listener, but very kind. His intention was to stay
sober and assist my efforts in that direction as well.

Over the next couple of years, Diane and I worked at temporary jobs, and then Diane started getting consulting work on various
public health-related projects. She was still into adopting a child and
trying to save money for it, since private adoptions were expensive.
At the time, I was more or less neutral about it. I wanted to do it if
it made Diane happy, but I knew those feelings could change if we
actually had a child.

We were both in recovery and learning how to live like normal
people, doing simple things like having friends over for brunch or
dinner. In early 1988, we had a potluck to celebrate 20 years since
we first met. It would have been unthinkable just a few years before
that 50 people would come out in the rain to wish us well and fill our
small apartment with music, food, and laughter.

In July 1988, we went to Mendocino for a long weekend during
the town's annual music festival. The first morning, as we strolled

down Main Street, an onshore wind carried the unmistakable scent of wine through the town. It's not unusual for Mendocino to be over-run with visitors during the summer and fall, but we had never seen so many people walking around with wine glasses. Then we realized it was not only a music festival but a wine-tasting event as well. As the day wore on, the air became even thicker with the smell of wine and we finally couldn't take it anymore. What a crazy time for some-one in early recovery to be there. Alcohol wasn't my drug of choice, but it could trigger all sorts of feelings, even cravings. We did the only thing we could. We found an AA meeting where we met a lot of other people, grateful for a safe place to be during the unexpected challenge of being in otherwise mellow Mendocino.

DIANE

June 2, 1989 was a beautiful, warm, sunny Friday at the Oakland Rose Garden. The air was thick with the sweet and spicy fragrance of thousands of roses bursting into bloom. We had decided to get married for the second time (making me wife #2 and #4) with just enough time to get clothes and rings and ask the judge if he would officiate on his lunch hour. We invited all of our friends. Ed called it a "brown bag lunch" wedding.

We were married by Alameda County Superior Court Judge Gordon Baranco, who had granted Ed's Certificate of Rehabilitation (which restores civil and political rights of citizenship to ex-fel-ons who have proved their rehabilitation) in March of that year. Coincidentally, Judge Baranco had been a student at U.C. Davis law school when I worked there. At the end of the ceremony, we formed a circle, joined hands, and recited the simple but profound Serenity Prayer.

ED

That night we went to an AA Convention in Oakland. It seemed fitting to spend part of that day with friends who were helping us to grow into the people we wanted to be.

Hearing that we had just gotten married for the second time, someone exclaimed, "Oh, how romantic! Just like a fairy tale!"

Actually, no. It never was and never will be a fairy tale. Slaying several dragons would have been far easier than all the work we had to do before we even thought about getting married again. The work part is never over, not for us, not with our history.

DIANE

It wasn't like we walked through a door marked "Recovery" and by the next day everything was magically changed. The pink cloud of early recovery lasts only so long but it was an important first step, a time of softness. We had never before been happy or lived one day to the next without being certain that it was only a matter of time before some other shoe would drop. We had to learn how to be with each other from scratch. At the least we had to start to trust each other. Without lying, cheating, stealing, shame, and secrets, it seemed there was endless open space to build on.

ED

It helped to have the common ground of Twelve Step programs. We were speaking the same language, using the same framework, and learning to share life as two separate people. For the first time, we were doing things and going places to have fun instead of temporary escape. At times we would look at each other in disbelief that we had come even this far. Our relationship was solidifying in ways it never could before, and that was something we would need as recovery kept forcing us to confront long-standing issues that we had not yet dealt with. There were many issues, like my pawning Diane's jewelry, stealing checks from her checkbook, the untrue stories I had told her that needed to be untangled. I had to become, as AA put it, honest, open, and willing. Whenever I found myself lying to cover up something that I was ashamed of, I'd have to confess the truth, go to a meeting, talk about my failures, and return filled with relief. That is what would make or break us. Continuing to lie would lead to relapse.

DIANE

By now, the children born to my friends when I had tried to get pregnant a few years back were no longer babies and I saw the unending commitment and time it took to have and raise children. I wasn't at all sure I had what it took to do what they were doing every day of every week of every year. I resented the loss of time with my sister and close friends who recently had children and were continually distracted and interrupted. The demands seemed endless, the patience needed beyond my capacity. Most concerning, I didn't know if, for me, having a child would be yet another way to get lost in someone else, especially a very dependent little being, and that worried me.

To be honest, by then I no longer felt left out of the childbearing experience as much as I felt free—and maybe a little bit guilty about it. What I did know was how good it was to be with Ed. Still,

I was a little scared because I'd never been so happy with anyone before; indeed, I had never really been happy at all.

A door had opened to all sorts of dreams, even as we were also trying to find our way in territory that could be treacherous. For the first time in eight years, we were again sharing a bed and, aware of the huge load of sexual baggage we each carried, we went slowly, shy and apprehensive, not wanting to jeopardize what we had.

We worked at temporary jobs while we figured out what direction to go next. One day as we were walking to meet each other after work in downtown San Francisco, a Sam Trans bus jumped a curb and went out of control, plowing down trees, killing three people, injuring at least a dozen others, and pinning a car partly underneath it with two or three people trapped inside. Crumpled bodies lay on the street near the bus. Shoes and long loaves of fresh bread were scattered everywhere. Just ordinary people going home after work; whoever they were, whatever their dreams, whatever they had been thinking or feeling had ended in that moment. If it had been just five minutes later, either one of us would have been crossing that same street. That day, I understood how nothing is promised and how limited our time here is.

When we had talked about adoption a few years before, Ed said he was willing to adopt because I wanted to. Now, as a married, interracial couple, we didn't have to look at expensive private or international adoptions. We could have any baby, or just about any child for that matter, through the county child welfare system.

Yet, after our first home study meeting with a county social worker, all I could feel was ambivalence and apprehension, thinking about all the things we had missed doing in the last 21 years. For Ed at 60 and me at 45, the long-term responsibility of raising a child would certainly dominate the rest of his life and most of mine.

Four months after our first visit with the social worker, someone called about a friend whose daughter was having a baby—a so-called "crack" baby—that would be put up for adoption. She wondered if we were interested. That threw us both. We didn't really want a drug-exposed baby. Somehow, Ed and I avoided talking about it. But a decision had to be made.

As I became more scared and unable to sort through my feelings, I noticed how I was disconnecting from myself. I would wake up thinking about children and then get stuck and upset. But sitting down at the computer, I'd be lost in whatever I was working on within minutes. It was a masterful fix, distracting enough to distance myself from the confusion and feel better until the next day when I woke up remembering and the whole thing would start all over again. The simple act of paying attention to how I was freezing my feelings, altering my mood, and disconnecting from myself broke the spell. There it was again. I went to a Workaholics Anonymous meeting in Oakland and confirmed what I already knew.

Ed and I were each working through many issues to make our relationship healthy. At times it felt so fragile that it seemed counterproductive to take on more than one big thing at a time. What I was certain about was that I liked my life as it was. I didn't want it to change. Neither, as it turned out, did Ed.

ED

I was in early recovery and concerned about getting real work. One day, my sponsor's wife, Rose, told me to apply for a job where she was working as a counselor at Thunder Road, an adolescent drug treatment program in Oakland. I was hired after talking for a while with the program director, Sylvia Ritchie. Six months later, after observing my work, she handed me three well-used sheets of paper that she called an outline to use in a new job, which came with a raise in salary. I would be the head of family meetings that parents attended once a week to learn about addiction and recovery. When I left Thunder Road a few years later and went to work for Kaiser Permanente in their substance abuse treatment program, I did separate education classes for family members and for addicts. During the 20 years I was at Kaiser, out of those original few sheets of paper that had been handed to me at Thunder Road, I developed an eight-part lecture series that I call "The Art and Practice of Living Well."

Over time, I stopped talking about alcohol and drugs as "the problem" and focused instead on the person using alcohol and other drugs and developed a series of questions: Who am I? How did I become myself? What is my purpose? What do I want? Where am I going? What help do I need? What kind of people do I want in my life? One of the biggest surprises I learned about myself is that, as I got deeper into the recovery process, I discovered that I actually knew very little about myself.

The job of recovery is to become "inner-directed" and that task requires re-directing your attention from others to the self. But as a child, I had been accused of selfishness and told that I should be ashamed of myself for thinking of this "ME" thing. So I became a "people pleaser." When the people I was with suggested drinking or using drugs I often spoke up to say it was a bad idea, but I was always voted down and ended up following the "gang." I went to prison twice following someone else's idea. I married two women I did not care for (even marrying Diane the first time was Georgina's idea). I bought a very expensive car that I hated and fantasized committing suicide in it because someone else thought it was cool.

In recovery, we try to clarify our intentions and not be led by someone else's thinking without careful thought about our own self. We work on speaking about ourselves with "honesty, openness, and willingness," or HOW, as AA puts it. We practice being unafraid to say what is true for us. We go to meetings and talk about ourselves and our negative thoughts so we don't have to act on them.

All this helped me to approach the work I do in treatment programs in a unique way; I talk to people, not about alcohol and drugs, but about themselves and the choices they made that got them into the revolving door of jails, prisons, and treatment programs in the first place. And while I do this work, I am also working on my own growth and development.

24

I Really Want to Smoke

DIANE

Where you are in an earthquake is strictly up to fate. There's no warning, it just happens and then the aftershocks keep happening and there is no warning about those either. After our marriage, the Loma Prieta earthquake was the second big thing that happened in 1989, on October 17. While it wasn't *the* big one, it was a 6.9 quake that shook the entire Bay Area, leaving collapsed freeways and bridges, fires and death in its wake. Having just experienced my first major earthquake, I felt like I had lived in California for 25 years in complete innocence.

In mid-November, as strong aftershocks continued at random, Ed and I quit smoking together as part of a stop smoking program at Thunder Road where Ed was working. That was the third big thing. Almost from the first day, anything could set us off and we started fighting, a lot. Two weeks after quitting, I had an enormous meltdown, crying uncontrollably and giving vent to more anger than even I guessed could live inside of me. We were like shards of glass, cutting each other with hurtful words over the slightest thing. Anything could set either of us off. While I alternated between outbursts of anger and grief, Ed gloated endlessly about how easily he was sailing through and not feeling a thing. Worse, he even seemed to enjoy seeing me be so out of control.

We swung wildly from one extreme to the other. One day he suggested that we go to Wilbur Hot Springs and soak. Then he backed off. "I don't know if I want to be locked in a car with you for two hours," he said. That was something we would ordinarily have howled about, except now there was no humor between us at all. We had become hostile strangers. I started thinking the relationship couldn't be saved after all, which gave birth to a new grief since I had come to trust life with Ed during the past three years. Oddly enough, the harder it got, and the more I wanted to, the stronger my resolve was not to smoke.

I went to Nicotine Anonymous meetings where I knew I would find support. It was there that I learned how nicotine cuts off feelings, an interesting fact because in those days, smoking was ubiquitous at all Twelve Step meetings and in treatment programs. People with 20 years of sobriety from alcoholism or heroin addiction, the ones who might have ridiculed the notion that smoking was a real addiction, now conceded that quitting smoking was harder than quitting any other drug, including heroin. One man, who came every week, had been repeatedly committed to mental institutions where he'd be drugged into semi-consciousness. Though desperate to stop, smoking was the only thing that stood between him and the next dreaded involuntary commitment, the only thing that kept him "sane" when he was back in the community. Everyone loved that he kept coming back, even smelling of stale cigarette smoke.

There's a funny saying in that program, "Have a feeling, have a smoke." I had smoked for any and all reasons—when I was happy, sad, stressed, relaxed, or angry. People said regaining the ability to fully and clearly feel was one of the best things that happens when you quit smoking. I knew there must be some merit to that but, at the time, all I felt was dreadfully vulnerable. I had to learn how to do everything all over again—wake up in the morning, have coffee, talk on the phone, work, drive, socialize, celebrate, and grieve—all without a cigarette.

After the first month, the tension between us started to abate, and there were occasional glimpses of humor. At least we could joke about how we were both gaining weight, each eating a bag of cheddar cheese popcorn every night watching TV or rented movies. I had smoking dreams, dangerous dreams where I would absolutely convince myself that it would be okay to have just one cigarette. I knew I could handle it and didn't even think it important to tell anyone. I would smoke in the dream and then wake up in a full-blown panic, convinced that I had relapsed.

Six weeks after quitting, on Christmas Eve day, a block of wax Ed was melting to make a candle got too hot and caught on fire. We had a ridiculous fight that resulted in Ed completely shutting down, convinced that we shouldn't be together, and unwilling to talk about it.

Everything escalated from there. I needed to detach but felt abandoned by my best friend. I spent much of a mostly sleepless night wondering what was the good of being in recovery when these things can happen on Christmas Eve, especially when you've been trying to communicate better and think you've been making progress.

We had bought expensive gifts for each other but on Christmas Day they remained unopened. It was a beautiful, sunny December day. I finally drove to Thornton Beach in Daly City and sat on the headlands all afternoon, scanning the water for whale spouts and watching hang gliders sail silently by over a sparkling ocean. Then, I started tripping. That morning the only thing he said to me was that he wanted all his money. I sat there looking into the ocean and had a fleeting thought. What if he uses? But that was the least of it. If he used, there was nothing I could do about it except take care of myself. I got home in time to find him dressed up in his now opened Christmas presents getting ready to go to a meeting, presumably to share how awful a day it was and how crazy he got.

I cried for a long time when he left. It felt like all the anger and pain from the very beginning of our relationship had come up all at once. I had a terrible fear that he got peacocked up because he was seeing someone, just like right after the first time we got married 20 years before. The more I thought about that possibility, the hotter my rage grew. I really wanted to smoke.

ED

We got married, stopped smoking, and a lot of difficult feelings came up. They say that you get emotionally stuck at whatever age you were when you started seriously using alcohol or drugs. That meant when I stopped using I was the emotional age of a teenager living in the body of a 57-year-old. But the truth was that until I left home at 17 to join the Army, sometimes the only way I could cope with my mother was to shut down.

When I was a child, my mother would tell me to sit there and shut my mouth. So I shut my mouth. She'd ask me a question and I wouldn't answer. "Did you hear what I asked you?" I wouldn't say anything.

She would get very frustrated, and then I'd feel like I had some control. There would be another one of her "what's wrong with you?" queries and I'd say, "You told me not to say anything so I'm not going to talk." And I would quit talking.

I could see how it got to her and I continued to do it because it gave me power. But short of exploding, which was not a pretty sight, I didn't know how else to handle anger and frustration. I didn't know what to do with the feelings. I thought someone or something else made me feel so awful.

My mother told me, "You make me sick." So I would stop talking to her because making her sick was wrong. I would do stuff that I hated and kept swearing that I wouldn't do it anymore and then kept doing it anyway.

The thing about Twelve Step recovery is that quitting drinking or drugging is not a cure, just a beginning, a beginning for a new life. I learned that I wasn't even sober yet, in an emotional sense. When I stopped using substances, I was left with myself, my beliefs, and the harsh past I had never learned to let go of. I had tried to fix the habit of painful suffering by drinking and drugging, smoking and sexing. But what meetings and my sponsor taught me was that I had a choice. I could openly walk into the pain and the struggle, and start to unpack my life, and work to understand and heal myself. Or I could continue to hide from myself, keep my secrets and be a "dry drunk," living in the same misery as before except without the drug—a process that had a short life before using would likely begin once more.

Recovery, as we would learn, is an inside job. It's not easy to be left with the feelings that drove you to self-medicate in the first place. When Diane and I got into struggles before I stopped using, I'd deal with it by shooting dope. That would only make things worse, but at least I didn't have to feel. It was a different story after getting into recovery. Anger was a terrible place where I would be scared and lost. I had no tools to have a healthy argument and didn't know how to handle conflict. So I did what I knew how to do. I shut down. I denied having anger for a long time in recovery, even though it started coming out right from the beginning, even though I would beat myself up for not knowing how to handle feelings.

There were so many reasons to be angry from my earliest years, starting with getting beaten up going to school. Not being able to go to the Cleveland Air Show. Told to go to shoe shop when I wanted to join the Debate Society because the school counselor said that Black people had nothing to debate. Running away and joining the Army. Getting locked up for using drugs and put in a system that existed with the intention to re-enslave people. And of course, one of my earliest memories of betrayal was waking up to find my parents stealing money from my piggy bank. They never apologized for taking my money and they never returned it. I now believe that their behavior gave me permission to lie and steal when I grew up. I had so much anger all I could do was turn it inward, towards myself. I never expressed it outwardly. I never gave it words, until I got to the point where I'd explode, and then I would shut down or shoot dope.

At least now, when Diane and I had arguments that ended with me shutting down, I would go to a meeting and be ready to talk when I got home. It was reassuring to know that there was always a meeting somewhere when I needed one.

Meetings were where I shared my discomforts, which used to lock me up with no way to respond. I was learning that talking about what was going on freed me, the feelings of being lost and powerless were gone, and I wouldn't feel imprisoned. I didn't feel alone, either, but felt that I belonged to a community of people who, like me, were finding they weren't alone either. This gave all of us courage.

I went back for therapy with Louise, who I had been seeing before I left Walden House. Over time, as we worked together she helped me to see myself, and that it wasn't so much what life brought to me that mattered, but what I was doing with what life brought to me. She helped me to see that I could let go. I worked with her to understand my experiences with my mother, especially the anger, which was much more difficult than I imagined and would take a long time. For many years, I continued to curse the beautiful picture of my mother as a young woman that we keep on the mantle. Louise helped me begin to understand that my life was largely the consequence of my choices. That concept has been a very important underpinning of my entire recovery process.

25

No More Secrets

DIANE

I needed something more than meetings to help me with the anger I couldn't control. By then there were many therapists with first-hand, lived experience in their own recovery process, and I found Chris, who was a black belt master in cutting through denial and opening unhealed wounds.

I finally told her about the affair with my uncle so long ago, and how I purposefully lost touch with all my friends from high school and college, too ashamed to tell them what had happened when I went to California that summer. And how, for so long, before I could trust that a new woman friend that I liked, liked me, I had to tell this most awful thing about myself so they would know what kind of person I really was. I continued to carry the shame of that disastrous affair, and even when I started going to Al-Anon—one of the safest and most nonjudgmental places for people to talk about soul-killing experiences—I still couldn't tell the story about my uncle.

Chris was gentle, but firm. "The shame and guilt you feel and the need to keep it secret tells me you've been molested. When you finally grieve about that episode in your early life, you'll need to get in touch with how helpless you were in that situation, something you have done everything to avoid in all the years since."

It was true that I had always dismissed any suggestion of molestation. I had been a young, inexperienced 20-year-old, but still old enough, I believed, to take responsibility for what I had consented to. And even though my mother would always insist that she never blamed me for what happened with my uncle, how could I trust that? She herself had told me when I was growing up that it's always the woman's responsibility, that men can't control themselves. None of those voices in my head had ever stopped.

I closed my eyes and found my 20-year-old self. There was no need to say anything, just hold her close, to finally forgive and protect her. And, as the 45-year-old woman I was, I understood in a flash that my aunt knew her husband well enough to have known what was likely to happen if she left me alone with him for a week. At that moment, the narrative I had lived with for so long—that it was all my fault—began to crumble.

Chris pressed me to tackle the complicated, guilt-ridden baggage I carried about my mother. It was past time to confirm what I had long suspected—that no one on my father's side of the family knew anything about me and Ed. One obvious clue was that they didn't know my last name. They sent birthday cards and checks to me through my mother, using my maiden name. It was a sickening feeling to know that at some level I, and by extension Ed, was a family secret. That knowledge was made even worse when I faced the truth, that I had been passively complicit in sustaining it.

Around that time, after every trip to Connecticut, I would return home with the flu or a bad cold as if my body was trying to wake me up to what my mind wanted to keep buried. But this time, the growing dread I felt about an upcoming visit forced me to want the truth or not go. I couldn't ask my father. He had passed away a few years before. So I called my mother.

"Does Dad's family know about Ed?" It was a question she had hoped I would never ask.

"No."

"Do they even know I'm married now?"

"No." It was a peculiar relief, hearing that truth out loud.

"Why not?"

"Your father made me promise that I would never tell his family." I felt cold, like all the blood had drained out of me.

"But why?"

"He didn't think they could understand or accept it."

I wrestled with myself, and then let it go. What I had to do was stay in the present.

"You know, Mom, right now I have nothing in my life to hide or feel ashamed about. Why should this continue to be a secret? I'm happy. I have a great life. Ed and I are proud of all that we have accomplished. Why do you need to keep holding onto this?"

"Please, Diane," she sighed heavily. "I'm not going to live forever. Just wait a few years. Please. Wait until I'm dead."

I was shocked, then furious she would even think continuing to keep this secret was something that was all right to expect from me.

Then I understood that her expectation was the unspoken debt to be extracted for the uncle affair. The consequences from that alone had been unthinkable enough, and my parents were still reeling when I told them about Ed. Having a Black boyfriend and then an interracial marriage was more than they could handle. They had expected me to know that and to ask no more from them. And that was how one difficult incident had become hopelessly entangled with another. In the dark hidden place where secrets fester, and after years of practicing my mother's "you should know, I shouldn't have to tell you" expectation that I read her mind, I had understood and let it stay buried.

"We've always had such a good thing between us," she continued. "Let's not lose that."

I couldn't change what had already happened, and while I didn't expect her to change, it wasn't my job any longer to protect the secret that was about me.

"Yes, of course. But a lot of that 'good thing' depends on not talking about Ed."

"I accept Ed," she said stiffly. "If I didn't I wouldn't have had a daughter for the last 20 years."

I thought about the times she had called my house and hung up when Ed answered the phone.

"Your acceptance has too many conditions," I finally answered. "I don't want to hurt you, but I don't know how not to hurt you without hurting myself even more."

I told my sister that I couldn't—no, I wouldn't—pretend any longer that it was normal to keep my marriage secret.

"How would you feel if it was you?"

It took a minute. "Oh," her voice was tinged with sadness. "I hadn't thought about how all this affects you."

I finally worked up the courage to tell Ed the truth. The enormity of what he considered a major betrayal took some time for him to process.

"I hate that I'm your mother's dirty secret," he said, bitterly. "How could you not have told me years ago?"

I hadn't wanted Ed to know this terrible thing about my family, especially because his family had always accepted me without reservation. And I saw how my need to protect Ed from knowing how poorly my family had chosen to handle our relationship complemented my need to hide that knowledge from myself while being complicit in keeping the family secret.

But I had made a big mistake trying to spare his feelings, when what we both needed was honesty.

I canceled my trip to Connecticut, and for a few months spoke only infrequently with my mother. She called just before Rosh Hashanah.

"I don't like what is happening between us," she began.

She wanted to make amends, as is traditional during the Jewish New Year. She said that whatever I wanted to do would be all right.

"Talk to whoever you want," she said. "Just don't ask me to."

I didn't want to lose her any more than she wanted to lose me. The compromise she made with herself to keep her promise to my dad and release me was the best I could hope for.

Soon afterwards, I called Aunt Fanny, my father's youngest and only remaining sibling. She had been the Auntie Mame of our childhood, a tall, thin, zany force who loved that her crazy antics made us laugh. She was funny, stubborn, and strong-willed, though her stubbornness, or close-mindedness, sometimes backed her into unfortunate corners. When her oldest son married a woman who wasn't Jewish, Aunt Fanny made him promise to raise his children

as Jews. Several years later, after one of her young grandsons innocently revealed that they went to church with their mom every week
and hardly ever went to synagogue, Aunt Fanny cut off all contact
with her son and his family. My mother, who had been longing for
a grandchild of her own, was baffled. "How could she do something
so foolish that she doesn't see her own grandsons? How could she
punish herself like that?"

So, I had no expectations when I called Aunt Fanny, who was
in her late eighties. She listened quietly, and then said in her heavy
New York accent, "You know what, darling? If you had told me ten
years ago, I couldn't have accepted it at all. But as I grow old, I am
learning that love between two people is the only important thing."

She and Ed finally met at our nephew's Bar Mitzvah in 1997
(along with the rest of my dad's family who were there). They bonded
effortlessly and warmly, enjoying each other's company, kibitzing,
teasing, and laughing as if they had known each other for a very long
time. With him, she was still the Auntie Mame of my childhood.

ED

As Diane and I were trying to work through many of the issues
we hadn't been able to talk about before, I slowly came to understand
that if you live, you will keep encountering situations you didn't even
know existed.

From the reading I was doing about relationships for my
classes at Thunder Road, I found an interesting process about setting
rules to settle conflict and brought it home for us to try. It goes like
this. When one person gets angry or upset about something, they
tell the other they want to talk and both agree on a time to talk about
it later. It shouldn't be in the moment while emotions are running

high. We would agree that when we sat down together, only the person with the problem would talk, while the other says nothing, just listens. Then we would stop for some agreed-on period of time, up to 24 hours, when it would be the other person's turn to respond, while the first one remained silent and listening.

We found it to be a brilliant process. If you are the one who has to listen and not talk, you actually hear what the other person says rather than spending time while they are talking thinking about what you'll say, which would probably escalate the conflict. Sometimes the time between one person talking and the other responding was enough to lessen the tension making it possible to talk through rather than fight through what happened. It worked so well with us that it became an exercise I used a lot in my classes.

Over time, I worked as a consultant, trainer, and lecturer for many drug treatment programs in the community, in hospitals, in jails, and in prisons with both clients and staff about the art and practice of living well. I got a grant from The California Wellness Foundation to take my "Art and Practice of Living Well" series into San Quentin and the women's prison at Chowchilla. There, I did the eight-part workshop over two months with pre-release inmates to give them some tools that would help prepare them for release from prison into the community.

One day, when I had been clean and sober for more than three years and still working at Thunder Road, I was walking down the hall and heard a guitarist playing "Laura," one of my favorite tunes. The sound was coming from a counselor's office. I knew and loved the tune and I sang it whenever it came into my thoughts. The guitarist was really good and when he finished, I knocked on his door. He invited me in. I told Alex Markels how impressed I was with his playing and how much I'd appreciate singing with him and his guitar.

That meeting was the beginning of my singing again in public. During the 1990s, Alex and I played at all sorts of Twelve Step events, in Bay Area restaurants, and an occasional club. In 2005 I attended Jazz Camp West in La Honda, California where one of the faculty members heard me sing and, in my late seventies, put me on a trajectory that I hadn't at all expected.

Los Angeles, 2004

Bill Henderson invited Ed to sit in with him at The Vic (Santa Monica)
and sing "A Sleepin' Bee." When he asked what part of L.A. our zip code
was in, Bill was shocked to learn we had traveled from
the Bay Area just to sit in with him on one tune!

Jazz Camp West, 2006

A week like none other in the redwoods. Round-the-clock vocal, instrumental, and dance classes, rehearsals, and performances with the best teachers from the Bay Area and beyond. (Left to right: Ed, Albert "Tootie" Heath, Nancy Nisperos, and Donald Dean.)

Ed Reed Sings Love Stories, 2006

At Bay Records Studio in Berkeley after two days of recording our first CD in February. (Left to right: Bud Spangler, Eddie Marshall, John Wiitala, Ed, Gary Fisher, Diane, Peck Allmond, Dan Feiszli.)

Marians Jazzroom, Bern, Switzerland, 2009

This is where the seeds for *Born to Be Blue* were planted...by the third night, the music was so good we were all talking about this amazing Bern quartet making a new CD. (Left to right: Randy Porter, Robb Fisher, Akira Tana, Ed.)

Bern, 2009

After dinner on the garden patio of the hotel where Marians Jazzroom is located. (Left to right: Akira Tana, Diane, Ed, Randy Porter, Carolyn and Robb Fisher.)

Yoshi's San Francisco, 2009

In the Green Room with Ernestine Anderson. By the end of the second night,
as she and Ed traded stories and got to know a little about each other,
Ernestine's initial aloofness had melted into a sweet affection.

In the studio recording I'm a Shy Guy, 2013

Special thanks to photographer Chuck Gee for this set of photos
Recording band on Ed's fourth CD, his love letter to the Nat King Cole Trio.
(Left to right: Akira Tana, Anton Schwartz, Ed, John Wiitala, Randy Porter, Jamie Fox.)

Ed listening to the previous take.

Ed and co-producer Laurie Antonioli.

Ed and "I'm a Shy Guy" jazz angel Marge Slabach.

The "I'm a Shy Guy" Gang

(Left to right: Marge Slabach, Akira Tana, Ed, Diane, Anton Schwartz, Laurie Antonioli, John Wiitala, Jamie Fox, Dan Feiszli, Randy Porter.)

Happiness is being in a studio recording a new CD!

Patricia Silva, 2014

Patricia's stunning oil portrait of Ed's photo on the cover of *The Song Is You.*

Bud Spangler, 2014

With Susan Muscarella of the California Jazz Conservatory and Ed.

TEDxSantaCruz. 2014

The topic of this TEDx Talk event was "Radical Collaboration."
Ed's talk was aptly titled, "There Is Nothing Wrong With You."

L.A. Film Festival, 2014

Q&A after the premiere screening of *Sound of Redemption,* the Frank Morgan documentary for which Ed was interviewed. (Left to right: Ron Carter, director NC Heikin, Roy McCurdy, George Cables, Ed, Mark Gross, Grace Kelly.)

The day after the screening, the band gave a concert at the Grammy Museum. Pianist George Cables (far left, not visible in photo) invited Ed to sit in on a few tunes. (Left to right: Ron Carter, Ed, Roy McCurdy, Mark Gross, Grace Kelly.)

Dizzy's Club Coca-Cola at Jazz at Lincoln Center, 2015

Three pinnacle nights in this iconic venue with the dazzling
New York City nighttime skyline behind the band.
(Left to right: George Cables, Ugonna Okegwo, Ed, Akira Tana.)

With Bette Midler who, along with Aretha Franklin, had performed in
another part of Jazz at Lincoln Center that night, came to
Dizzy's afterward for dinner during Ed's last set.

Piedmont Piano Company, Oakland, 2019

Ed's 90th birthday concert at a favorite East Bay venue.
Piano Company owner Jim Callahan, holding Ed's birthday cake.
(Left to right: Jim Callahan, Adam Shulman, Ed, Anton Schwartz.)

Bird & Beckett, San Francisco, 2019

Another 90th birthday concert at a legendary
San Francisco bookstore and intimate concert space.
(Left to right: Adam Shulman, John Wiitala, Lorca Hart, Ed.)

Adam Shulman and Ed, 2019

"I love to tease pianists, and sometimes try to lose them by stringing the lyric out or changing the tempo. But with Adam, no matter where I go in a tune, I've never been able to lose him. He's always there. He always finds me, seemingly effortlessly."

Ed and Diane in their garden, early 2000s

Part Five:

Dessert

26

Into the Unknown

ED

My earliest memories of my mother—her singing voice and the feelings of experiencing her great talent—have stayed with me all my life. As a little child, I was always singing along with Mom or singing as she instructed. She was firm—what I called "nagging" as I got older—about things like stage presence, attitude, facial expression, physical posture, diction, pronunciation, tonality, and dress. It was fun in my early years, but as I grew older I got angry at her insistence that I sing and recite something nearly every day. Before holidays, we began daily preparation for upcoming performances at church and school at least a month in advance. Christmas and Easter were landmarks for which we spent the whole year getting ready. Preparedness was the keystone to dignity, honor, and success. Because my mother was so highly respected, it was necessary for me to become a shining example of her prowess in each breath I took.

As a young child in Cleveland, I had become a jazz fan at Aunt Lois's house. She had a large record collection and a huge wind-up Victrola that she taught me how to use properly. The jazz players and singers of my youth got into my heart—Billie Holiday and Lester Young, Duke Ellington with alto saxophonist Johnny Hodges and singers Herb Jeffries and Ivie Anderson. I loved the guitars of Charlie Christian, Django Reinhardt, and countless other jazz players. To my classical music-loving mom, some of the music was just unacceptable, especially the use of "scat" singing in jazz bands. And she wouldn't ever let me sing the blues at home because so many of the lyrics were unkind, violent, chauvinistic, and otherwise too negative for her sensibilities.

Like my mother, I nearly always have a song in my heart that won't leave me alone until I can sing it satisfactorily. I've always known I could sing a song, but felt inferior to the instrumentalists because I had no formal musical education and didn't read music. I would defer to them in everything and was grateful that they even let me on the bandstand with them. To me, they were the "real" musicians and I didn't think I could hold my own with them. I had no theoretical foundation in music which, to me, was mystifying and left me feeling inadequate. Hanging out with pianist George Lewis, trumpeter Dupree Bolton, and tenor saxophonist Boogie Daniels in Los Angeles in the 1950s, living down the street from and talking to saxophonist Buddy Collette every day, I was always in awe of what they did instrumentally.

But because I never learned to play an instrument or read music, I felt like my parents hadn't taken me seriously. Though my mother had insisted that I learn to sing and perform, maybe she really didn't want me to be a jazz singer. I often wonder, and don't understand, why my mother didn't give me the chance to get formal

musical training, especially in light of her strict and repeated instruc-
tion about my speech, diction, posture, dress, and facial expressions
when I performed as a child. Perhaps she was thinking more about
social acceptance and her dream that I go to law school and didn't
want me to get sidetracked. But I was already on a "side track."

My sense of inferiority changed when I got into recovery.
Some of that feeling came from what I thought other people thought
of me, something that had been so important to my mother, who
always said, "What will people think?" But in Alcoholics Anonymous
recovery, one of the first things I heard was "what other people think
of you is none of your business." Operating on that principle, I could
get up on the bandstand and talk to musicians. But, even today, they
have a language I can't speak, and I still feel a little "less than."

As a child, I used to listen to jazz on the radio and pretend
that I was leading the band. By the time I was a young teenager, my
fantasy was that Duke Ellington would knock on the door with an
offer to be the band's vocalist and join him and Billy Strayhorn on
the road.

Well, that didn't happen, but 60 years later, I did get slowly
pulled back into the jazz world. One summer afternoon in the early
2000s, I was at an AA recovery birthday party which was held in
the large beautiful backyard of a friend. They had hired a local jazz
trio and a vocalist, Stephanie Bruce. We talked after the first set.
She invited me to sit in with the band and sing a couple of tunes. I
was instantly interested when she said she gave voice lessons. I took
some classes from Stephanie, including a couple that she taught at
the Jazzschool in Berkeley (now the California Jazz Conservatory).
At the end of each class, she would sponsor a class recital with a
trio at the Terrace Room at Lake Merritt in Oakland. One year she
offered students a chance to professionally record a tune in the

home studio of one of her friends. Diane and I met her there and I recorded "A Sleepin' Bee" for the first time. After hearing me sing at one of Stephanie's student recitals, Susan Muscarella, president and dean of the Jazzschool and Conservatory, gave me a scholarship to take a couple more classes.

In 2004, Carla Kaufman, a bassist who occasionally played with guitarist Alex Markels and me at some of our gigs, invited me to sit in with her group at the Cheeseboard Pizza Collective. The Cheeseboard is at the "Gourmet Ghetto" end of Shattuck Avenue in Berkeley. They not only make incredible vegetarian pizza, but also support live music during the lunch and dinner hours. It is a perfect European-style venue, with an open front so that all who pass by can stop and listen to the music—or get in line for pizza, a line that often snakes all the way up the street and around the corner.

After singing with Carla's group a few times, one of the Collective members, Patricia Silva—also a hot Flamenco singer and accomplished artist—offered me a regular booking with an existing jazz duo. That began a five-year gig for me every Tuesday night at the Cheeseboard with the piano/bass duo of Brian Cooke and Robb Fisher. Sometimes we added a drummer.

Cheeseboard Pizza is one of the older iconic eating places in Berkeley. Originally housed in a narrow rectangular room with an upright piano tucked into the corner by the door and four or five small tables, it was always crowded with people lined up against the wall waiting to order pizza. That tiny room was very noisy, but a fun place to be. After my first couple of years there, Cheeseboard Pizza moved into a larger space next door that accommodated more tables. It was always full of Cal students, along with families and people stopping on their way home from work to pick up a fast dinner. Often our friends came to hang out and hear free live jazz. We were at the Cheeseboard on election night of 2008 when we learned that Barack Obama would be our next president and Shattuck Avenue erupted in a frenzy of excitement with crowds of exhilarated people dancing, singing, celebrating in the street.

The three of us, Brian, Robb, and I, were a good match. We loved and thrived on the "Great American Song Book." Each of us was always bringing an obscure, beautiful tune to the gig, and I don't think we ever got completely stumped by any one of them. As a team, one of us would always have a piece of the tune, and together we would work it out even as we performed it. In a sense, those years were like an ongoing workshop for us, rehearsals for the gigs we played together outside of the Cheeseboard.

During those years, I met and played with some great musicians at the Cheeseboard and worked with many of them in other venues, including pianist Laura Klein and her guitarist husband Tony Corman. Laura recently told us about how she remembered the day we met.

"I was playing at the Cheeseboard with Carla Kaufman when Ed asked to sit in," Laura said. "This was before he had a gig there. Often singers would want to sit in and most of them weren't very good. But Carla quietly said, 'Don't worry, this guy is really good!'

"So I asked Ed what he wanted to play and he handed me a little piece of paper with hundreds of song titles and keys in tiny lettering. I can't remember what tune we played, but I do remember that as soon as Ed started singing, the whole place went quiet, and everyone turned to listen! That was the beginning of our musical relationship and our friendship."

When I went to Jazz Camp West for the first time in 2005, I met and worked with some wonderful faculty members and jazz luminaries from around the world. One of them, jazz vocalist and teacher Rebecca Parris, helped me to understand that I could become the singer I wanted to be. Another faculty member, New York-based multi-instrumentalist Peck Allmond, asked where he could find my CDs. When I said I didn't have a CD, Peck paved the way for me to meet Bud Spangler, legendary Bay Area drummer, jazz radio host, and producer. Peck would later recall in an interview with *DownBeat*, "I really couldn't believe what I was hearing. The maturity of his phrasing, the spontaneity and the depth of harmony. I told him, 'You've got to record, man!'" Thanks to Peck, six months later we were in a studio, Bay Records in Berkeley, with Bud and the stunning quartet he brought together—New York-based pianist Gary Fisher, bassist John Wiitala, drummer Eddie Marshall, and of course Peck, who wrote the arrangements and played trumpet, tenor saxophone, flute, alto flute, clarinet, bass clarinet, trombonium, and kalimbas on that first recording. On some tunes, Peck overdubbed, or recorded one or more of his instruments over the original, resulting in a layering of sounds and creating beautiful harmonies.

DIANE

It was the year of our first recording project—2006—and it felt like we were poised, almost on tiptoe, about to fly off the edge of the world into a great unknown. We had made a major financial investment with no idea about what was to come. Sometimes it felt like the beauty of Ed's first recording would take the world by storm and we'd be swept into exhilaration without anchors. We tried to stay grounded even as we felt ourselves plummeting into a new bottomless world where every step led to another that cost us more in money, time, and serenity.

People had said Ed should make a CD as casually as others would later say that we should write a book and tell our story. Now we were doing it, climbing a steep learning curve from recording studio to mixing, mastering, graphic design, manufacturing, licensing, distribution, website, publicity, radio promotion, interviews, sales, gigs, and travel. We were like blind newborn kittens needing a lot of support and guidance from people who knew what to do, and we were unbelievably fortunate to have a musical and production team that seemed to fall into our laps.

Even as the dream unfolded, a lot of the time I felt that I was coming unglued with so many competing demands. Much as we wanted to slow down around our "day jobs" and focus solely on the music, we couldn't afford to. There would be no retirement and definitely no pensions with both of us working as consultants. Unless, that is, *Ed Reed Sings Love Stories* did it! That hope, like a stream swollen with spring runoff rushing down from the Sierras, was driving us forward to more music and the chance to work together doing something we both loved.

Ed has always lived in the field of all possibilities. He dreams big and never stops wanting to change the world at large—and our own smaller world too—not incrementally, but all at once. Even as the first CD was still in production, he was already thinking about which Bay Area hill we would build our new house on. And even I, the more practical of the two, felt swept away. Regardless of what happened, this would always be one of the best decisions and investments we had ever made together. We were sure that his parents would have applauded using $25,000 that Ed had recently inherited from a small family trust to pay for the CD.

What would become *Ed Reed Sings Love Stories* officially began on February 26, 2006 with a rehearsal in Bud's basement studio. It was coincidence, or not, that it was my mother's birthday, the first since her passing the previous year. I put her picture on a shelf in Bud's studio so she could be there too.

While some people close down in old age and shrink their worlds, my mother opened her heart. Slowly, over time, she and Ed got to know each other. When we were in Connecticut, they sat together at the kitchen table and Ed sang to her. They would put their heads together and whisper. She grew to love him, unexpectedly and fully. She also loved the promo CD that Ed had recorded with Alex several years before, and played it all the time. During our visits and on the phone, she always asked Ed when he was going to make a full-length CD. So, her photo needed to be there for his first one.

ED

During my last time at San Quentin in 1964-66 when I was singing with the Warden's Band, I heard a new tune, "A Sleepin' Bee" sung by Bill Henderson, on KJAZ, the then-Bay Area's jazz station. No one sounded like Bill Henderson and no one else consistently sang the great tunes that he chose. As the late jazz journalist Leonard Feather was quoted in *Variety* (April 6, 2016), "Henderson's phrasing is virtually his own copyright. He tends to space certain words as if the syllables were separated by commas, even semicolons, yet everything winds up as a perfectly constructed sentence."

I loved "A Sleepin' Bee" and worked on learning the lyric along with the other singers who loved jazz. In those days, we were only allowed to listen to jazz radio for a limited time every week, so if we heard a tune we wanted to learn, we had to wait, sometimes for months, until it was played again. Then the instrumentalists would write the musical chart and the singers would concentrate on getting the words down on paper. The day I finally finished writing the lyric, I was listening to the radio in the band room with Art Pepper, who had gotten the tune with his horn weeks before. Art and I were in the Warden's Band together and he played on nearly everything that I sang. Despite our musical closeness, the band room was the only safe place we could talk because of racism and the de facto segregation of races in prison. The day we finished "A Sleepin' Bee" was beautiful as Art and I launched into the song simultaneously, and that gave us such joy.

Forty years later, in 2004, I met Bill Henderson at my cousin Sandi's memorial in Los Angeles. Sandi had been married to the late great bassist, Andy Simpkins. Someone asked Bill to sing "A Sleepin' Bee," which had become one of his signature tunes, when he suddenly stopped. "I forgot the lyric!" he laughed. Something inside me made me yell, "I know that tune!" Everyone gasped, including me. My God, I was yelling at one of my favorite singers in the world. They're going to throw me to the lions! But no, Bill just smiled and asked me to come up and take the lead. We sang a duet. I nearly fainted. But we did it. And the audience loved it.

A few months later, Bill called to invite me to sit in during his gig at The Vic in Santa Monica and sing "A Sleepin' Bee" with him again. We booked a flight to L.A. for this unexpected honor and thrill. Between sets, Bill invited Diane and me backstage to the Green Room for dinner and to talk. As he got ready to go back on stage, he asked, "What part of L.A. is your 510 area code in?" He was shocked to learn that we live in the Bay Area and had traveled all the way to L.A. just to sit in with him on one tune! After that, Bill and I stayed in touch until he died in 2016 at age 90. He sent me some of his CDs, along with handwritten lyrics to a couple of tunes I had asked him about.

When I recorded my first CD in 2006, there was no question that "A Sleepin' Bee" would be a part of it. Over time, I also covered other Bill Henderson tunes—"The Song Is You," "Old Country," "Don't Like Goodbyes," "Never Kiss and Run," and "It Never Entered My Mind."

A few years later, I emailed Bill as we were preparing to record *Born to Be Blue,* our third CD. "I'm in the studio next week and must confess that I'm doing another cover of your stuff. It is amazing to me how much your singing has pointed the way for me. By now, though, I may have found a way to escape your phrasing and use my own!"

He answered in his own gracious way, "Hey Ed, Keep stealing!!! Just make sure you give it all you got, go all the way and make a touchdown. That's right, we are on the same team, the singing team. We are the few that are still around doing what we do! Keep singing and be well. Bill."

There were, of course, other greats who influenced me— composers Duke Ellington and Billy Strayhorn; instrumentalists like John Coltrane, Thelonious Monk, and Miles Davis whose music, at one time, I listened to exclusively for months; and vocalists Shirley Horn, Nat King Cole, Billy Eckstine, Sarah Vaughan, and Carmen McRae—whose music I love to sing and have included on many of my projects.

Of the band members on *Love Stories,* I knew Peck Allmond, whom I had met the year before at Jazz Camp, along with bassist John Wiitala and drummer Eddie Marshall. Back in the early 1980s, before I got clean and sober, I occasionally sat in with John Wiitala, pianist Jessica Williams, and drummer Bud Spangler when they played at Mimosa, a small restaurant off Grand Avenue in Oakland, not far from Diane's apartment. The band on my CD had a long history working together in the Bay Area. Years earlier, Peck had a group with John Wiitala and Gary Fisher, the pianist on *Love Stories*, and they would jam in a garage in San Francisco. One day, the story goes, drummer Eddie Marshall was walking down the street and heard them practicing. Eventually they started gigging. Now, the four of them were playing on my first CD!

During the pre-recording rehearsal at Bud's studio, Eddie cracked up over my singing "A Sleepin' Bee" in dialect.

"Did you actually just sing: 'And I walks with my feets off the ground?' Did I really hear you say 'feets'?"

He had a great laugh over that. We all did.

DIANE

I know nothing more exhilarating than walking through the door into the magic of a recording studio. You feel it the minute you cross the threshold into a space where sound is denser, the lighting is darker and softer, and the ambience is full of expectation. It is a world apart from ordinary life, a place that can transform sound into something new, unexpected, and extraordinarily beautiful. Like the popular tune that Al Jarreau, Tuck and Patti, and others have sung, to me that experience is "better than anything—except being in love."

Two days in a studio must be comparable, at some primeval level, to a birth canal, where each tune begins a new voyage into the world. Leaving that womb-like space after a day's session and driving home is always a sensory shock—the world outside is too bright, too noisy, too chaotic, too jolting, too discordant, too raw.

I always sat in the control room behind the producer and recording engineer who worked the complex console that records each artist on a separate track. Often I couldn't see Ed or the other musicians who worked in separate, mostly darkened isolation booths during the session. Sometimes I listened on headphones where the sound is pure and flows into and through every pore, every cell; sometimes I listened to the sound coming from speakers in the control room.

I smiled and floated through those days.

In the weeks and months following the session that would become *Ed Reed Sings Love Stories*, our sound engineer, Dan Feiszli, did his alchemy, mixing each tune. By the time he was finished, and after endless listening, I could sing the entire recording, just about every note, solo, and lyric. Any phrase that Ed wanted changed, or any solo that one of the musicians wanted to redo, were re-recorded or dubbed at Dan's studio. Long gone were the days when a band recorded only one take on a single track with no way to go back and change anything without re-recording everything. Today, technology is so sophisticated and precise that, with separate tracks, anything—a phrase, a note, even a single brush stroke—can be tuned, added, or taken out. It is even possible for someone who is completely tone deaf to "sing" an entire song in monotone and have it transformed into a pitch-perfect melody.

27

Ed Reed Sings Love Stories

ED

ove Stories was officially launched in early 2007, just before my 78th birthday. The first CD release concert took place at Anna's Jazz Island in Berkeley on February 10 with the full recording band. Anna de Leon, an accomplished jazz vocalist in her own right, had been one of my earliest champions. She always encouraged me to reach for the best in myself and in the musicians I chose to work with. After hearing me sing for the first time, she said, "Why aren't you famous?" It was a question that was asked repeatedly during that year as *Love Stories* circulated through the jazz world. "Where has this cat been all this time?"

Anna came to the studio at the end of the second day. She and I handwrote the lyrics from memory to "Sometimes I Feel Like a Motherless Child," an old Negro spiritual that I had decided to sing at the last minute. It was released a cappella on the CD, and I continued to perform it without accompaniment in many subsequent concerts through the years, which seemed to leave audiences quietly stunned.

Our producer Bud Spangler brought two friends to that sold-out event at Anna's, where people stood outside to listen in the cold winter night. At the end of the show, he introduced me to Terri Hinte. Terri had recently left Fantasy Records after 30 years as one of the most highly respected publicists in the world, and was working independently. Bud also introduced his long-time dear friend and colleague Merrilee Trost. She had worked at Concord Records for over ten years as Vice President of Publicity and Promotions. She continued to be as engaged with the music as a jazz concert producer as on the day over 40 years before when she reportedly "fell down the rabbit hole into the magical world of jazz." Over time, each of these women would open doors to infinite possibilities on my behalf. But on that night, in the middle of that hot room at Anna's, full of excited, noisy concertgoers pushing towards me, I asked Terri if she would represent me. She smiled and instantly agreed.

DIANE

And so, Blueshorts Records was born. That was the "label" we created when Terri recommended that we have a name for this first and future CDs. Ed instantly said, "Blueshorts." That idea had come from his daughter, Denyce, a few years before on one of her visits. She and Ed had been talking about a project they could do together and, seemingly out of nowhere, she suggested that he call it—or call something else—Blueshorts. And that is what he decided to name our new label.

With Terri's vast connections in the jazz review world of print, and our radio promoter, Neal Sapper, who got radio stations to play a sensational new CD from an unknown vocalist on the air, Ed was quickly spun off into the wider world of print reviews and radio interviews. The word about this new but old singer who seemingly just burst into the jazz world from nowhere had everyone wanting to talk to him. Ed told one interviewer, "This stuff is coming so fast, I haven't had much time to think about it. I just wanted to make a recording, and all hell broke loose!"

Captivated by his phrasing and skill in bringing alive the story inside the lyric, critics and audiences alike sensed they were listening to something unusual, something not found in many vocalists. But to Ed, it was as natural as breathing. "When I'm singing," he would say, "the question for me is: who is this in the song? Who would say these things, and why? I really have to know what the lyric is about. What's the point of standing up in front of an audience if you're not saying anything?"

That first year we would learn a lot about the highs and lows of the unpredictable jazz business. Terri introduced us to Maxine Harvard, veteran booking agent and promoter whose clients have included Freddy Cole, Bobby Broom, Mary Stallings, Jimmy Scott, Andy Bey, and Arthur Prysock. After listening to Ed's CD, Maxine said, "There's something in his voice that says to me this man is going to be a great favorite of fans. I'd like to be part of making that happen."

Maxine booked Ed at Yoshi's in Oakland and arranged an East Coast tour in the fall of 2007. The much-anticipated CD release concert at Yoshi's was on August 29 (coincidentally also the birthday of Charlie "Bird" Parker). The gig was highly publicized in most Bay Area newspapers and was the feature story on page one of the *San Francisco Chronicle*'s Datebook section, along with a color photograph of Ed that took up three-fourths of the page. When Ed came out onto the stage, he shaded his eyes, looked out in amazement into the sold-out audience, and laughed. "Did you see the story in the *Chronicle* with that huge photo? I thought it was a Wanted poster!"

Both sets sold out, so we made a lot of extra money on top of the guaranteed amount. Most amazing, we sold nearly 100 CDs after the show, making for a deliriously profitable night. In those early concerts, we brought a little cash box to gigs, but it was so clunky and pretentious that I soon stopped using it, preferring instead to go home with my pockets stuffed with $20 bills. We never had another night like that for CD sales, though, not until jazz historian Nat Hentoff wrote an article about Ed that was published in the *Wall Street Journal* in 2008. Something like 300 CDs flew off the shelves, which all but wiped out our remaining stock.

The success at Yoshi's left us feeling invincible and overly confident. Just six weeks later we were humbled, having to pay the band out of pocket after a gig in Carmel. We had naively promised the musicians more money than we had been guaranteed and didn't make enough in ticket and CD sales to make up the difference. It took a couple of years and the Great Recession for us to learn to be cautious in what we promised and, especially, that success in one venue is neither cumulative nor promised in the next.

Even before the radio campaign officially began (when we would receive weekly reports tracking the number of spins, the stations playing the CD, and where Ed placed on JazzWeek's top 50 list), Bay Area jazz station KCSM had already played tracks from the album over 40 times. Ed called to thank the station and ask them if they would wait until the tunes they played from the CD could be counted by JazzWeek. In reply, radio announcer Michael Burman said that while he understood the concern, the music was so good he "just couldn't help" but continue to spin it.

Ed made his New York City debut in the fall of 2007 at the Jazz Standard—one of those classic jazz clubs where you walk down a long flight of stairs from street level into a long, dimly lit rectangular room. Behind the bandstand, at the far end of the room, is a floor-to-ceiling wall of red acoustic sound panels. Our publicist Terri Hinte was there. So was our agent, Maxine Harvard, a fiery redhead wearing spiky-heeled knee-high boots, whom we met in person at that gig for the first time. Most of my family who lived in the New York City area, many of whom I hadn't seen in years, were there as well.

By the end of 2007, the Bay Area's jazz station, KCSM reported that *Love Stories* ranked #1 among the top new releases they had played that year. Plus, the CD was chosen as one of the ten most memorable new releases in California by jazz journalist Andrew Gilbert, who also did a wonderful piece about Ed on NPR's *California Report*. When Ed thanked him for the radio story, Andy replied, "It's definitely my favorite of the pieces I've done for California Report so far. I was even able to listen to myself from beginning to end without changing the station!"

No matter how many superlative reviews Ed received during the first year, and forever more, he never stopped asserting two truths. "There's a lot of literature about fame and how it's like birds that come and pick you to pieces," he would explain. "People change, but I don't think I have, because it's not about me," he would say of his newfound singing career. "It's about the gift. And the gift is to be shared or it'll kill you. I believe that."

His second truth was that the music was "dessert"— the main meal was his ongoing work with recovering addicts and their families, using "The Art and Practice of Living Well," his ever-evolving series.

"I'd be willing to spend two or three years just singing," he said. "But I'd always go back to helping people connect with themselves. That work is what is so exciting to me. I think it might be better than the applause I get from a performance. It might even be better than a standing ovation."

28

The Song Is You

DIANE

The instant the first CD was finished, mastered, packaged, and sent off into the world of jazz critics and radio airwaves, we were ready, no, aching to get back into the studio. And so it happened that in late 2007, we spent two days recording with a six-piece band at Bennett Studios—a renovated old railway station—in New Jersey. This time, we added guitar and violin to the standard rhythm section of piano, bass, and drums along with Peck's wind and brass instruments. At the end of two days, 16 tracks had been recorded and the second CD, *The Song Is You,* was born. It was released in May 2008.

This one had a rough beginning. The day we should have received the shipment of eight boxes containing 1,000 CDs came and went, but no CDs arrived, even though UPS said they had been delivered. The following morning a woman who lived a block away rang our doorbell. She had found those boxes at the end of her driveway by the garbage bins which, if it had been pickup day, could easily have been taken away with the rest of the trash.

With relief and gratitude, we packaged, addressed, stamped, and mailed 450 promotional CDs only to start getting calls a few days later from journalists and radio stations reporting that some of the tracks were skipping. We pulled a CD at random from each of the boxes and found that the skipping problem was happening on some discs but not others. Even worse, our Bay Area station, KCSM, was already playing the new CD and, to our horror, we actually heard one of those bad tracks malfunction on the radio. The remaining 550 CDs were returned to the manufacturer who replicated another 1000 and re-sent 300 replacement discs to radio stations with a letter explaining what had happened.

The CD release concert at Yoshi's on August 25, 2008 happened just about a year from our first huge success there. But it coincided with Michelle Obama's speech at the 2008 Democratic National Convention. Not many other events could have successfully competed with that historic moment, so the sold-out house we had hoped for was only half full.

Then, in late September as we were starting a two-night gig at Seattle's Jazz Alley, the financial markets that were already swinging went wildly out of control. Lehman Brothers had collapsed the week before, setting off a worldwide financial crisis. People stayed home and held onto their money. Our disbelief was matched only by our stunned, shaking heads not knowing whether to laugh or cry that we had actually brought along a small suitcase stuffed with CDs, expecting to sell out!

We tried to settle into the idea of living with uncertainty, and feeling grateful that we still had our "day jobs." By then, we suspected that the music would always be an act of love, more than a path to riches. What lifted our spirits when we worried was the flood of reviews and articles about Ed, though after a while, we were ready to read more about Ed and his music than his long dark journey through addiction and incarceration that journalists and critics couldn't stop writing about.

Some of the titles used for many of the reviews were attention-grabbing in their own right, ranging from the wonderful to the weird.

Some were cool and sublime:

"A Stunning Debut at 78"

"Blue Arrival: at 78, Ed Reed is soaring

in a new career as a singer"

"Jazz singer's long road to intersection with destiny"

Some were melodramatic:

"Ed Reed beating the odds"

"Better late than never"

Others highlighted the drugs/prison connection:

"From San Quentin to the spotlight"

"Singer and ex-addict finds redemption

in a CD and gigs"

"Former prisoner Ed Reed releases debut album"

And some were plainly ridiculous:

"Seasoned crooner dodged obituary"

"Love on lockdown"

"Behind bars is better than bars for meeting musicians"

Happily, none of that seemed to stop people from coming to concerts or keep Ed from getting bookings. One of our favorite evenings was at the Monterey Bay Aquarium where Ed sang along with other Bay Area jazz artists during a Monterey Jazz Festival fundraiser for a Santa Cruz jazz club. Between sets, we wandered through the wide halls, listening to the duos and trios strategically placed through the labyrinth of the Aquarium, playing against the backdrop of a universe of sea creatures swimming in various-sized glass-enclosed displays, some right up against the open sea.

Then we saw the giant red Pacific octopus. It swayed gracefully, reacting to the beat it felt, maybe even heard, in the music being played by the group across the aisle from its huge tank. We stopped in our tracks, hypnotized by the enormity of this creature that hatches from an egg the size of a grain of rice, moving so effortlessly, so perfectly synchronized to the music. We watched as this master of disguise playfully charged around the walls of the tank and then squeezed into a tiny rocky corner of its den, simultaneously shrinking to a fraction of its size and changing its skin color from deep brick red to grayish white that blended with the rocks. The magical dance of that giant denizen who lives a solitary life in the sea, a creature that we could see was watching us even as we watched her, totally eclipsed everything else going on that night.

ED

One of the highlights of those next few years was when I was a guest on Marian McPartland's *Piano Jazz* program on NPR. Merrilee Trost, whom we had met at Anna's Jazz Island the night of the first CD release concert in 2007, was a close friend of Marian's and visited her regularly at her home on Long Island. During one of her trips in early 2008, Merrilee called and asked us to overnight my first CD to Marian who was intrigued by my story.

Merrilee later told us, "I remember that weekend so well, sitting in her kitchen, listening to the CD when it arrived and watching her face as she 'got into it.' She always told me she could decide in the first 30 seconds whether someone was good or not. She listened to your whole CD and decided, then and there, to have you on *Piano Jazz*."

Marian and I hit it off right away. She had just celebrated her 90th birthday. Though frail and in a wheelchair, she remained a powerhouse on the piano. I had been warned that Marian no longer accompanied her guests on piano as she used to, but she surprised everyone when she insisted on playing a favorite Ellington tune, "All Too Soon," with me. That was a gift.

DIANE

During the recording of the show with Marian McPartland, I sat in the control room with the sound engineer, the program director, and Seattle-based jazz critic and author, Paul de Barros, who had just begun writing Marian's biography, *Shall We Play That One Together? The Life and Art of Jazz Piano Legend Marian McPartland*. Eight years later, in 2016, Paul described that session in an article he wrote for the *Seattle Times* to promote Ed's upcoming concert at The Triple Door.

"Back in 2008, when I was working on a biography of Marian McPartland," he wrote, "Marian and I went into the Manhattan studio, where every month she would record a couple of episodes of 'Marian McPartland's Piano Jazz,' to wait for the arrival of a new singer named Ed Reed. I say 'new singer,' but Reed was 78 [*sic*] years old at the time. That's right. Marian had turned 90 in March, so I suppose in some respects Ed really was a young singer to her. My, how they flirted! Marian loved that guy! She didn't stop talking about him for a couple of weeks."

It was because of Paul de Barros that Ed was booked at the Jazz Alley in Seattle a couple of months after the *Piano Jazz* session. "During the show, which was a knockout," he wrote in the *Seattle Times* article, "I called the Jazz Alley from the control room and said, 'You've got to book this guy. He's amazing. Sounds like a combination of Nat Cole and Joe Williams. Just turned up out of nowhere, like some ghost of some guy from the past we never knew existed.'"

ED

One of my big thrills was when I opened for Ernestine Anderson during her two nights of sold-out shows at Yoshi's San Francisco in 2009. I had loved her music ever since I used to see her in Oakland during my teenage years in the Army—she was not that much older than I. There I was, 60 years later, spending time with Ernestine in the Green Room before and between our sets. By the end of the second night, as we traded stories and got to know a little more about each other, her initial aloofness had melted into a sweet affection.

29

Born to Be Blue

ED

In September 2009, we traveled to Bern, Switzerland for five nights at Marian's Jazzroom (another Marian). It wasn't our first trip to Europe, but it was the first time I sang professionally outside of the U.S. We had an exceptional trio with us—Grammy-nominated pianist and Steinway artist Randy Porter; Akira Tana, whose intuition and sensitivity made him a singer's dream drummer; and bassist Robb Fisher, with whom I was still working every week at the Cheeseboard. Up until then, because of the high cost of traveling with musicians, we always used local sidemen for gigs and tours outside of the Bay Area. But this contract covered all the expenses for me to bring my own trio and Diane to Bern.

Being on the road with musicians is its own unique experience. Even the most weathered travelers in our group were jet-lagged for a good part of the week in Bern. I stayed "upside-down"—sleeping most of the day, up most of the night. In between, we rolled out of our rooms in the morning in time to eat together, feasting on the extravagant European-style buffet of breads, cheeses, granola, yogurt, eggs, meats, fruit, pastries, and strong coffee in the hotel's breakfast room. It was beautiful Indian summer weather. Every evening before the first set, we all met and had dinner together outside in the garden patio of the hotel that was built on the side of a mountain. After dinner, we headed down to the hotel's old wine cellar where the Jazzroom was located.

It's sad but true that touring musicians rarely have time or energy to explore whatever new place they're in, no matter where in the world they might be. At least in Bern, we were lucky to be staying in one place for the entire week, which made overcoming jet lag and playing two sets a night a little easier than having to pack up and travel every day from city to city.

DIANE

I had the added joy of spending most of that week in Bern with my high school friend Heidi, who had taken the train from Berlin to hang out with us. Heidi and I had reconnected nine years earlier, after she got her first computer and tracked down her Stamford High School friends. She flew to California to visit us a few months later. The following year we made the first of several trips to Paris, London, and Berlin, meeting up at some point along the way with Heidi and her husband Lutz, a conductor who taught at the Berlin Academy of Music and toured the world. Heidi and I took long walks around Bern's lovely Old Town with its charming cobblestone lanes and twice-weekly farmers' market with fresh local produce, fish, meat and baked goods, cheeses, clothing, and handcrafted products. We spent one afternoon at the Paul Klee Museum just outside Bern, and another on a ferry on Lake Thun, surrounded by massively beautiful Alps whose peaks were shrouded in fog.

Heidi, herself an accomplished classical pianist and piano teacher, was made an honorary member of the band. She had dinner with us every night and came to all the performances, immersing herself in the world of jazz, with which she was completely unfamiliar. In trying to understand how jazz works, she had the difficulty common to many artists trained in classical music technique. Improvisation is rare in a form that relies on playing exactly what is on the page. In contrast, a jazz chart might have nothing but chord changes and no written melody. An orchestra playing classical music relies on the conductor as the focal point to provide direction and interpretation of the written music. But a jazz musician, during a solo, might compose a whole new melodic line on top of a chord progression played by the rhythm section. During our conversations at dinner, the musicians would demonstrate for Heidi what jazz is by singing an excerpt from Beethoven or Chopin and then reinterpreting it, improvising on chord changes and making it swing.

It was a special week, spending so much time hanging out with the band. One day I asked Randy if it was boring to play the same sets night after night. "Not at all," he answered, "because we never play a tune the same way twice. We improvise; we stretch; we get better."

By the third night, the music was so good we were all talking about this amazing Bern quartet making a new CD. The question, as always, was how we would do it without going into debt.

At minimum, it costs about $25,000 to rent the studio, pay the musicians, producer, sound engineers, publicist, radio promoter and photographer, mix, master, and manufacture 1000 CDs, and license every song for physical and digital formats. Over 150 CDs with bio and press release is sent to jazz critics and nearly 300 CDs go to domestic and some international radio stations. That automatically reduced our inventory by 450 CDs, for which we would never be paid. (Many of those CDs would end up for sale on the internet as used as well as new CDs, sometimes for twice our selling price). Even so, there is no point doing this without investing what is needed to get it out into the world—and that is a stretch for many indie artists who, after recording and manufacturing a CD, could not afford a publicist or radio promoter.

From the beginning, we had been told that to stay on the charts and keep getting gigs, we would need to release a CD just about every year. That was realistic in the days when a contract with a label was still possible before the internet and YouTube and the many ways to listen to music for free changed the music industry forever. For us to stay in the game, we had to do it ourselves. In an ideal world, we would have used the money made on gigs and CD sales to pay for the next project, but we never broke even, not even during the first few years when people were still buying CDs and before everything went digital. To fund a new project, we would have to be creative. For the third and fourth CDs, we mixed and matched a mortgage refinance, held a house concert fundraiser, did a crowd-funding campaign, and, when we were completely out of ideas and money, used the credit card.

When we got home from Switzerland, we tried to convince ourselves that a third CD was not realistic, but couldn't stop hoping for a sign. Then, our first jazz angels, Harvey and Lynn Sande, fans from the Cheeseboard who were always asking Ed when he would make another record and how much we would need to do it, handed us a check for $10,000. That was enough to get us into the studio for two days, and pay the musicians, recording engineer and our beloved producer Bud Spangler.

ED

We added tenor saxophonist and composer Anton Schwartz to our original Bern quartet of Randy, Robb, Akira, and myself. Bud had talked a lot about Anton, the brilliant Ph.D. student who had walked away from his studies in artificial intelligence at Stanford in the mid-1990s to play jazz saxophone. Soon after I released *Love Stories*, Anton invited me to do a concert at his loft in Oakland and I started asking Anton to sit in on some of my gigs. When Anton and Randy played a duo concert in 2010, I knew I wanted Anton to be on this new project. I loved his versatility—his solos, especially the blues, are poignant and whimsical, as well as fiery.

Rehearsals started in the summer of 2010 for what would become *Born to Be Blue*, our third CD. These are the liner notes that I wrote:

> The title track and name of the new album, *Born to Be Blue*, speaks to so much of my life experience. The lyric reminds me about the importance of the blues—what I think of as the wisdom that speaks of the heartbreak in all life experience. Most often, though, we might not get to understand the lessons inherent in the heartbreak of the living process.
>
> These songs continue to assist my understanding of the saying, "the good stuff takes care of itself"—that "good stuff" only needs a little timely acknowledgement from us to make

itself useful. Sadness, on the other hand, requires a great effort of ownership and acceptance.

I love to sing songs about grief, lost love, and loneliness because those songs keep teaching me about my humanity and its illusion of grand complexity, its ongoing saga, and its resilience.

On October 24, we had a dress rehearsal concert at Piedmont Piano Company in Oakland, two days before going into the studio to record. This turned out to be one of my more memorable concerts. It was a stormy Sunday afternoon. Rain had been falling hard all day and we arrived at the affectionately nicknamed Piano Store to find there was no power in the neighborhood. Despite the floor-to-ceiling glass windows enclosing the large showroom filled with grand pianos, the light that reached the stage at the back of the room was dim. Someone ran out to buy candles.

And yes, I sang and the band played a concert in a blackout by candlelight. No power, no sound system, all acoustic. I looked out to the full audience and saw beautiful patterns of shadows and light on people's faces. The encroaching darkness, the music, and the flickering of candles created a sweet closeness in the room and a feeling that all of us—the band and the audience—were part of an unexpected but magical turn of events. The concert had sold out. Over time, it became one of those legendary afternoons that people who were there still talk about and marvel at how strong and clear the 81-year-old singer's voice projected without a microphone.

DIANE

Two days after the dress rehearsal at Piedmont Piano and feeling invincible, we carpooled over to the studio in Menlo Park. As we unpacked, the musicians loaded in, and decisions were made about who would be in what isolation booth, Ed looked at me and asked, "Where's the music?"

I was stunned. "What do you mean where's the music? *You* should have it."

"No, I don't. I thought you did."

That wouldn't be the first or the last time we left something of vital importance at home on the way to a gig or recording. Once, when we got to the Oakland Airport on the way to Los Angeles for a weekend of gigs, Ed discovered he didn't have his wallet. He was miraculously checked through security without an ID, partly on the strength of my vouching for him as his wife, but mostly because of his photos on the jacket covers of his CDs that we had brought with us to sell. Another time, after we landed in Seattle for a series of weekend concerts and workshops with Anton and a local trio, the first thing we had to do was find the nearest Macy's after realizing that Ed's performing clothes were still hanging on the outside of the hall closet by the front door. And on one of our many East Coast trips, while inching through early morning Manhattan traffic on a Megabus with Randy, Akira, and Anton for a show that evening at Scullers in Boston, we got a call from our friend who had dropped us off at the bus stop saying he found Ed's garment bag (with all his performance clothes in it) in the trunk of his car. Another quick stop at Macy's when we got to Boston.

It sometimes felt like life was imitating those inevitable travel dreams of being on a plane going halfway around the world, and discovering you forgot to get dressed or take a suitcase. But on the *Born to Be Blue* project, I had a much more unique one. I dreamed that I came home to find a garden hose in the living room with the water running. In a panic, I called out to Ed to help get the water out of the house, which by then was making its way into the hallway. But when I looked down, my shoes were completely dry. The message in that dream became our reality check. When unexpected things happened, before losing it, we'd look at each other and one of us would say to the other, "Are our feet wet yet?"

We knew we had come a long way. In the years since the struggles of early recovery, Ed and I had learned how to work together in situations of stress or conflict. If we ever needed those skills, it was now. Our confidence grew as we became more and more immersed in this new, unpredictable world and each of us did what was natural—Ed made the music happen, I became his de facto manager and took care of the business end.

By the time I made the two-hour roundtrip drive from Menlo Park to the East Bay for the music charts we had left at home and returned to the studio, they had already recorded "Wee Baby Blues" and "All My Tomorrows" without charts. It had been a productive morning. I was back in time to go get lunch for everyone.

Often after a concert when people come to the table where we're selling CDs, someone trying to decide which one to buy will inevitably ask what my favorite is. And I always tell them that question is like asking me to pick my favorite child, which I cannot do. Each of Ed's CDs has its own character and each touches me in a different way. Some are more romantic, some are sad, others are more fun, and certainly each varies instrumentally. But in truth, this one, *Born to Be Blue*, has always been particularly special to me.

Perhaps it's because Ed (who co-produced the recording with Bud) and I were much more involved in making musical and production decisions with *Born to Be Blue*. We felt a much greater share of ownership and pride in the finished recording than after we made the first two CDs when we had been inexperienced and needed to rely more on the expertise, guidance, and decisions of others.

Perhaps it's because some of my very favorite tunes are on that CD. "Inside a Silent Tear," about lost dreams, sadness, and disappointment, and "Throw It Away," about letting go, say so much about each of us and our journeys.

Perhaps it's because on the front jacket cover we used a photo of Ed as a serious (and unhappy) child about which jazz journalist Andrew Gilbert wrote:

> A morose little boy with heavy-lidded brown eyes looks out from the cover of Ed Reed's revelatory new album *Born to Be Blue*, and with every song Reed tells the story of how that 5-year-old went out into the world with a raw wound in his soul ... Given his track record of exponential creative growth over the past four years it might be premature to say that *Born to Be Blue* is Reed's definitive statement, but his third album possesses all the distilled emotion and narrative coherence of a jazz masterpiece — *Mercury News*

Or, maybe because on the back of the jacket, we used a photo that captured a fiercely intense Ed Reed, microphone in hand, singing a story. This picture had sparked a mild controversy with Bud and some others who felt that Ed looked too confrontational and unwelcoming, that the photo should be of an adult who has realized his dream and was extending an invitation to the listener to join him on his musical journey. Maybe they were right, but we loved that photo. To us it was a portrait of a man who had become strong from all he had overcome, a perfect counterbalance to the unhappy child he had been.

Or, maybe because we felt we must have done something right when *DownBeat* magazine featured *Born to Be Blue* as an Editors Pick the month after its release, in its July 2011 issue. The reviews were stunning.

> Reed has developed a jazz voice that is distinct—full of the pain, sorrow, love and beauty that go along with taking that long, hard trail through life. All of that is on full display here. When Ed Reed sings ... look for an intimate story every time ... *Born to Be Blue* is the kind of record that makes you happy that this life offers people more than one chance to offer their gift to the world — *DownBeat*

> Stylistically harkens back to the elegant tenderness of Johnny Hartman ... richly insightful ... intensely moving ... hypnotic renderings — *JazzTimes*

> Reed has a marvelous knack for knowing just how much room a lyric needs to breathe, timing his pace and pauses to build emotional impact — *San Francisco Examiner*

> His vocals are warm, mellow, nuanced and extraordinarily expressive. He gets deep inside a lyric. When Reed sings, he's telling a story — *Mercury News*

But mostly, even before the critical acclaim poured in, I loved this recording because it's so incredibly beautiful.

30

I'm a Shy Guy

ED

In late 2011, I began thinking about the King Cole Trio tunes that I used to sing to girls over the phone in the 1940s. As a young adolescent, I felt like the most lonely, shy kid on the planet. I was listening to the King Cole Trio on the radio all the time and when I heard Nat sing "I'm Lost" and "You're Looking at Me" I was struck dumb because they perfectly described my feeling of never fitting in anyplace.

Nat was my hero. He was everything I longed to be—calm, cool, sophisticated, elegantly dressed in a gray chalk-striped suit that fit like a glove. But I was young and my self-confidence around girls was so very low; I had no words to express my feelings. Even though I couldn't bring myself to talk to them in person, I knew every ballad Nat Cole and the Trio had recorded and I sang those tunes on the telephone to the girlfriends of other guys, who in turn threatened to knock me out. But they didn't, so I kept on singing to Ozella, Delphena, Dorothy, Sissy, and Carmel. The worst part was when I would see one of them the next day at school, and she would look right through me.

I was singing in the choir at Jordan High on 103rd Street in Watts when Nat came to visit in 1943 or '44. The Trio performed in the auditorium and then they spent time in the choir room. Nat walked around the room talking to the students but when he spoke to me and offered his hand, I was too shy to open my mouth or even shake his hand.

Seventy years later, as I started to work on our fourth recording project and performed so many of the tunes I used to sing to girls over the phone, I remembered the pain of being young, shy, and self-conscious. Somehow reliving that long-ago trauma was unexpectedly therapeutic. Singing those beautiful, sad songs about loss and heartache took me back to some of the unhappiest experiences of my life. But this project helped me to let go. Nat was a romantic and I had always followed him. Now, it was time to go out on my own.

DIANE

The King Cole Trio project became our new obsession. Ed bought just about everything the Trio recorded and we listened to at least 300 songs, at home, in the car, on vacation to put together a list for the project. By February 2012, Randy was already writing arrangements, and we started believing this would happen, even though we still needed to figure out how we would pay for it.

In June 2012, Ed and Randy played a duo gig in Oakland, to try out some of the tunes. Then Anton hosted a King Cole Trio concert in September at his Oakland loft as part of his house concert series, along with Randy, Akira, and bassist John Wiitala (who was on Ed's first CD, *Love Stories*). The band was already cooking on those tunes and the response in the packed hot room was overwhelming. The audience was smiling, laughing, unable to keep themselves from singing along on some of the tunes that everyone knows—"It's Only a Paper Moon" and "Straighten Up and Fly Right," stomping their feet to "Is You Is or Is You Ain't My Baby," swooning to "Unforgettable," and loving the softness of "Nature Boy." Dawn, Anton's wife, and I stood together at the side of the room, holding hands, laughing, bursting with excitement. It was clear this would be our new project, though in reality it was still just a dream.

Once again, welcome help came from two new jazz angels. The week after the loft concert, our friends, Marge Slabach and Dianne Safholm, asked when we would be recording and if $10,000 in seed money would be enough to get us started. That was all we needed to move ahead with Ed's love letter to the King Cole Trio. We'd figure out the rest as we went along.

ED

Born to Be Blue was the last CD Bud would help us to produce. In late 2011, he was diagnosed with a rare form of lung cancer. The initial prognosis was positive but turned out to be wrong. Though he was producing a CD for another vocalist as we began to record our King Cole Trio project, he was as always, no matter what, still with us and there for us just about every step of the way.

By now, we felt we knew enough to produce this fourth CD ourselves and we asked our good friend Laurie Antonioli to co-produce the musical part of the project. Laurie is a fearless and

eclectic master vocalist, lyricist and educator, and the Vocal Program
Director at the California Jazz Conservatory (CJC) in Berkeley. I had
met her in 2006, after my second summer at Jazz Camp West when
I hung out with the great singer Sheila Jordan all week. Right after
camp, Sheila came to Berkeley to perform at the screening of a new
film, *Brotherly Jazz*, about the Heath brothers (saxophonist Jimmy,
bassist Percy, and drummer Albert "Tootie" Heath, who had been
on the Jazz Camp faculty that year). The screening and concert was
a benefit for CJC. Sheila took my hand and put it in Laurie's, urging
us, as two people in recovery, to become good friends and to support
each other.

The day before our now-ritual dress rehearsal concert at
Piedmont Piano in February 2013, Diane wrote to Bud: "Just wanted
to let you know we're pretty stressed out. Ed's had a nasty respira-
tory virus the last 11 days. His uncontrollable coughing has finally
stopped, but we're not sure what will come out tomorrow when he
opens his mouth at the Piano Store. No rehearsal and no singing
since the Ellington gig at Freight and Salvage two weeks ago. Please
say a prayer."

Bud wrote back: "Hey Sing-ah man. My prayer's definitely
yours. I heard a good old Yiddish saying today that applies to all of
us who are required to SHOW UP. 'Man plans—God laughs.' That
sounds all too familiar to me. PS: I'm asking my angels to share their
largess with youse guys. Love ya, Bud."

Our two days in the studio were as smooth as cream. And,
thankfully, so was my voice. No other recording session had ever
been that easy or fun. The night before we went into the studio, I
called Jamie Fox, the golden-toned guitarist (who also recorded with
me on *The Song Is You*) and asked him to write a quick chart with
written musical notations for "I Just Can't See For Looking," an old

King Cole Trio favorite I suddenly wanted to sing. First thing in the morning, Randy, John Wiitala, and Jamie—a true instrumental King Cole Trio of piano, bass, and guitar—huddled around the piano with me to try it out. We ran through it once, and then signaled Dan to record. It was a first take and we liked it so much, it became the lead tune on the CD. The rest of the songs seemed to fall out of my mouth just as easily. It must have helped that this music had been a part of my emotional makeup since I had been a young teenager.

Maybe Randy said it best after listening to the final mixed and mastered CD in September. In a quick email, he wrote, "The CD is absolutely stunning. Cindy [his wife] couldn't wipe the stupid grin off her face. And me too!"

You have to hear the music to understand the "stupid grin" part. Though the recording has its fair share of my usual sad songs, those were balanced this time by many others that have you laughing, even singing along, like the scatting birds in "'Tis Autumn."

DIANE

Two months later, at the end of April, we began another East Coast tour, first in Chester, Connecticut, then Boston, and ending in Brooklyn. This time we traveled with a quintet, including Randy, Anton, and guitarist Jamie Fox, along with Nigerian/German bassist Ugonna Okegwo and drummer Willard Dyson (who was part of the *Song Is You* recording band). The latter two were always our first choice East Coast bass and drum sidemen. We still talk about Willard's unforgettable solo when he played the entire melody of "Bye Bye Blackbird" on his drums, something I never knew drums could do. It left the audience spellbound, and then erupting into wild applause.

During the few days between the Chester concert and Scullers Jazz Club in Boston, Ed, Randy, and I stayed at my sister's house, a charming 100-year-old New England-style farmhouse on two acres of lush, green, forested land in rural Deep River, Connecticut, southwest of Hartford. Unlike the previous two East Coast tours we had taken during frigid January weather, this time we traveled in a warm spring sun. Trees and plants were bursting with new vibrantly colored growth, and everyone everywhere was giddy with happiness that winter was at long last over. In Boston, the great jazz singer Rebecca Parris brought a half dozen students to Scullers and joined Ed onstage to duet playfully on "It's Only a Paper Moon." All the while, she bantered with Ed and the band members, keeping the audience in stiches, while the musicians tried not to lose their composure. "This is quite the band, look at him over there," she teased, pointing to Randy at the piano. "Just terrible! Terrible! No rhythm whatsoever!" As she lobbed quips at Anton in the middle of his solo, she said, "Look at him, trying not to laugh!"

After the concert, jazz impresario Fred Taylor, Scullers' artistic director, brought three bowls of chocolate ice cream to our room. He entertained us for a couple of hours with stories from his lifelong work of discovering and nurturing up-and-coming artists and his love for classic comedy. We laughed until our sides hurt, as he reenacted routines played by Mel Brooks and Carl Reiner in *The 2000 Year Old Man.*

Fred had been one of Ed's earliest supporters. After listening to the first CD, *Love Stories,* Fred had left an excited voicemail for our booking agent, Maxine Harvard. Fred and Ed were the same age, and Fred wondered, like so many people, why he had never heard of Ed Reed before. He booked Ed to sing with the *Love Stories* recording band at an annual gala fundraising event in Boston in late 2007.

The following year, Fred invited him back to Scullers after *The Song Is You* was released, and continued to host subsequent CD release concerts.

A few days later, we were in Brooklyn, the night before the last concert of the tour. Anton had invited us for dinner at his mother's apartment in Manhattan. We had met his mom the previous year at the Jazz Standard in New York during a *Born to Be Blue* CD release concert and were happy for the chance to spend an evening with both of them.

While not intentionally planned, we began the tour at a modern new synagogue in upscale Chester, Connecticut where my sister produced an annual concert series, and ended it at the historical 155-year-old Lafayette Avenue Presbyterian Church in Brooklyn. Founded in 1857, the church had been part of the Underground Railroad, a sanctuary for runaway slaves. It had recently come back to its roots with the hiring of our dear friend, Rev. Carmen Mason-Browne, as its first African American and first female minister. The concert was held in the sanctuary. The walls were adorned with magnificent murals showing the vibrant African American community in the neighborhood (for which actual residents had been used as models). Eight stunning Tiffany-art stained-glass windows were set along the east and west walls.

Of course the glaring omission in this series of three events featuring tunes from *I'm a Shy Guy* was the physical CD itself. It had been recorded only two months earlier and was still in the process of being mixed. It would be several more months of mastering and manufacturing before it would be available. The timing for the tour couldn't have been worse, but it was one of those things we had no control over. All we could do was shrug in embarrassed apology as people clamored to buy a CD after each concert. Just another missed opportunity to make a little money.

Once released, *I'm a Shy* Guy was chosen as an Editors Pick in the October 2013 issue of *DownBeat* magazine, the second of Ed's CDs to receive that distinction, and earned Ed glowing reviews:

> Vocalist Ed Reed knows how to find the sweet spot in a song and how to make it his own, as he proves on his latest recording. The ever youthful, 84-year-old Reed sings this material as if he's lived with it his whole life, which he has. These songs roll off his tongue with an understated grace and comfort. Here, we have Reed snuggling up to songs that Nat 'King' Cole's trio made famous in the 1940s. From the downbeat of "I Just Can't See for Lookin'," the record's first tune, there's no doubt that Reed has gentle yet firm command of this material. His voice is clear. His timing and intonation could be offered as a master class. And the band just slides into the groove of this classic trio ... — *Editors Pick, DownBeat, Oct. 2013*

> Welcome to *I'm A Shy Guy* which is one of those rare recordings that is made up of numerous "first takes" with the end result a fluidity of sound and swing ... Ed Reed's voice is distinctive with a slightly smokey elegance that embraces a note, a phrase, and the very lyrical essence of storytelling that turns an average singer into a vocal artist ... — *Bop N Jazz*

> Reed's is the voice of experience and hard-won wisdom. On this rounded collection of famous and lesser-known King Cole Trio sides, he takes his time with each lyric, singing

dependably behind the beat. Many singers have done Cole tributes recently, but Reed's is among the best. Without stooping to imitate, he captures the spirit of Cole's wry humor and charm. — *DownBeat, Dec. 2013*

ED

We had the first *I'm A Shy Guy* release concert at Yoshi's in November 2013. I love to come into a room with great players and a listening audience to see what happens when we meet each tune as if it is brand new, with all of its possibilities lying in front of it. It seems that even the tune itself awaits us anxiously to discover its new persona. Then we, the players, get to search it, seek it, play with it, and light it up like it has never been lit before. Then at the last note, the musicians and I grin at it like new parents, and that can be so beautiful. At Yoshi's, we were all as relaxed and joyful as we had been in the studio, swinging easy with the music.

DIANE

By the time *I'm a Shy Guy* was released in October 2013, Bud was on palliative care. We would go to his house with sandwiches for lunch, sometimes with Anton when he was in town. Ed had dedicated *I'm a Shy Guy* to Bud and gave him a copy during one of those lunches. From the first, both Ed and I felt joined at the hip with Bud. Out of the extraordinary musical relationship that developed, an even more extraordinary friendship grew that weathered some perilous moments we were all thankful to have gotten through. We are grateful to have had Bud in our lives. He was there always, and through all things. He approached everything with, at times, an unbelievably corny sense of humor and, always, with an open, gracious and generous heart that, like the drummer he was, kept the beat steady and supportive and loving. The last time we saw him was early in January 2014.

The previous year, our friend Patricia Silva from the Cheeseboard had been diagnosed with mesothelioma, a lethal form of lung cancer caused by exposure to asbestos, whose effects are latent for anywhere from 10 to 60 years before symptoms develop. A few years earlier, Pati had painted a stunning oil portrait of the photo on the cover of *The Song Is You*. It is one of the most iconic and best known photos of Ed, taken by a young professional photographer, Ashley Summer, who had generously offered to do an entire photo shoot at no cost so that she could try out a new camera.

In the photo, Ed wore one of his dark felt hats and a black jacket with a pure white silk handkerchief in the breast pocket. The red band that he ties around his hair at the base of his neck was just peeking out beneath the hat. He was posed sitting in a chair, bending forward, eyes closed, his left hand resting on his knee, his right hand touching the top of his hat as if he was getting ready to tip it. It is both elegant and sophisticated, a favorite photo, used again and again in journals and press releases.

Pati had given the painting to Ed on his birthday a couple of years before. We had it framed in late 2013 and took it to her house so she could see the simple but beautiful mahogany frame we had chosen, as she had suggested. We knew time was short. Patricia was very weak and on methadone for pain, but insisted on getting up and putting on makeup so she could have her picture taken with Ed, along with her oil painting. She laughed a lot and was happy, especially, to see Ed.

ED

Just a few days later, on the afternoon of January 16, we got two emails within an hour of each other. Bud was gone. Pati was gone. It was a Thursday, the day I taught my afternoon class for addicts and evening class for family members at Kaiser in Vallejo. Somehow, I don't know how, I got through those two classes without remembering anything that happened there or on the drive home. The next day we flew to Seattle for a long weekend of concerts and an "Inside the Lyric" master vocal workshop that I also taught at the Jazz Conservatory in Berkeley. At least we were staying with Anton and his wife Dawn, who were as close and dear to Bud as we were. While the two deaths left us in shock, unable to process so much loss, we had to get through concerts and workshops that weekend, and couldn't let the loss of these cherished friends really sink in while we were working.

31

Rising Star

DIANE

The loss and sadness that marked the beginning of 2014 slowly dissipated and the year unexpectedly became one of Ed coming full circle back to his San Quentin connection, although it wasn't the first time. In the late 1990s, Ed had returned to San Quentin to teach classes based on his "Art and Practice of Living Well" series for pre-release groups at San Quentin and the women's prison in Chowchilla.

The new connections were related to his music. Ed had received an email from Ralph Bravo's nephew, Henry. Ralph Bravo was the guitarist Ed had met and jammed with the last time he was incarcerated at San Quentin in 1964, the guitarist Ed always says was the best he ever heard. Henry Bravo was using Google to search for his uncle, who had disappeared after leaving prison in the late '60s, never to be heard from again. He found mention of his uncle in a story on Ed's website about Ed hearing Ralph playing his guitar in the Lower Yard at San Quentin and then singing with him—the moment that inspired Ed to think of himself as a singer. While Ed didn't know what had happened to Ralph, it was comforting to his family that someone who knew Ralph and loved his music, as they did, was keeping his memory alive.

Then in June, we were invited to attend the premiere screening at the L.A. Film Festival of a documentary, *Sound of Redemption*. It was about alto saxophonist Frank Morgan, who had spent the better part of 30 years in and out of San Quentin for using heroin and committing crimes for money to buy drugs. A couple of years before, one of the film's producers, James Egan, and the director, award-winning filmmaker NC Heikin, had found Ed through the publicity his late-life jazz career had generated and, knowing about Ed's drug and San Quentin connection to Frank, had interviewed him at length for the film. The filmmakers invited Ed to its premiere screening in L.A. because what he said about his own personal and professional experience with addiction and recovery helped to explain how Frank Morgan's heartbreak and pain led him to spend a lifetime trying to find comfort using drugs.

ED

I had been extensively interviewed for the film *Sound of Redemption* because of my longtime association with Frank Morgan as a drug user and crime partner, and because I'd sung in the Warden's Jazz Band during my last time at San Quentin in 1964. Frank had spent the better part of 30 years in and out of San Quentin and was a regular in the Warden's Band, though he and I never managed to be there at the same time.

I met Frank through a mutual friend on 5th Street in Los Angeles in the 1950s when we were both buying and shooting heroin. Soon, we began to hustle together. We would go into a store and one of us would distract the cashier while the other would stick his hand in the cash register and walk off with the money. We were good together, and sometimes would team up when we happened to run into each other. Once, on the way back to the car, we were walking by a theater. Right in front of the box office, Frank threatened to punch me in the face because he thought I had shortchanged him. We weren't that far away from where we had stolen the money. I said, "That's stupid, we can't fight here, man. We'll get arrested." Plus, I hadn't done anything wrong. I managed to talk him out of a fight. As a part of the film, a tribute concert for Frank Morgan, who died in 2007, was held at San Quentin with many of the jazz greats Frank had performed and recorded with after he left prison for the last time in 1985. The concert was performed in a room packed with inmates and became the centerpiece of the film. Most of the musicians who were in that band were also in Los Angeles for the premiere screening of *Sound of Redemption*. The day after the screening, the band gave a concert at the Grammy Museum, and the great pianist George Cables invited me to sit in on a few tunes.

After the screening, director NC Heikin led a Q&A that I was a part of. As NC talked about Frank and his problems, I had a sudden epiphany, remembering the fight Frank and I nearly had in front of that box office. I couldn't be 100% certain, because construction of the Convention Center had destroyed so many familiar landmarks, but because the box office of this theater was so distinctive, I had the weirdest feeling that it was the one we nearly fought in front of. And there I was, all those years later, such a different person, in a film about Frank Morgan, and his ultimate redemption.

DIANE

Ed got an email from a German journalist and correspondent, Arndt Peltner, who was working on a lengthy feature for a German radio station about San Quentin. He had just read "The San Quentin Story" by Warden Clinton Duffy and was trying to access some of the recordings of the long-defunct Jazz Band mentioned in the book. Arndt knew that some reel-to-reel recordings were in storage at the prison, but hadn't yet received clearance to go inside the vault to look for them.

After he interviewed Ed for his San Quentin research, Arndt told us he had pitched another idea to his radio station. He had found Ed's story to be compelling and inspiring, and one that he thought should be told. His pitch about the magazine article he wanted to write was accepted for publication right away, and the radio station gave him the green light to produce a feature piece. Arndt interviewed both of us to get a more complete story of each of our experiences.

His script for the radio feature began with us speaking in English, fading out and replaced with German-speaking voice over actors. Ed's music was interspersed here and there. It was aired on German radio the following year. My friend Heidi listened and sent us a Google translation.

That year, 2014, it felt like recognition for his life and music just poured in. Later in the year, Ed was voted #1 Rising Star in the Male Vocalist category in the *DownBeat* magazine critics' poll—a rather astonishing honor at age 85!

In early 2015, Ed was invited to give a TEDx talk in Santa Cruz. The theme of that session was "Radical Collaboration." Ed talked about the radical collaboration he had with himself as he struggled with addiction and getting into recovery. In his ten-minute talk, he sang portions of two songs and told a nutshell version of his life. It was, in many ways, a similar but condensed form of what he did in both his classes and on the bandstand, blending his "Art and Practice of Living Well" teachings with songs that spoke strongly to his experience. The people in his drug treatment classes always loved it when he sang the sad tunes of sorrow and loss that described their lives. And his concert audiences loved and appreciated his courage in sharing so much of his story with them between songs.

Ed's TEDx talk, appropriately called "There Is Nothing Wrong With You," was bookended by two of his favorite songs. He began the talk singing the first part of a Blossom Dearie tune, "Inside a Silent Tear," a cappella. It is a song that Ed says epitomizes his despair about his drug addiction and unhappy relationships. He ended the talk with a portion of Artie Butler and Phyllis Molinary's "Here's to Life," a beautiful tribute to the power of gratitude and hope.

ED

On December 15-17, 2015, I performed at Dizzy's Club Coca-Cola, at Jazz at Lincoln Center in New York City. Those three evenings were pinnacle experiences of a lifetime. Never had I been in such a great room, let alone been the featured performer in a space with such a beautifully dramatic background and history, along with a great cast of character actors, backstage, onstage, and in the audience.

I don't usually get nervous or very excited before a performance because my mother would not allow it when I was growing up. I've talked before about how determined she was that I would be the performer that she had dreamed of being. Until recently, I was not aware of how much of what I do now I owe to Ruth Reed, my beautiful mother, who prepared me for my joyful life onstage today, both in music and my lecture series.

Ruth would say in a calm and very proper manner: "Edward, I want you to stand there comfortably with all the dignity that you can muster because what you're about to do has nothing to do with the audience."

Then she would say that I was there to perform whatever the song or recitation was "with the perfect diction and grammar that you have practiced, with an expression on your face of peace, joy or sadness, excitement or anything else that the selection calls for. You are to do that with dignity, and a keen and buoyant enjoyment of life. No one else can do what you are about to do."

During those nights at Dizzy's, all that she taught me served me well—until I looked out of the floor-to-ceiling window behind the bandstand. Then it all became dreamlike. That huge window was filled with gigantic skyscrapers lighting the dazzling New York nighttime skyline. From where we were, five stories above Columbus Circle, was a view that, to me, was reminiscent of a film set from a Humphrey Bogart/Lauren Bacall movie drama or a Frank Sinatra show at the top of his game. And there I was, performing on that magnificent stage.

I loved the band members. George Cables is, to me, somehow different from all of the many pianists I've worked with over the years. I first heard him in the 1970s when Diane and I went to see jazz trumpeter Freddie Hubbard at Pasquale's, a beach club in L.A. George was the young guy there playing piano. We had to catch a plane so I didn't get to meet him that night but Freddie, with wide-eyed sincerity, told Diane and me that we looked very much alike, which completely floored us. Not too long afterwards, Art Pepper introduced me to George Cables at The Great American Music Hall in San Francisco. George and I met again in 2012 at a Healdsburg Jazz Festival fundraiser, but we never performed together until 2014 during the L.A. Film Festival after the release of the Frank Morgan film, *Sound of Redemption*.

My dear friend and longtime bandmate, drummer Akira Tana, came to New York from the Bay Area for the gig at Dizzy's. Akira and I first performed together in October 2007 at the Sonoma Jazz and Wine Festival and we have been at it ever since, including our week in Bern, Switzerland at Marian's Jazzroom. Akira was in the band for my last two recording projects, traveled with us on several East Coast tours, and played on many of my gigs. He has become a good friend and is a fantastic musician, drummer, and bandleader.

I first met New York bassist Ugonna Okegwo when I was at the Jazz Standard in 2012. Since then, we have worked together every time I come to the East Coast. I'm always happy to see Ugonna and really like his playing. He's present and knowledgeable, and his playing is so flexible. He is always there for me musically, anywhere I go.

As we went through each tune, George, Akira, and Ugonna became magical for me. I say magical because it can't be easy for the players to follow what I do. I never sing a song the same way twice. I don't even try, because I'm always searching, seeking more beauty— harmonically, rhythmically, lyrically. For instance, I'd been working on the Bronislaw Kaper tune "Invitation" which to me is so mysterious. It had taken me a long time to figure out what I wanted to do with the song in various tempos. George, in particular, seemed to grow physically larger as we reached out into the music. I'm not sure how to express the joy, amazement, gratitude, and friendship I feel for George Cables. I'm grateful for all the great pianists I've worked with, but my connection with George is special.

Backstage at Dizzy's before the show, the tension was thick enough to cut with hedge clippers. Akira always tells hilarious stories, Ugonna is always good company, and George Cables always smiles encouragement. My booking agent, Maxine Harvard, worked fiercely to protect my energy and keep everybody away between sets. That was an impossible task as well-wishers were coming and going in and out of the Green Room like in a train station, along with waiters from the club who brought refreshments, dinner, and anything else they could provide for us.

People had literally come from all over the country. Diane's good friend from high school, Cathy, drove up from North Carolina for the week. She and Diane had not seen each other in 50 years! Cathy was there each night lending a hand wherever she could, with a look of joyful amazement on her face. My dear sister-in-law Miriam and her partner, Mike, drove in from Connecticut and my wonderful nephew Kyle, whom I love a lot, and his spouse Amanda Blair flew in for the night from the University of Chicago where they were each finishing their doctoral dissertations. So many friends were there from California—Margaret and her partner from my AA meeting, our longtime friend Rita from Sacramento and her son, Chris, also a doctoral candidate. (His late father, Michael, and I had been students at U.C. Irvine in 1968 when I was very, very crazy.) Also in the audience was a singer and a bass player I used to work with years before I became "edreedsings," our friends Rev. Carmen Mason-Browne and her husband, Kenn, from the church in Brooklyn where we'd performed two years before, and a few other friends from the West Coast.

On the last night, ten minutes before going back onstage for the second and final set, we read the wonderful review I had gotten in the *New York Times*. Then, in the middle of the set there was a sudden commotion in the room. Heads turned and gasps were audible as in walked Aretha Franklin and Bette Midler with their entourage. They had just finished a show in another part of Jazz at Lincoln Center and had come to Dizzy's for dinner. The stage lights were too bright for me to see who had come in, and it was just as well because at that point I probably would have become very nervous. On the bandstand, between tunes, I pointed to Diane sitting on a stool against the back wall and talked about our upcoming 48 years together. Diane later told me that in the middle of the next tune, a blues, Bette Midler turned to her and, with that great Bette smile, gave her two thumbs up. After the show, they invited me to their table.

I said those nights were magical and I meant it, literally. From the opening note I sang on the stage that first night, up to the final note on the last night, I felt my mother's spirit standing next to me, telling me what I needed to remember, just as she did when I was six. I loved that she was there with me.

32

I Am Me

ED

In 2015, I began to work regularly with a trio of Bay Area musicians who would become the dream band that I had fantasized about since childhood—pianist Adam Shulman, bassist John Wiitala, and drummer Lorca Hart, and we often added Anton Schwartz on tenor saxophone. Our first group project was John Coltrane ballads, mostly from his classic 1963 recording with jazz vocalist Johnny Hartman. We put together a collection of tunes from that album, along with some of the beautiful songs from Coltrane's *Ballads* and performed at SFJAZZ and the Healdsburg Jazz Festival in the fall of 2016. As it turned out, the timing of those concerts coincided with Coltrane's 90th birthday. From there we dove into the music of quirky Thelonious Monk, and then Shirley Horn, one of my favorite singers, who unapologetically loved to sing the beautiful, sad ballads that I do—the ones I call "slow and slower."

Adam has been described as "one of the Bay Area's elite accompanists," which perfectly captures the breadth of his versatility. Jazz journalist Andrew Gilbert wrote that one night Adam could be "play-ing mean second-line grooves and rumbling gospel chords behind [a] rapidly rising jazz singer ... [and] a few days later, navigating ballads at molasses-drip tempos with the extraordinary 89-year-old crooner Ed Reed."

I love to tease pianists, and sometimes try to lose them by stringing the lyric out or changing the tempo. But with Adam, no matter where I go in a tune, I've never been able to lose him. He's always there. He always finds me, seemingly effortlessly. And at the end, when I turn towards him, we're both smiling, appreciating the intricate dance we've just done.

Lorca Hart always surprises me with combinations of cymbals and drum beats, both new and beckoning. I can be singing a song, and know where I'm going with it, and then Lorca plays something that grabs my attention and takes me to a place I've never been to or known about.

John Wiitala, who has played on my first and last CDs and many of my gigs through the years—going as far back as the 1980s—is the uplifting and constant heartbeat of the band. John and I lose ourselves in the psychology of living well. Our talks are fantastic.

It is, truly, a dream band.

DIANE

AA sets aside one night each month to celebrate recovery milestones, starting with 24 hours of sobriety. The room buzzes with excitement, along with the smell of coffee and birthday cake.

Seven months after those nights at Dizzy's Club Coca-Cola in New York, on July 8, 2016, Ed walked to the front of the room to accept his AA chip for 30 years clean and sober. As Anton Schwartz said, "Birthdays are fun and all, but THIS one is truly something to celebrate!"

And me? I think that if *this* can happen, then *anything* is possible.

ED

And then, in 2018, during a Sunday afternoon concert at the Back Room in Berkeley, something happened that I had always dreamed about.

For the first time in my life, I sang like I always wanted to sing.

This time I wasn't dreaming. I didn't think I was anyone but me.

THE END

Acknowledgments

ouble Helix is a true story—actually two true stories—from the best of our memories that stretch way back in time. Journals and other past writings have helped to trigger details of some events that otherwise would have stayed half-remembered or buried. Some names have been changed, and conversations have been re-created as accurately as possible.

So many people have been involved, directly or indirectly, in the birth of this book. We are indebted to our friends, family, and colleagues who read and gave us feedback on drafts as they were developed and changed, who helped us to fine tune *Double Helix* as it has evolved over the years, and who cheered us on, and gave us courage to keep going: Stephanie Bruce, Jan Bourret, Sue "Birdi" Burish, Galen Ellis, Miriam Gardner-Frum, Kyle Gardner, Andrew Gilbert, Dawn Hagen, Maureen Henry, Kate Karpilow, Jean Nudelman, Christian Pederson, Heather Pegas, Anton Schwartz, Patricia Scott, Barry Warren.

We are expressly grateful to our Memoir Writing Group whose honesty, insights, practical suggestions, and gentle prodding kept us moving forward. There was no extra mile they wouldn't travel with us, including indulging our request to read chapters of the book out loud during group time to test our idea of writing in an alternating narrative style. Very special thanks to the group's facilitator, and our mentor and good friend, Michael A. Kroll, who understands so much, asks the hard questions, never fails to make a rough spot smoother or more intelligible, and came up with the title for this book.

Profound gratitude to our editor, Elizabeth Fishel, whose exceptional care, skill, and probing questions helped to shape this book in ways that have substantially improved it.

Thank you to Irene Young for the cover photo. Irene believes that, "The key to photographing people is to do so with a wide open aperture of the heart, with no judgment, and with a true belief that everyone is beautiful." https://ireneyoungfoto.com/

Special thanks to Ian Carey for the cover design and for creating a most whimsical double helix graphic that makes us smile. http://iancareydesign.com/

We are forever grateful to the people of Twelve Step programs for their patience, support, and fellowship that helped us to become the people we are today and to have the courage to tell our stories.

We would never have dreamed that Ed would begin an entirely new career at age 78, or that his music would generate the excitement it did. None of that would have been possible without the magnificent team that has provided unending guidance, support, and friendship since the inception of Ed's professional jazz career in

2007 as a jazz singer, performer, and recording artist. Our publicist Terri Hinte ushered Ed's music into the world of print and online jazz journalism, resulting in articles and reviews in some of the most prestigious jazz publications and other media. Terri also helped to review and guide this book to completion for which we will never be able to thank her enough. Our tireless agent Maxine Harvard booked Ed into world-class venues and taught us most of what we've learned about being an artist in the jazz world. Our radio promoter Neal Sapper worked with dozens of key radio stations across the country that spun Ed's music into the top 10 of the jazz charts.

We're so proud to be a part of the welcoming, generous, and close-knit San Francisco Bay Area jazz community. We have made many new friends and been thrilled to work with many great musicians and vocalists on both the West and East coasts. Special thanks to Susan Muscarella and Laurie Antonioli at the California Jazz Conservatory in Berkeley for opportunities over the years to perform and conduct workshops. Our endless thanks and deep appreciation to the incredible musicians in the Bay Area, New York, Seattle, and Los Angeles who have worked with Ed over the years. We are indebted to the San Francisco Bay Area's 24-hour jazz radio station, KCSM, whose announcers play Ed's music, have interviewed him on-air multiple times over the years, and are always supportive and kind to us. It's truly been the gift of a lifetime to be embraced by this diverse community that loves with all of its collective heart.

About the Authors

E D REED was a heroin and cocaine addict for 40 years. Since beginning his recovery in 1986, Ed has worked with addicts/alcoholics, families, and programs as a health educator, lecturer, program developer, trainer and consultant inspiring others to change their lives through recovery. He uses an 8-part series that he created, "The Art and Practice of Living Well," as the foundation for his workshops and lectures with diverse populations in treatment programs, public health clinics, schools, jails, prisons, and the workplace. Ed has conducted his series at Kaiser Permanente's Chemical Dependency Recovery Program, New Bridge Foundation in Berkeley, and other treatment programs, as well as at California's San Quentin and Chowchilla Prisons, and jails in Alameda, Contra Costa, and Solano Counties.

In 2007, long after his release from prison and his hard-won recovery, Ed began a late-life career as a jazz singer, performer, and recording artist. He has released four critically acclaimed CDs, performed on world-class stages nationally and internationally, and has been extensively interviewed by print journalists and on jazz radio stations. In 2014, at age 85, Ed was voted #1 Rising Star in the Male Vocalist category by *DownBeat* critics, and was awarded the "Local Jazz Hero" award in 2011 by the Jazz Journalists Association. He was a featured interviewee in *Sound of Redemption: The Frank Morgan Story*, a highly acclaimed documentary released in 2014 about a great alto saxophonist who spent the better part of 30 years in prison and, like Ed, played in the now-defunct San Quentin Warden's Jazz Band. In 2015, Ed was invited to give a TEDx Talk entitled "There Is Nothing Wrong With You" that combined his story of recovery with his music.

DIANE REED has over 30 years' experience as a consultant providing policy analysis, research and writing, evaluation assistance, and grant writing services to public and private agencies, and community-based organizations. She has worked in a wide range of areas, including child welfare, domestic violence, nutrition, tobacco, alcohol and other drug problems, perinatal health, HIV/AIDS, tuberculosis, criminal justice, and community-based service collaboration. She holds a Master of Public Health degree in policy and planning from U.C. Berkeley and has co-authored academic articles published in the *Journal of Public Health Policy* and the *Health Education Quarterly*. In addition, she and Ed co-authored an article about the children of incarcerated parents that was published in *Social Justice*. After making her living writing, Diane is now exploring the joy of finding her own voice as a creative nonfiction writer.

Ed and Diane live in the San Francisco Bay Area with four cats and an ever-emerging and beautiful garden.

www.reedswrite.com
www.edreedsings.com